CHARLES PRENDERGAST

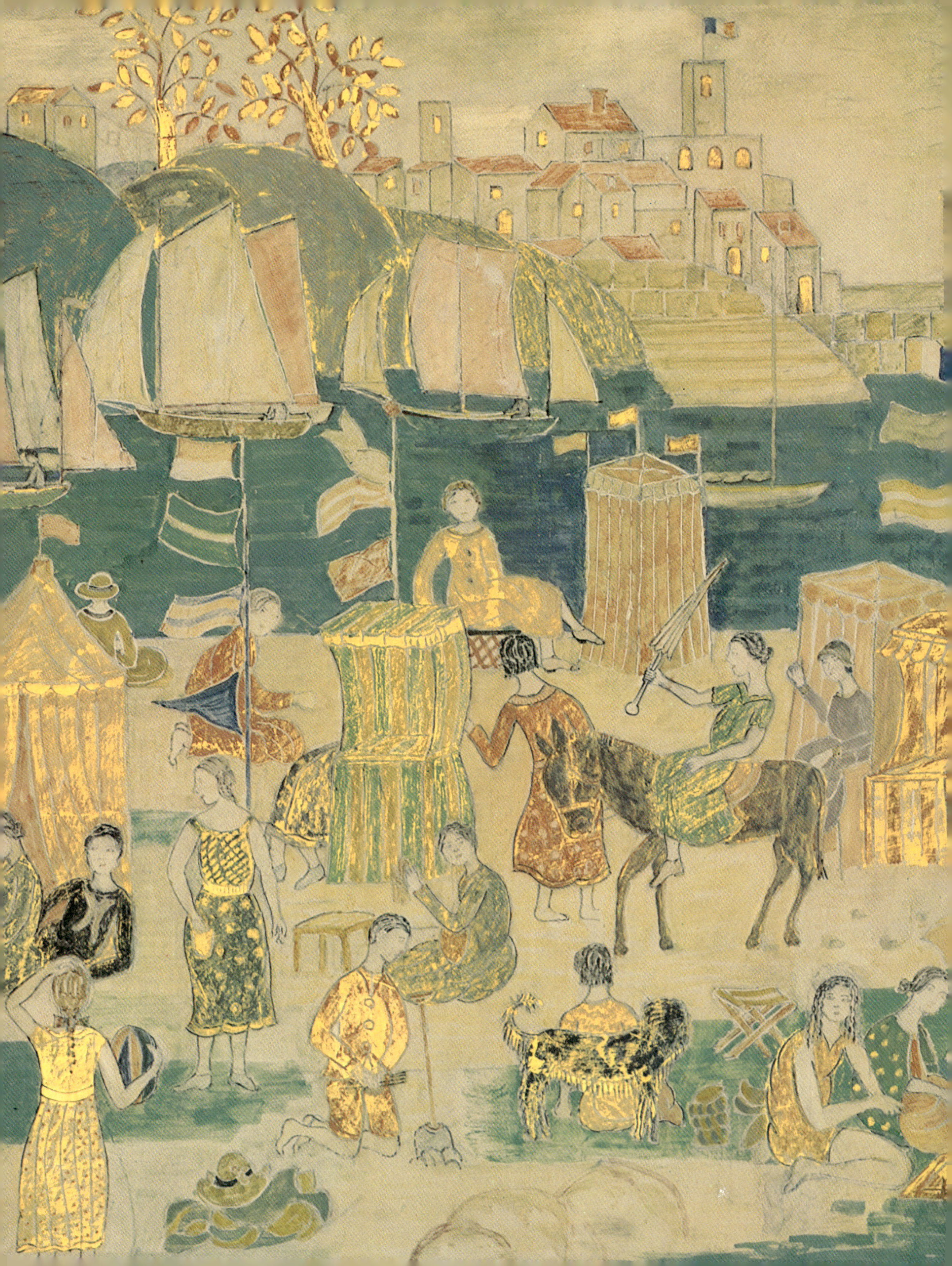

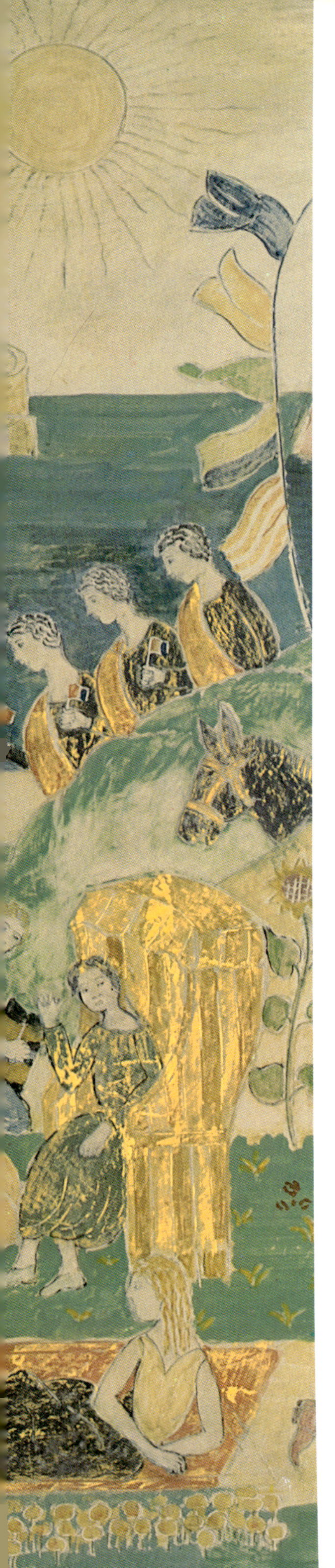

THE ART OF CHARLES PRENDERGAST FROM THE COLLECTIONS OF THE WILLIAMS COLLEGE MUSEUM OF ART & MRS. CHARLES PRENDERGAST

Nancy Mowll Mathews

WITH AN ESSAY BY

Marion M. Goethals

AND CATALOGUE ENTRIES BY

Vivian Patterson · Marion M. Goethals · Ann Ugast Greenwood
Claudia Hill · Molly Donovan · Anne Dowling
Susan Imbriani · Rachel B. H. Petrik · Linda Reynolds
Stefanie Spray

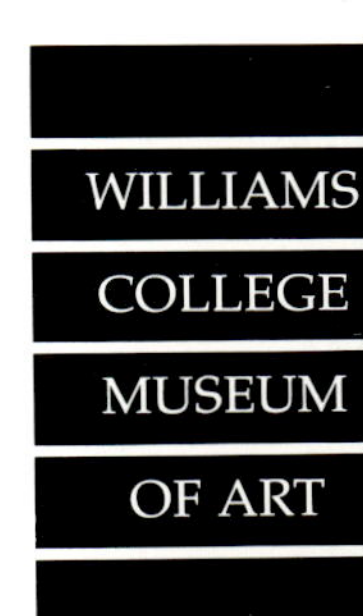

Library of Congress Cataloging-in-Publication Data

Mathews, Nancy Mowll.
The art of Charles Prendergast from the collections of the Williams College Museum of Art and Mrs. Charles Prendergast/Nancy Mowll Mathews; with an essay by Marion M. Goethals and catalogue entries by Vivian Patterson . . . [et al.].
p. cm.
Exhibition catalog.
Includes bibliographical references.
ISBN 0-913697-16-8
1. Prendergast, Charles, 1863-1948—Exhibitions. 2. Prendergast, Charles, 1863-1948—Criticism and interpretation. 3. Prendergast, Eugénie—Art collections—Exhibitions. 4. Art—Private collections—Massachusetts—Williamstown—Exhibitions. 5. Williams College. Museum of Art—Exhibitions. I. Goethals, Marion M., 1946- II. Williams College. Museum of Art.
N6853.P73A4 1993
709'.2—dc20 93-22826
CIP

ISBN: 0-913697-16-8

This catalogue accompanies the exhibition "'Beauties . . . of a Quiet Kind': The Art of Charles Prendergast from the Collections of the Williams College Museum of Art and Mrs. Charles Prendergast," presented at the Museum from August 14, 1993, through January 9, 1994. The exhibition, one of a series organized for Williams College's Bicentennial (1793-1993), honors a decade of patronage by Mrs. Charles Prendergast. This volume is also the first in a series of catalogues documenting the permanent collection of the Williams College Museum of Art.

COVER: Detail of *Fairy Story*, ca. 1922 (reworked ca. 1942-46), incised gesso, tempera, pencil, and gold leaf on panel (22 x 31 in.), Williams College Museum of Art, Gift of Mrs. Charles Prendergast (86.18.26)

FRONTISPIECE: Detail of *Holiday Beach Scene*, ca. 1931-32, incised gesso, tempera, and gold leaf on panel (27⅞ x 59 in.), Williams College Museum of Art, Gift of Mrs. Charles Prendergast (86.18.63)

Williams College Museum of Art
Main Street
Williamstown, Massachusetts 01267

To Mrs. Charles Prendergast

CONTENTS

FOREWORD

Linda Shearer
DIRECTOR

Since my arrival at the Williams College Museum of Art in 1989, I have become intimately acquainted with the art of Charles Prendergast. It has been a pleasure for me to discover the many facets of his work as I have examined objects in our collection, from delicate watercolors to gilded panels, from decorated boxes to hand-carved frames. I have been so struck by the unique character and whimsy of his work that I have felt, as many others have before me, that I have happened upon a rare hidden treasure. The year 1993 marks the Bicentennial of Williams College; it is very fitting, therefore, that we have the honor of presenting this exhibition and catalogue as a tribute to one of the many treasures of Williams College.

None of this could have occurred without the generosity of Mrs. Charles Prendergast, who in 1983 endowed the Prendergast catalogue raisonné and simultaneously began donating selected works by her husband to the museum. Today, WCMA boasts sixty works by Charles Prendergast, including many of the extraordinary hand-carved frames for which he is well known; we have been honored by Mrs. Prendergast's designation of her own collection of sixteen Charles Prendergast works as promised gifts. These holdings are especially gratifying in light of the relatively small output of this artist, who produced only 250 identified works, not including the frames. His works are now primarily in the hands of private collectors and are seldom seen by the public. The Williams College Museum of Art, consequently, is the only site where Charles Prendergast's art can be studied and appreciated in depth.

My heartfelt thanks go to Mrs. Prendergast for her generous gifts, as well as her ongoing support, to the Williams College Museum of Art. I have the highest professional respect for her stewardship of the Prendergast estate, which fell to her upon the death of Charles Prendergast in 1948; I also have the highest personal admiration for this remarkable woman, and I value our friendship. Thanks also go to members of the board of the Eugénie Prendergast Foundation—John Boyd, Joseph Butler, and Harold and Catherine Genvert. I would like to express special gratitude to Antoinette Le Bris Maynard, whose close friendship with the Prendergasts dates from 1939 when she arrived in Westport from France for a summer visit and ended up staying a lifetime in this country. She has been most generous with her recollections and her mementos of Charles Prendergast.

We have been aided in our research over the years by many different individuals and institutions, but I would like to acknowledge the special help on this project from Erika Passantino and Eliza Rathbone of The Phillips Collection; Deborah Chotner of the National Gallery of Art; Linda Foss, Anne Havinga, Darielle Mason, Karen Otis, and Jerry Ward at the Museum of Fine Arts, Boston; Richard Wattenmaker of the Archives of American Art, and Etolia S. Basso, and her son, Keith Basso.

Closer to home, Gary Burger, director of the Williamstown Regional Art Conservation Laboratory, and conservators at the lab—Leslie Paisley, Michael Heslip, Hugh Glover, and Ingrid Neuman—have been invaluable in helping us assess and protect the Prendergast works in our care. At the Clark Art Institute Library in Williamstown, Susan Roeper, Paige Carter, and Elizabeth Kieffer freely lent their expertise to the research effort such a project engenders.

As a college museum, we have the good fortune to be closely involved with students; we relish every opportunity to further our involvement, and this undertaking has been no exception. In this case, students from the Williams College Graduate Program in the History of Art—Molly Donovan, Anne Dowling, Susan Imbriani, Rachel B. H. Petrik, Linda Reynolds, and Stefanie Spray—have contributed catalogue entries as well as a great deal of additional research that will be added to the files housed in the Prendergast Archive and Study Center here at the Williams College Museum of Art.

But an undertaking like this must rely heavily on the skills and talents of the museum staff who see it through from beginning to end. Guiding all our Prendergast activities is Nancy Mowll Mathews, Eugénie Prendergast Curator, whose dedication to and knowledge of Maurice and Charles Prendergast and their art is boundless; I am very grateful to her. Ann Greenwood, Prendergast Administrative Assistant, has shown her usual calm and conscientiousness at each step of the project; on behalf of myself and Nancy, I would like to express my appreciation for her hard work. Ann is also one of several staff members who contributed texts to the catalogue. Marion M. Goethals, Curatorial Coordinator, wrote the informative essay on Charles Prendergast's methods and materials and the entries on his sketchbooks, and Vivian Patterson, Associate Curator, Collections Management, and Claudia Hill, 1992-93 National Endowment for the Arts Curatorial Intern, each wrote entries for several objects. Since this catalogue draws on the extensive research files amassed for the Prendergast catalogue raisonné, I would like to acknowledge the work of Carol Clark, Nancy Mathews, Gwendolyn Owens, Carol Derby, Marion Goethals, and Charles Parkhurst from 1983 to 1988 that has provided us with such a valuable scholarly legacy.

This catalogue inaugurates a series of publications focusing on various aspects and strengths of the museum's permanent collection. Susan Dillmann, the museum's editor and public relations coordinator, is ably overseeing this long-term effort, setting the standard in this first volume with her characteristic eye for detail and style. Susan has relied on the capable help of her graduate assistant, Frances Lloyd, in preparing the manuscript. Jonathon Nix at The Studley Press has done an admirable job designing the catalogue, which also serves as a model for the collection catalogue series.

The museum is inextricably linked to the larger community of the college. I must mention the ongoing participation we enjoy with Robert C. Volz, Custodian of the Chapin Library of Rare Books, truly one of the great treasures of Williams College. Bob and Wayne Hammond, Assistant Chapin Librarian, frequently share with us not only their knowledge, but also the exquisite volumes in their care. Finally, I want to express my gratitude to Francis C. Oakley, President of the College, and his administration for their enthusiastic support of the museum, its programs, and projects. I am pleased that this beautiful exhibition and accompanying publication will be presented in the last year of his presidency; his personal appreciation of the art of the Prendergasts has been a continuing source of encouragement to all of us at the museum.

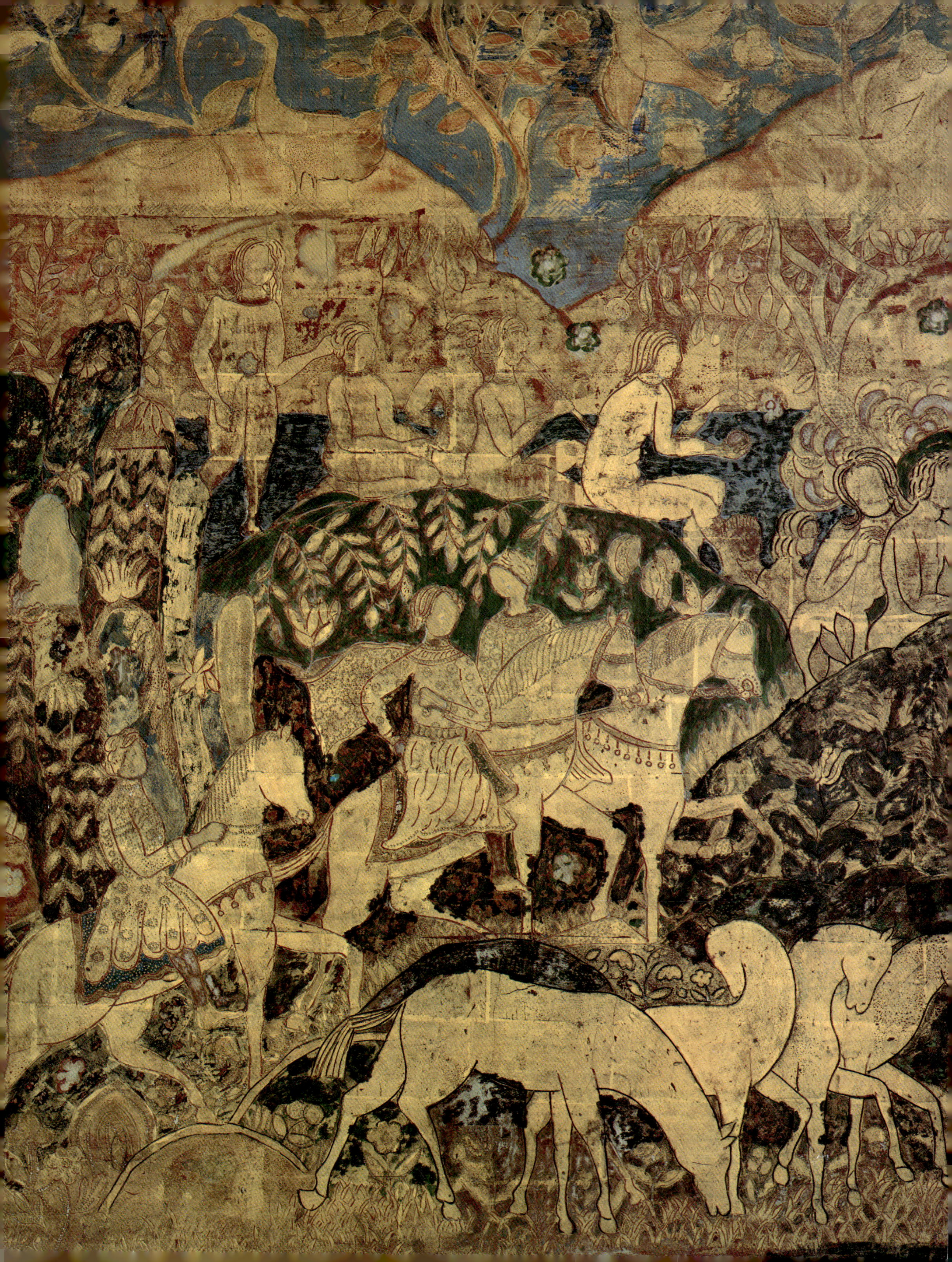

"BEAUTIES . . . OF A QUIET KIND": THE ART OF CHARLES PRENDERGAST

Nancy Mowll Mathews

CHARLES PRENDERGAST, A THOUGHTFUL ARTIST, produced just slightly more than one hundred finished pictorial works. Based as they were on ancient motifs and contemporary folk art subjects, these painted and carved objects have so few parallels in the art of Prendergast's time that they stand outside the established history of American art and have earned their creator only a small—but very passionate—following among connoisseurs and art historians. His works will probably always be the province of the very few because, by their very nature, they are fragile and precious, beautiful to look at and elusive in meaning. But when examined carefully, they reveal a rich world of wit and symbol that is unexpectedly universal in its appeal.

The pictorial works are also exceptional because they constitute a second career for Charles Prendergast who first rose to prominence as a craftsman and framemaker. It is more common for the reverse to be true—for an artist to start out as a painter and then later switch to the decorative arts, as did Louis Comfort Tiffany (1835-1910) and John LaFarge (1835-1910). But Charles Prendergast, born in 1863, established himself as a premier American framemaker by the age of forty-five and then began a second career as a fine artist (painter and sculptor) when he was in his fifties.

The transition to Prendergast's second career was smoothed by special circumstances. First, Prendergast was already part of the fine arts world—known to artists, dealers, and patrons by virtue of his activity as a framemaker as well as the prominence of his brother, Maurice Prendergast (1858-1924), as an American progressive artist. Second, Charles Prendergast capitalized on his skill and reputation as a woodcarver and gilder by creating "paintings" that employed framemaking devices—areas of gold leaf and supports of carved or incised wooden panels. The dialogue between Prendergast's pictorial compositions and the abstract decorative motifs of his frames was ongoing and creative. However in spite of the boost these factors gave to Prendergast's switch to the fine arts, it was his ability to delineate a fresh and original vision in a pictorial format that accounted for the success of his second career.

Baptized Charles James Prendergast in the Roman Catholic Basilica of John the Baptist in St. Johns, Newfoundland, the artist was the youngest of six children born to Maurice and Malvina Germaine Prendergast. The family was solidly middle or upper middle class with the father the owner of a general store and the mother the daughter of a Boston physician. Of Charles's five brothers and sisters, only the two eldest, Maurice and his twin sister Lucy, survived childhood, and only Maurice survived with Charles into adulthood. The family business failed and the Prendergasts moved to Boston in 1867 when Charles was four years old. Charles's father never reestablished himself in Boston; Charles remembered that during his childhood his father occupied himself with "odd jobs"[1] and in the Boston City Directories from 1867-1875, Maurice Prendergast (Sr.) is frequently listed as a laborer. Nevertheless, the educated lifestyle of his mother's family, the Germaines, undoubtedly kept the Prendergasts in a middle-class orbit even though money was short and the children received only a public school education until the age of fourteen. Both Charles and his older brother Maurice had developed refined tastes as children, were known to be facile with drawing pencils,[2] and gravitated to artistic circles when they left school. Maurice found his way into a commercial art firm and by 1879 (at age twenty-one) was a professional designer.[3]

Charles, by his own admission, was less directed than Maurice. He became an errand boy for the art gallery Doll & Richards when he was in his teens,[4] but left to make two voyages to England as a hand on a cattle boat. When he settled back down in Boston in 1887 he recalled working for another (unnamed) art gallery and was listed for the first time in the Boston City Directory as "clerk." In 1890 he shipped out again, this time to Paris with Maurice where the two brothers began taking art classes. Maurice, although now in his thirties, applied himself to the art student regimen, studying at the well-known academies of Colarossi and Julian. Charles, a handsome young man in his late twenties (fig. 1), was less dedicated to his studies and soon returned to Boston.

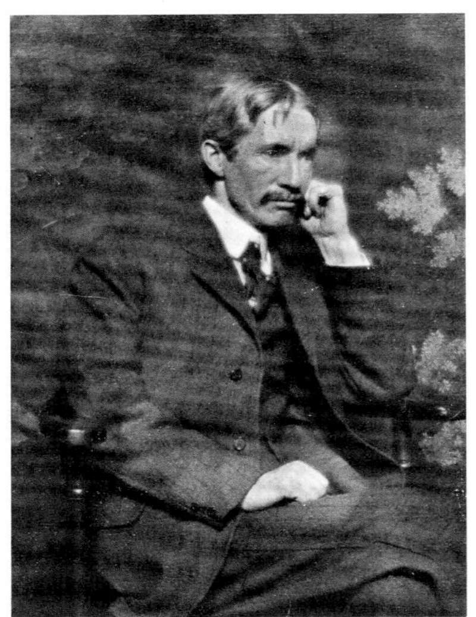

FIGURE 1. Anonymous, *Charles Prendergast*, ca. 1885, photograph (9¾ x 8 in.), Williams College Museum of Art, Prendergast Archive and Study Center

Charles may have been discouraged from pursuing a fine arts career after seeing the high level of work done in the classes in Paris and seeing his brother's career quickly take off in that competitive atmosphere. Charles, unlike Maurice, had not developed his early talent in drawing by working in the commercial arts, but had instead gained more experience in the business side of the fine arts. When he returned to Boston Charles entered into a partnership with a firm that produced decorative wooden moldings, especially for fireplace mantels. He may have joined the firm as a salesman, since his experience lay in that field,[5] but by the time his brother came back from Paris in 1894, Charles had gravitated toward the manufacturing side, gaining experience in all aspects of the carving of decorative wood objects.

The change in Maurice's life after four years in Paris inevitably caused a change in Charles's. Maurice moved back into the family home, which now consisted only of Charles and their father (their mother died in 1883). The two brothers, both in their thirties, found that living together was more than a convenience; it offered support and stimulation that they couldn't find anywhere else. When Maurice returned from Paris, therefore, his new status had a great impact on Charles. Maurice had entered the world of high art: his pictures were now on view at Charles's former employer, Doll & Richards, and his friends were the artists whose work Charles had handled and sold. In comparison, Charles's woodwork business seemed unbearably mundane and, as he told his biographer, he slipped into a depression: "I was so *damn* miserable, so *damn* unhappy, so *damn* aggravated, that I plain got sick of having myself around."[6]

Maurice and his painter friends ultimately suggested a solution to Charles's dilemma. They needed frames; they particularly needed frames made by someone "artistic," someone who understood what effect they were trying to achieve in their paintings and had the skill and the creativity to carve a frame that would enhance that effect. Maurice's new artist-friends, such as Hermann Dudley Murphy (1867-1945) and Sarah Choate Sears (1858-1935), were also independently wealthy and could afford to pay for handmade frames for their own works and the works of the other artists they collected. The art world in Boston, with its aristocratic make-up and its emphasis on refined taste was perfect for an artist-framemaker such as Charles.

However, a fine art framemaker needed to solicit the business of others besides artists in order to establish himself. In this regard, Charles's connections with Doll & Richards and the other art galleries of Boston must have been extremely helpful since dealers traditionally framed the works turned over to them by the artists they represented. The existence of frames on works by such Boston artists as I. M. Gaugengigl (1855-1932) may be the result of commissions by dealers rather than by the artists themselves. Furthermore, Boston's Museum of Fine Arts was steadily growing in stature since its founding in 1879, and, since its move to a grand new building on Huntington Avenue, was frequently in need of new or replacement frames for its masterpieces.[7] Not far away, Isabella Stewart Gardner had opened her home on the Fenway to occasional public viewings and also commissioned frames for her collection of old and new masters from Charles Prendergast.[8] Commissions from dealers, museums, major art collectors, and, occasionally, business corporations, supplemented Prendergast's work for the artists themselves and made framemaking a viable occupation by about 1897.

Since Charles needed to devote as much time as possible to frames for paying clients, it is likely that Maurice made the frames for his own paintings, or exchanged time helping Charles with outside commissions for Charles's help with the occasional special frame. As a rule Maurice charged for the frame when he sold a painting, and thus the brothers were paid for their labors. But frames needed to be made for exhibitions whether the works sold or not, and thus the time invested in each one needed to be carefully calculated. Charles later estimated that a "big" frame took him six or more weeks to produce while "little" ones took about two.[9] Maurice's first major exhibition in Boston in 1897[10] required about twenty small frames for monotypes, for which Charles and Maurice must have designed a simple frame that they could produce relatively quickly—more quickly than the standard two weeks apiece.

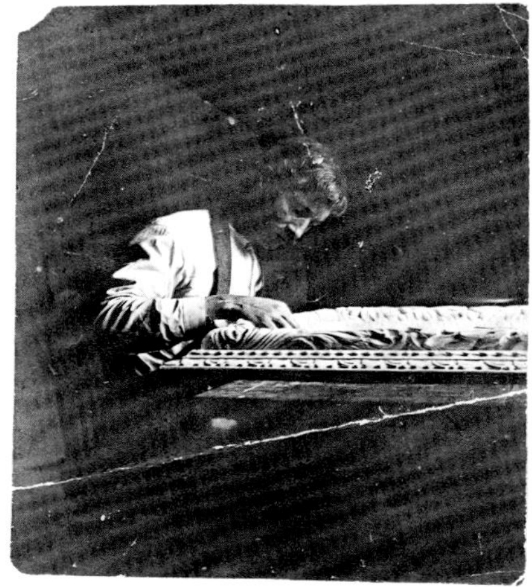

FIGURE 2. Anonymous, *Charles Prendergast*, ca. 1895-1905, photograph (3⅜ x 2⅜ in.), Williams College Museum of Art, Prendergast Archive and Study Center

In this way Maurice was drawn into a framemaking partnership with his brother that lasted for at least twenty years. Maurice became skillful with woodcarving tools and learned from Charles the secrets of gesso, glue sizing, and gold leaf. In return, Maurice kept Charles engaged in the artistic ferment that was bringing modernism into the American cultural consciousness and which Maurice sought out in Boston, New York, and Paris. As Maurice's colleague, Charles, like few other professional framemakers, saw his craft as part of a larger movement that was affecting the way people saw and thought about art. While modernist ideas had invaded the circles of craftsmen like Charles and spurred the Arts and Crafts Movement of the turn of the century, Charles had the added advantage of an intimate acquaintance with modernist painting.

Both Charles and Maurice believed in copying frame designs from American and European sources and used pattern books as well as their own volumes of hand-drawn notations of observed frames as guides. Thanks to the emphasis on "originality" in modernist aesthetics, Charles took the patterns as merely suggestions and turned them into compositions of his own design. He emphasized the fact that he designed as well as carved his own frames, in contrast to the typical framemaker who tended to mechanically reproduce whatever pattern was put before him. The craftsman, he believed, "must become an artist as well."[11]

To Charles Prendergast (fig. 2), being an artist meant adopting many of the ideas currently in vogue among modern painters. Not only must the woodcarver go beyond rigidly duplicated patterns to the actual flowers, vines, birds, etc. they are based on, the true artist must not imitate nature either, but instead adopt and modify the "forms of nature to suit the method of his work."[12] Charles Prendergast's description of the qualities to be achieved in woodcarving are strongly reminiscent of the qualities his brother sought in painting: "A piece of good wood-carving seems to have motion, so full of life is it. It should have a crispness, and energy and freedom which comes from knowledge and appreciation of material. . . . We want men who will take up their own work as artists, that is, and will not be satisfied to be mere copyists, supplying imitations of all styles."[13] Furthermore, Charles Prendergast absorbed the current idea in modernist painting that traditional standards of perfection were stifling art and that the artist must recapture some of the freshness of childlike or primitive vision. In Paris in 1907, Maurice had been bowled over by the primitivism of the Fauves and other radical experiments in painting and had since adopted a more spontaneous and colorful style. For Charles, this concept could be applied equally well to craftsmanship: "As we grow up, the primitive instinct seems to be all knocked out of us, and when we take up the crafts in after life, they seem to be labored and uninteresting. . . ."[14] The creative necessity of nurturing one's childlike or primitive side would become more and more evident in Charles Prendergast's later pictorial work, but it is important to recognize that it was already formulated during Prendergast's career as a framemaker.

By 1912, when Charles Prendergast executed his first carved and painted pictorial panels, he had already begun to introduce areas of pure color onto his frame moldings, making frames that were only a step away from being actual paintings. Yet long before that, he had manipulated color and pattern in traditional gold frames in a way that was recognized as painterly. Charles and his frame collaborator, Hermann Dudley Murphy, had developed a keen sense of how to use traditional framemaking materials and methods to continue the artistry of the painting onto the frame. Murphy described how important it was to study the painting first so that one could choose a frame design to complement its composition and character: "If there are large planes in the picture, the ornament must possess correspondingly large planes; if, on the other hand, the facture is minute and delicate the 'profile' and carving of the frame must be light and delicate, while strong, forceful subjects require bold relief in ornament and 'profile.'"[15] After the frame is carved, the framemaker must decide on the colors of the gold leaf (of which there were at least eighteen available) and then tone the gold with a colored varnish. For a Monet painting, for instance, Murphy said he chose a "very pale, greenish gold, which [he] 'toned' with violet grey."[16] In the Murphy-Prendergast approach to the frame, color plays a subtle but important part, noticeable only to the most discerning eye. As Prendergast put it, "Wood-carving is a beautiful art, and it requires a refined taste to appreciate it. Its beauties are all of a quiet kind."[17]

Charles Prendergast found that his artistic approach to framemaking coincided sufficiently with Murphy's that they agreed to form a frame business in 1903. Called Carrig-Rohane, the workshop employed assistant woodcarvers and provided its clients with frames based on a variety of historic styles; but Charles Prendergast appears to have tackled the more original or custom commissions. One of these was for Thomas Lawson, a wealthy financier, who wanted specialized frames for two large paintings of his bulldogs[18] (fig. 3). For this commission, Prendergast and Lawson decided to include incised drawings of bulldogs by themselves and at the sides of little girls in a whimsical departure from traditional frame decoration. Maurice's hand can be clearly seen in the drawing of the little figures and the frame is signed with both of their names.

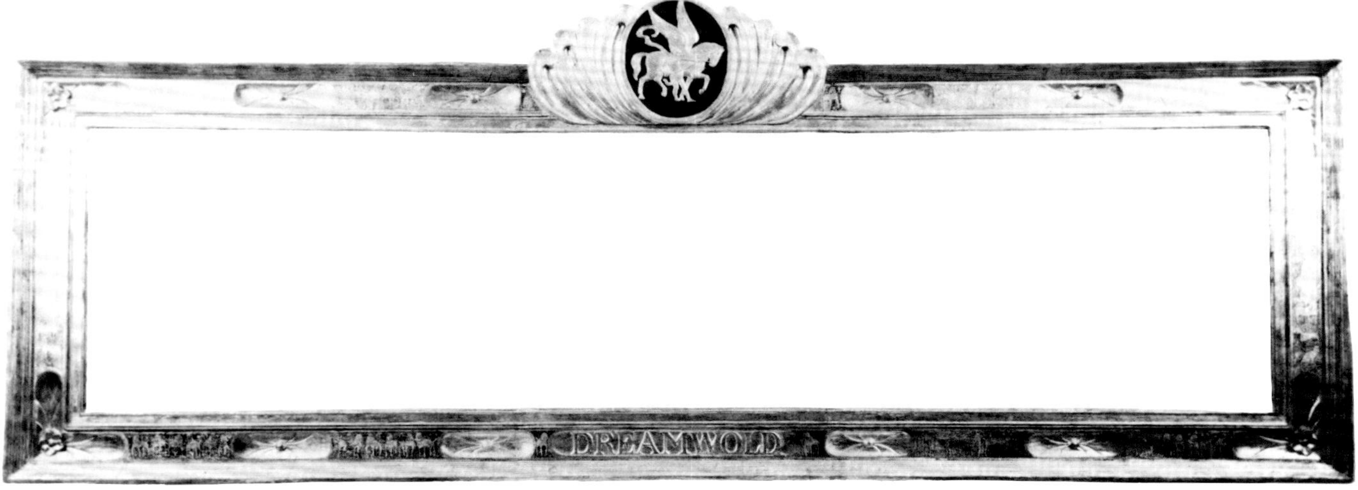

FIGURE 3. Charles Prendergast, *Dreamwold Frame*, 1908, 23-karat gold leaf and tempera on bass wood (40¾ x 108 x 3 in.), Gift of Salander-O'Reilly Galleries, Terra Museum of American Art, Chicago, M1988.1

Charles does not seem to have continued as an active participant in the Carrig-Rohane workshop beyond 1903, particularly after he and his brother moved back into Boston from Winchester where Murphy and the workshop were located. Murphy and Prendergast may have found that although their philosophy of the artistic frame was shared, their approach to the making of frames was not. Prendergast, as far as can be documented, believed in making the entire frame himself (or with the help of his brother) while Murphy immediately employed not only carving assistants but the decorative arts specialist Walfred Thulin (1878-1949) who later took over the entire enterprise. Prendergast's emphasis on the hand of the artist, perceptible in every facet of the frame's construction, made his frames highly prized and bolstered his reputation as an artist-framemaker, leaving the frame business on a large scale to Murphy and Thulin.

Charles Prendergast routinely listed his occupation as "artist" (rather than craftsman, framemaker, etc.) and in 1901 became a member of Boston's leading artists' association, the Copley Society, which his brother had joined in 1898. In 1908 he briefly joined the Boston Society of Arts and Crafts, probably because they held exhibitions of picture and mirror frames.[19] Such an exhibition was a tribute to the artistry of the contemporary framemakers working in the Boston area and was one of the few times frames were treated as fine art. By 1909 Charles Prendergast was considered the leader in the new frame movement and was described as "the first professional artist, so far as is known, to open a frame shop and to solicit work from other painters."[20] Although this description, which appeared in the New York weekly *American Art News*, may have conflated Maurice and Charles since it mistakenly implies that Charles was originally a painter, it nevertheless captures the image of an artist-framemaker that Charles had so carefully nurtured.

It is also significant that the published writings about Charles Prendergast in 1909 and 1910, when he was at the height of his fame as a framemaker, do not mention his brother. Although Maurice was well-known in the Boston area and had gained notoriety in progressive art circles in 1908 as a member of The Eight,

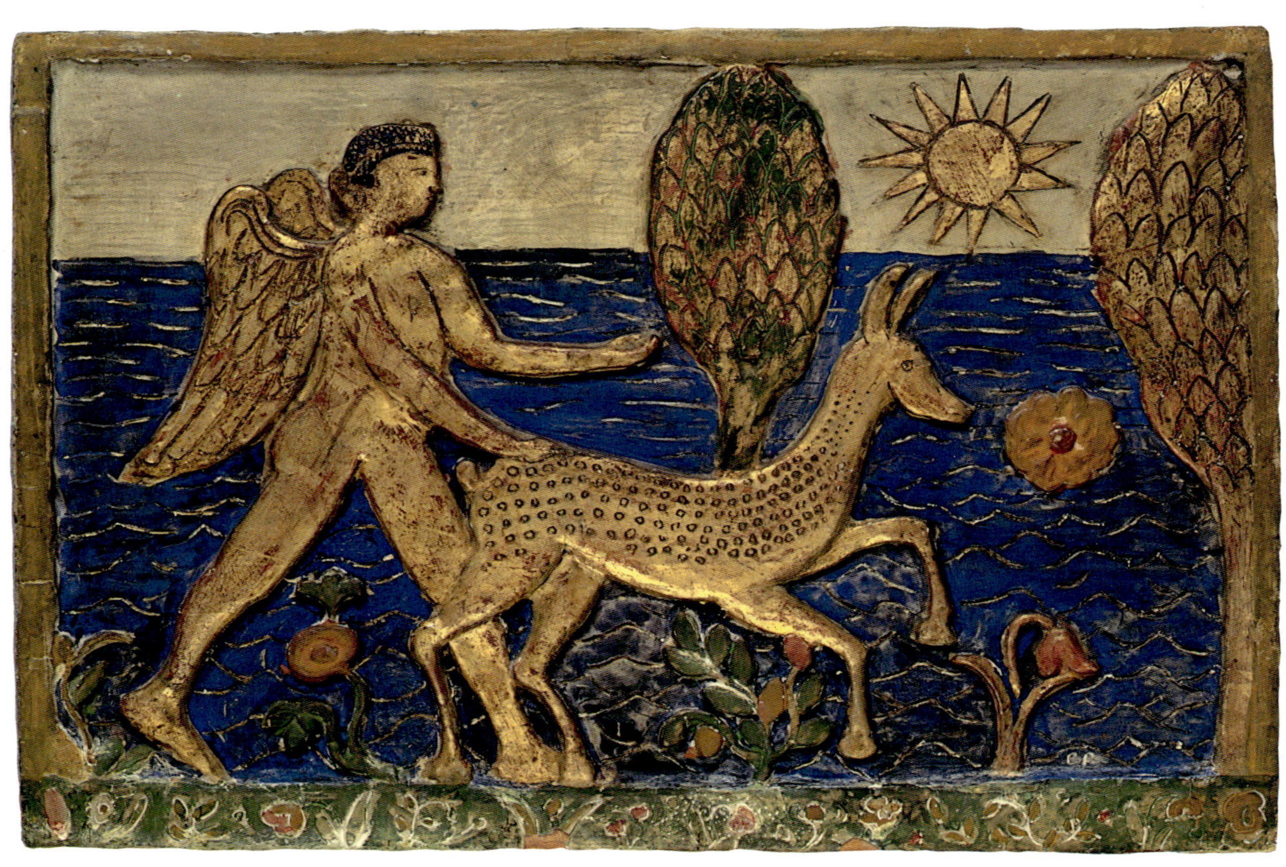

FIGURE 4. Charles Prendergast, *Rising Sun*, ca. 1912, Williams College Museum of Art (see p. 56)

he was apparently not well enough known at this point to have singlehandedly boosted Charles's reputation.

In 1911 Charles Prendergast decided to spend the summer in Italy. It had been years since he traveled abroad[21] and the trip signalled a new financial and professional security. Since Charles went without Maurice (Maurice joined him at the end of the summer), he was not merely accompanying his brother on a painting trip. As Charles's earliest surviving sketchbook ("Sketchbook D," CR 2409, Museum of Fine Arts, Boston) dates from this trip, we might postulate that he planned this trip to be a springboard into the pictorial arts. This hypothesis is supported by the fact that Charles's frames around this time broke new ground in using color (blue and gold and blue, rose, and gold) and in high sculptural relief of rosettes, birds, and angels' heads. This experimentation with color and naturalistic form in his frames brought him to the threshold of a new medium—the carved pictorial panel.

Italy was a revelation to him; he loved the sensation of stepping into the past. He studied the frames and woodcarving he found in antique shops and in the hands of local craftsmen, bringing several of them home with him. He bought photographs of Italian art, architecture, and design to add to the brothers' study collection. And after he returned he began his first panel, *Rising Sun* (fig. 4; CR 2212, WCMA), as if to capture the antique spirit so vividly conveyed in the rich Italian artistic tradition. For years afterward he experimented with overtly Christian subjects (angels, Madonnas, and other biblical subjects), and while he drew his actual motifs from a variety of sources once he returned to the United States,[22] the idea of the gilded pictorial panel that would give the viewer a glimpse of an exotic, timeless world was one powerfully communicated in the churches and museums of Italy.

Beyond the general notion that Charles Prendergast's 1911 trip to Italy was seminal, very little else is known about the origins, sources, and intentions of these new pictorial panels. He began producing them slowly, at the rate of three or four a year, dividing his days between work on the panels and his frame commissions. The first panels were done in Boston in the large studio he shared with Maurice at 56 Mount Vernon Street. It is not known whether he tried to exhibit them in Boston, or if he considered them more than just a casual departure from his professional frame work. But soon after he and Maurice moved to New York in late 1914, he was engaged to show two of his panels in a group exhibition of paintings, drawings, and sculpture at the Montross Gallery, and this led to an increasingly active schedule of exhibiting, selling, and participation in artists' associations. As if to signal his new identity, the American Art Annual's 1915 "Who's Who in Art" lists Charles Prendergast as a painter.[23]

In his first few panels such as *Rising Sun*, Prendergast attempted a sculpted relief effect that ties his panels to the tradition of relief sculpture and suggests parallels with contemporary work by artists known to him such as Paul Gauguin (1848-1903) and Raymond Duchamp-Villon (1876-1918). Another parallel exists in the art of carving of wood blocks for printing, practiced by many artists around Prendergast or known to him such as Arthur Wesley Dow (1857-1922) who had adopted the Japanese art of woodblock printing or, again, Paul Gauguin whose Tahitian prints bear a striking similarity to Prendergast's "primitive" compositions.

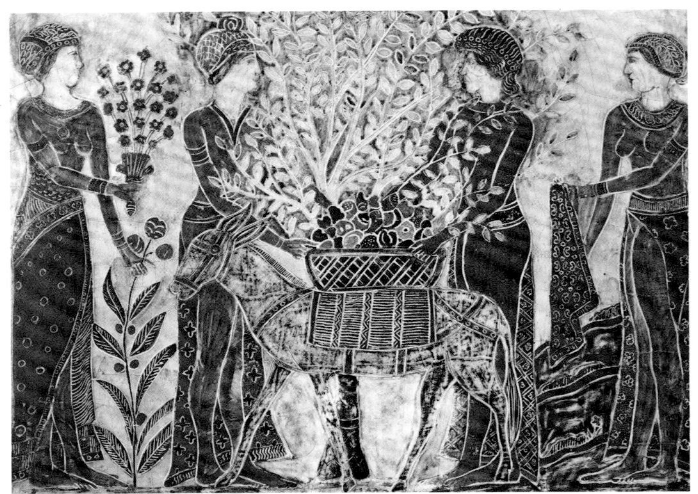

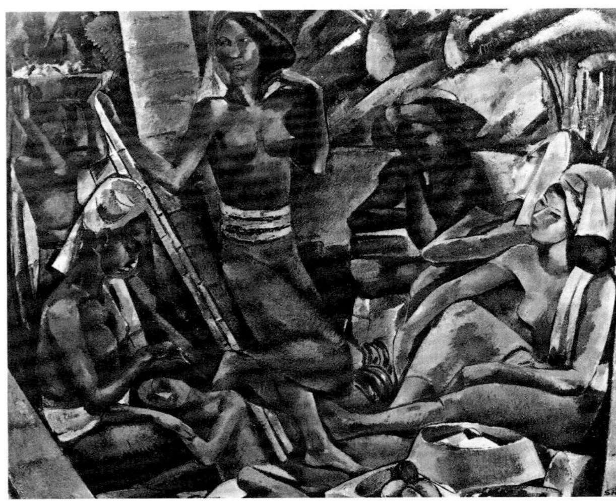

FIGURE 5. (left) Charles Prendergast, *Four Figures and Donkey with Basket of Flowers*, ca. 1915-17, incised gesso, tempera, and gold leaf on panel (17⅞ x 23¾ in.), Terra Foundation for the Arts, Daniel J. Terra Collection, 1992.60 (Courtesy of Terra Museum of American Art, Chicago)

FIGURE 6. (right) Maurice Sterne, *Resting at the Bazaar*, 1912, oil on canvas (26¾ x 31½ in.), Collection The Museum of Modern Art, New York, Abby Aldrich Rockefeller Fund

Charles Prendergast soon abandoned the high relief of *Rising Sun* for the use of incised lines to suggest low relief as in Egyptian or Mesopotamian mural reliefs (e.g., *Four Figures and Donkey with Basket of Flowers*, ca. 1915-17 [fig. 5; CR 2246, Daniel J. Terra Collection, Terra Museum of American Art, Chicago]). The lower relief and incised panels also relate to sources in two-dimensional media (rather than sculpture or carved woodblock prints) such as the one source Prendergast himself acknowledged: Chinese and Persian miniatures. Prendergast remembered studying them in the Museum of Fine Arts when he lived in Boston and was struck by the effect of miniaturization and colorful simplification. He responded to them first as a professional artist. As book arts, meant to accompany a text, miniatures had the advantage of being part of the decorative arts tradition, a tradition dear to Charles Prendergast. The non-Western, simplified anatomy and spatial constructions also suited an artist who had not undergone the rigorous training needed to master the Renaissance styles popular in art schools and in Western high art. With his keen eye and skill in decorative effects, this was a style of painting that was useful to him.

Beyond his professional interest was a delight in the aspects of the miniatures that have the most basic appeal to Westerners: the childlike response to the size of the worlds that are created and the anticipation of a story in the narrative pictures, even if it is not known to the Western viewer. Prendergast indulged his own childlike response to them in recalling the long-ago pleasure: "My, my!" he says. "I thought it was wonderful—those little animals, those little trees, those little houses, all painted so slick and fine. I couldn't get over them."[24]

Charles Prendergast's sources in ancient, "oriental," "primitive," and medieval art were not unusual among the artists in the Prendergast circle in New York in the teens. While there were no other carved panels in Charles's first exhibition, there were works that drew on some of the same sources. Maurice Sterne (1878-1957), for instance, had just returned to New York after traveling to Egypt, India, Burma, and Bali where he spent two years. In the spirit of Gauguin, Sterne painted large compositions of nude Balinese women in various contemplative poses (fig. 6). Sterne quickly established himself as a leading modernist in New York on the basis of this exotic subject matter and a stylized approach to form. There is more than an echo of Sterne in such works as *Four Figures and Donkey with Basket of Flowers*.

Even Prendergast's use of gold leaf in his pictorial compositions was not without parallel in the work of artists who exhibited with him. In a similar show at Montross the next year (1916), Prendergast was accompanied by such artists as Herbert Crowley, whose style was conservative enough to please critics who objected to the more extreme styles of Joseph Stella (1880-1946) and Max Weber (1881-1961, also shown in the exhibition), but who, like Charles Prendergast, was experimental enough to use gold leaf in his paintings. Other kindred spirits among the artists exhibiting with Prendergast were Arthur Wesley Dow, an old friend from Boston who had devoted two decades to the study of Japanese art, and Gari Melchers (1860-1932), who had an academic painting style but studied folk ways in Europe and America and particularly liked to portray peasant mothers and children in Madonna-esque poses.

Not surprisingly, the artist closest in style and subject matter to Charles Prendergast was his brother, although that was not always obvious from the works hung side by side in exhibitions from 1915 on. In 1916 at Montross, for instance, Maurice showed a richly painted tapestry-like "landscape with figures" which, although unidentified, was no doubt a park scene with nude and clothed figures. Charles's entry, on the other hand, was a flat frieze of four dancing women drawn against a white background of bare gesso now called *Trees and Dancers* (fig. 7; CR 2221, Collection of Mimi and Sanford Feld). It was eye-catching in its starkness and its evocation of the antique. The two works showed the vast gulf between Maurice and Charles in their approach to the pictorial surface. Maurice had spent years experimenting with the qualities of paint and color to make the surface resonate with movement and emotion. He had studied the tenets of modernism so that he could stretch the limits of traditional painting and arrive at his own unique pictorial form. In contrast, Charles, as a framemaker, had devoted his life to the carved, decorative surface with its repeating forms and use of schematic motifs to create a "period" look. His panel, *Trees and Dancers*, capitalizes on just these qualities now transformed into pictorial form so that the quaint dancers miraculously come to life in their white

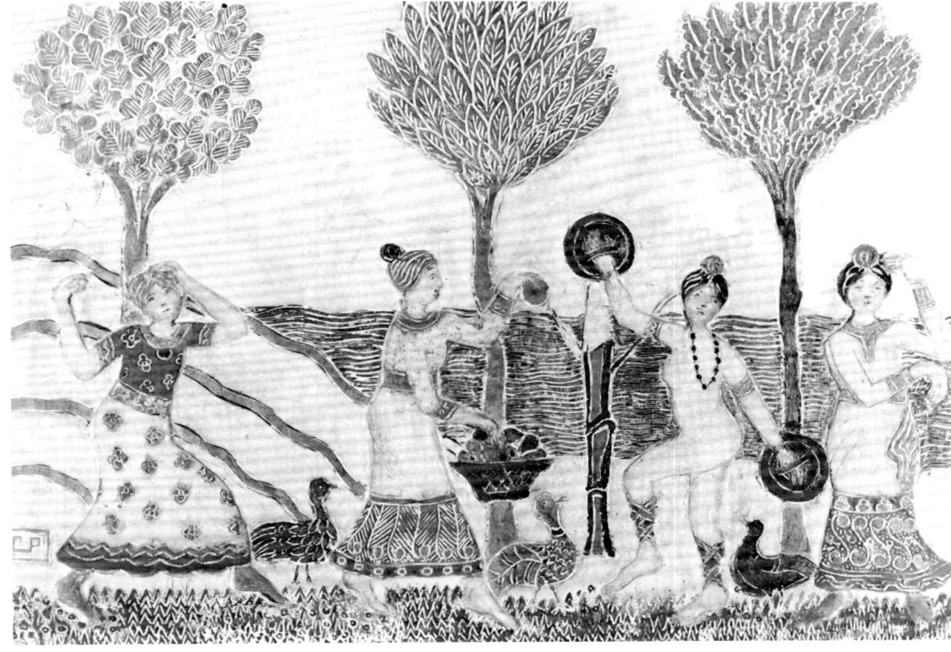

FIGURE 7. Charles Prendergast, *Trees and Dancers*, ca. 1915, oil and gold leaf on incised, carved, and gessoed panel (15½ x 22⅛ in.), Collection of Mimi and Sanford Feld

marmoreal atmosphere. When two such different works hung side by side it was obvious that the brothers had their own distinct artistic personalities; indeed Maurice and Charles probably chose works for public exhibition that would stress their differences.

However, if you were to go into their shared studio, it would become clear that overall there were many similarities in their work and that they relished many of the same ideas and motifs. From 1912 until 1915, they both explored the world of the antique and exotic, the childlike and the primitive. They drew on myriad sources gleaned from visits to museums and galleries as well as their avid reading of art books and periodicals. They both drew on these sources to evoke an idyllic world, a golden age that gave pleasure and solace to an audience increasingly burdened with the exigencies of modern life and the approaching world war.

Charles Prendergast in particular was drawn to subjects that symbolized fruitfulness, renewal, and rebirth as in *Rising Sun, Annunciation* (CR 2215, WCMA, p. 58), and *The Offering* (CR 2218, Last known at Christie's). One might speculate that his interest in these themes arose not only from the deteriorating world situation, but also from his own joy in his second career. To be reborn as a figural artist and painter at the time many of his friends were facing retirement was a blessing for which he never stopped being grateful. Furthermore, his skillful adoption of ancient and folk art motifs allowed this message to be communicated without the self-consciousness that marred similar eclectic efforts of such contemporaries as Arthur B. Davies (1862-1928).

The primary vehicle both Prendergast brothers chose for evoking the golden age was the monumental female figure shown either nude or semi-nude, or clothed with costumes from an antique or exotic culture. Both tended to distribute the figures in a rhythmic, frieze-like arrangement in poses that suggest group interaction or dancing. An example of this mutual interest is the similarity of Maurice's *Fantasy* (fig. 8; CR 385, WCMA) to Charles's *Dancers* (fig. 9; CR 2227, Museum of Fine Arts, Boston). The dancers take on similar poses and are both surrounded by stylized trees and foliage. In another example, Charles's *Flight of the Birds* (fig. 10; CR 2225, Addison Gallery of American Art) uses the same background as Maurice's *Blue Mountains* (fig. 11; CR 377, WCMA): a row of

FIGURE 8. (left) Maurice Prendergast, *Fantasy*, ca. 1914-15, oil on panel (22 x 26 in.), Williams College Museum of Art, Gift of Mrs. Charles Prendergast (85.45)

FIGURE 9. (right) Charles Prendergast, *Dancers*, ca. 1915, incised gesso, watercolor, and gold leaf on panel (23 x 31 in.), Gift of the Eugénie Prendergast Foundation, Inc., Courtesy Museum of Fine Arts, Boston (1971.23)

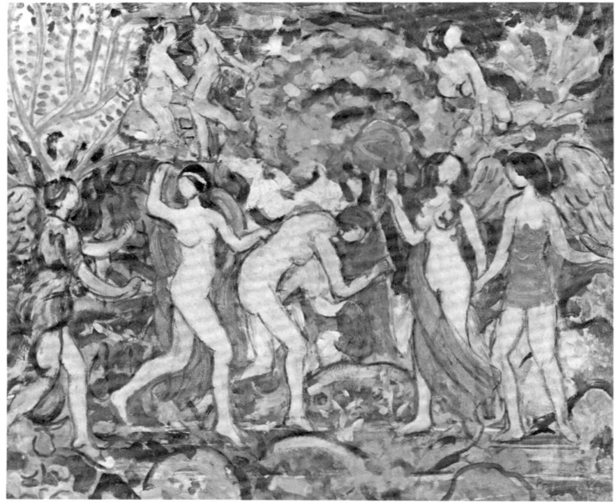

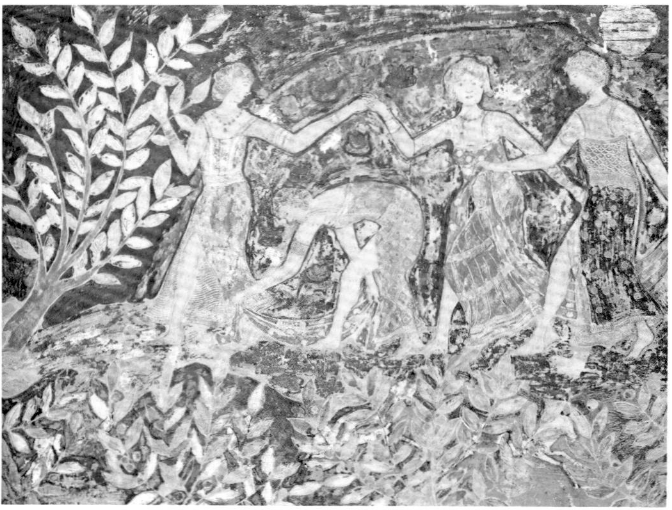

brilliant blue mountains striped by horizontal bands of clouds. The horse and rider are similar to another of Maurice's paintings of these mountains (*Rider Against Blue Hills* [fig. 12; CR 376, WCMA]). Basso mentions that Charles's *Flight of the Birds* uses elements from the illustrations for the Persian epic *Shah-nama*,[25] and thus the sharing between Maurice and Charles shows them both working from a Persian source. It is important to note, however, that in such cases the brothers have avoided actual duplication of each other as if conscious of protecting their own identities.

The Prendergasts also avoided collaboration except on occasional frames, and, after they moved to New York in 1914, even that seemed to decline. There are no hints of Charles taking a brush to help Maurice finish a large canvas or Maurice taking a chisel to work on one of Charles's panels. However, in one important instance the two artists worked together on a large panel to the extent that they both signed and documented it as a collaborative effort. Titled *The Spirit of the Hunt* (fig. 13; CR 1171/2251, Collection of Mr. and Mrs. Jon Landau), it is so

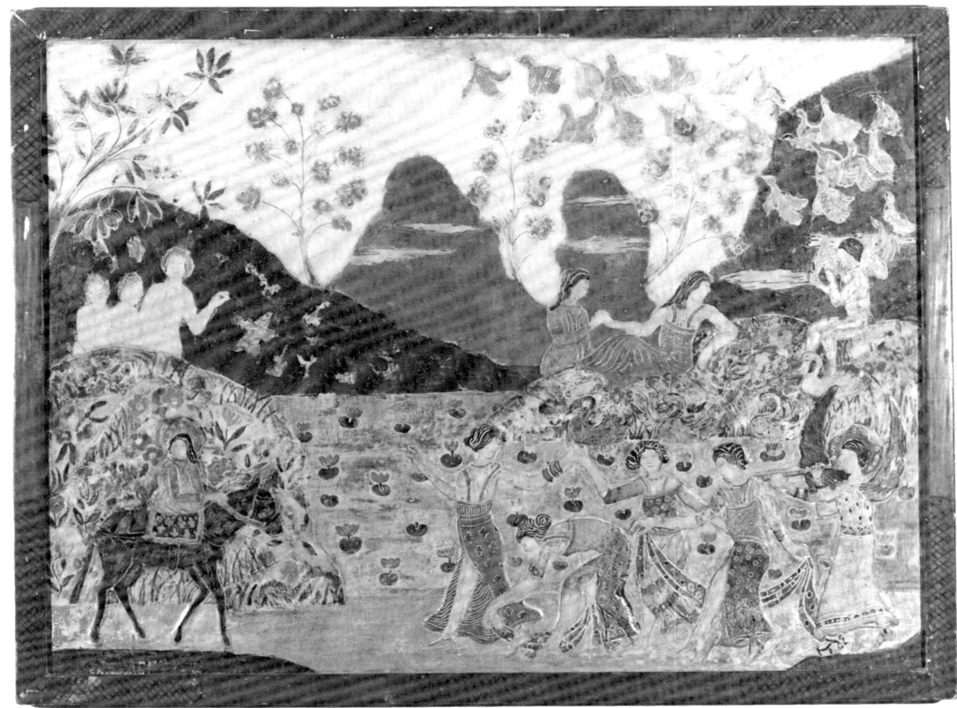

FIGURE 10. (top left) Charles Prendergast, *Flight of the Birds*, ca. 1915, tempera, pencil, gold and silver leaf on incised, carved, and gessoed panel (23 x 31 in.), Gift of anonymous donor, (1928.47) © Addison Gallery of American Art, Phillips Academy, Andover, Massachusetts. All rights reserved

FIGURE 11. (bottom left) Maurice Prendergast, *Blue Mountains*, ca. 1914-15, oil on canvas (16¼ x 25⅝ in.), Williams College Museum of Art, Gift of Mrs. Charles Prendergast (91.18.2)

FIGURE 12. (right) Maurice Prendergast, *Rider Against Blue Hills*, ca. 1914- 15, oil on canvas (20 x 30¼ in.), Williams College Museum of Art, Gift of Mrs. Charles Prendergast (86.18.10)

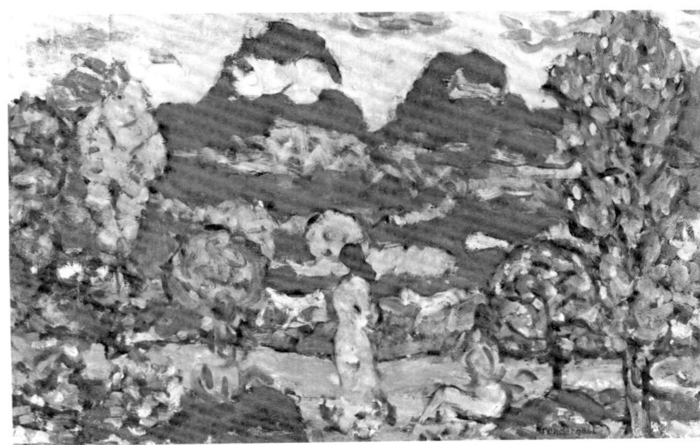

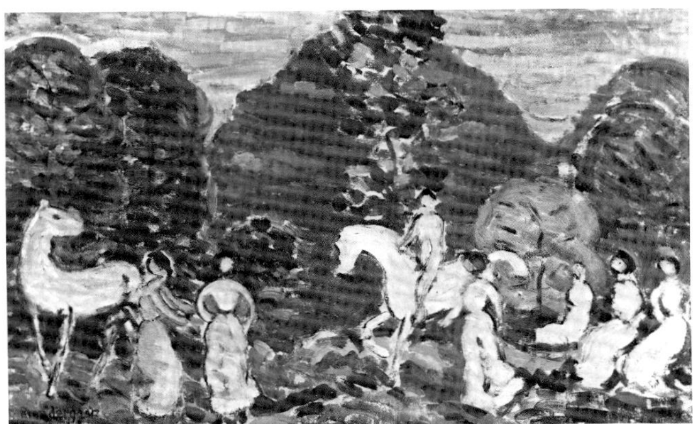

close to the style of Charles that researchers have looked in vain for any sign of Maurice's hand in either the design or the execution of the piece. Since Maurice's co-authorship was overtly proclaimed, we can only conclude that *The Spirit of the Hunt* is an excellent example of Maurice following Charles's style so closely that his own identity was completely subsumed—a skill he must have learned in the years of helping with Charles's frames.

Even though there is no detectable evidence of Maurice's hand in the execution of the panel, the work can be taken as a summary of the shared motifs that permeate the brothers' work throughout the teens. The central group of three women, a version of the three graces, was a favorite motif of Maurice's and could be seen in his most important work of 1915, *The Picnic* (fig. 14; CR 388, National Gallery of Canada) among many others. Other shared devices include the

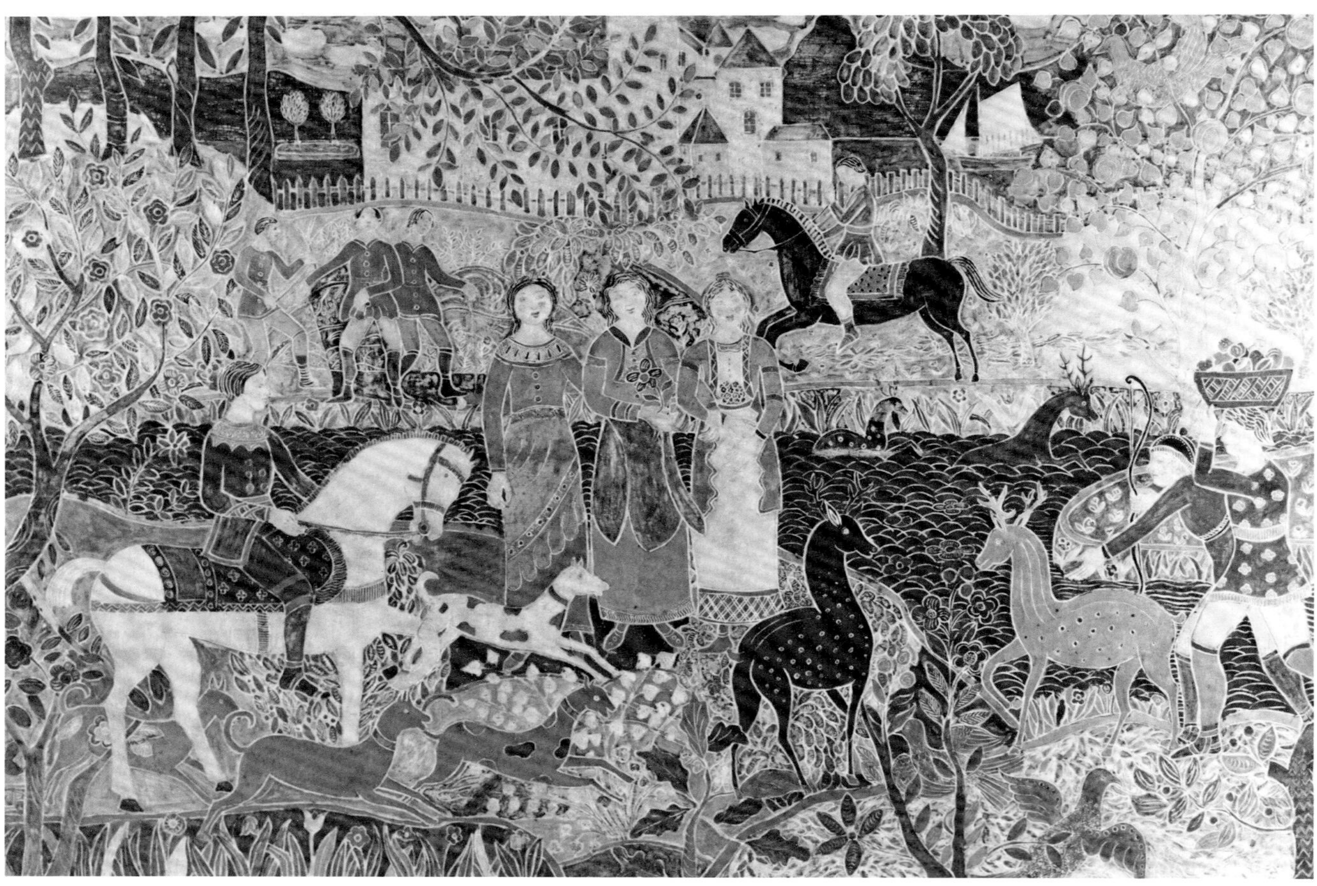

FIGURE 13. Charles Prendergast and Maurice Prendergast, *The Spirit of the Hunt*, ca. 1917, incised gesso, tempera, pencil, and gold and silver leaf on panel (55 x 80½ in.), Collection of Mr. and Mrs. Jon Landau, photograph courtesy of Salander-O'Reilly Galleries, Inc.

horseback rider approaching the women from the left, the lake, and the distant town as well as the stylized trees.

The panel is saved from being just another version of Maurice's typical idyllic composition by the inclusion of certain touches that were Charles's own: the folk costumes of the women, the castle-like architecture, and Charles's favorite animal, the deer. The composition even follows the story of St. Eustace who stopped short of shooting a deer when the sign of the cross appeared to him in the deer's antlers. Although Charles Prendergast omitted such an overt Christian symbol as the cross itself, the celebratory spirit that pervades the composition and the offerings presented by the three maidens as well as the man on the right carrying a basket of fruit on his head suggest that the spirit of *this* hunt brings salvation rather than slaughter.

Since it is so rare that two artists should work in the same studio year after year, it is important to understand the exact nature of the Prendergasts' professional relationship. The picture that emerges from a comparison of their work and from their letters and other documents is that of two men having strong

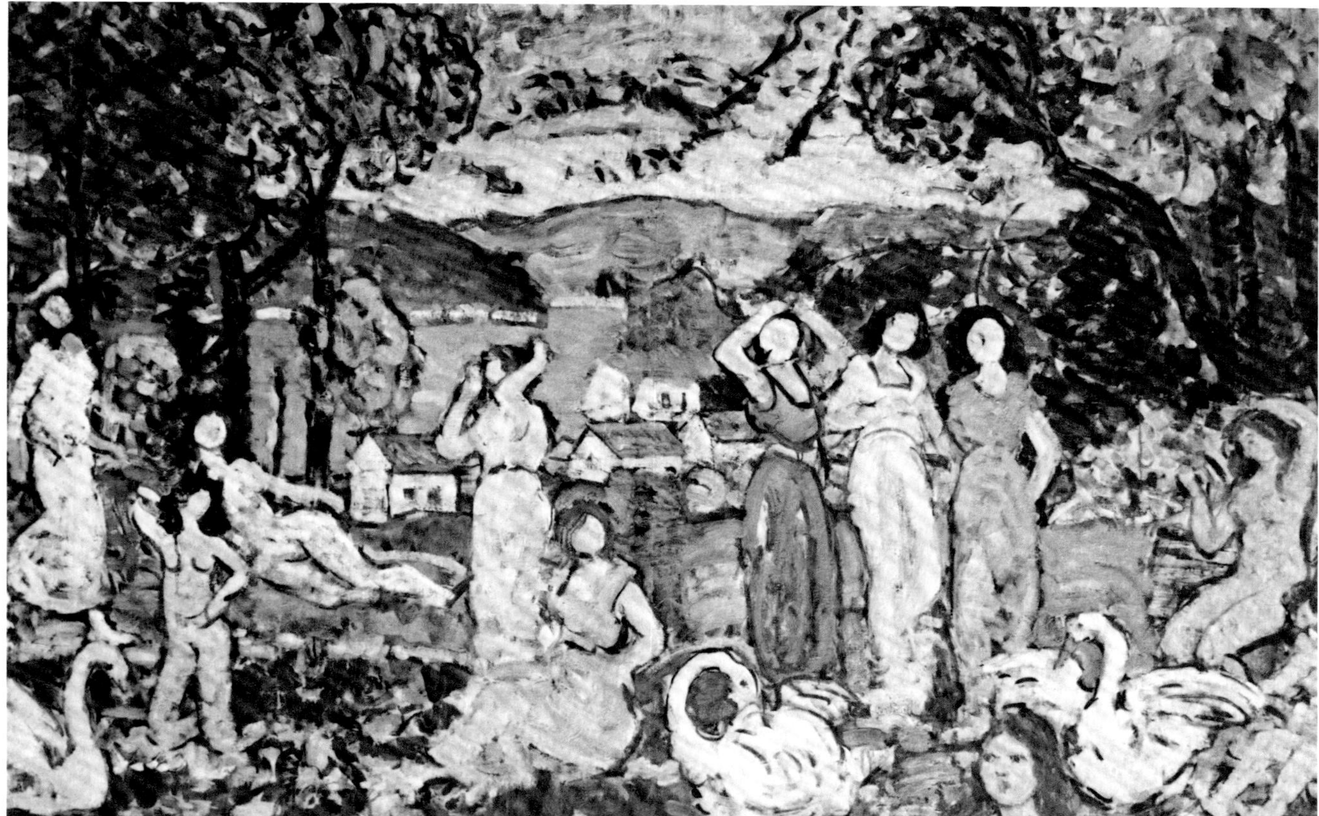

FIGURE 14. Maurice Prendergast, *The Picnic*, ca. 1914-15, oil on canvas (37 x 57 in.), Collection of the National Gallery of Canada (4528)

personal directions in art. That they shared ideas and interests, that they encouraged one another, is indisputable. But they also made their own decisions in terms of their creative process as well as their professional conduct outside the studio. For instance, neither one acted as a business agent for the other; if a collector or dealer wanted something from both, he had to approach each one separately (although they cordially passed on messages to each other). They had the same circle of personal and professional friends, but they did not necessarily join the same societies. Charles was an active member of the short-lived group called the Penguins in 1917 and 1918 while Maurice was only an exhibitor. When the Society of Independent Artists was incorporated in 1917, Charles was Vice-President and on the Board of Directors while Maurice again only exhibited. In 1919 their mutual friend, the writer M. D. C. Crawford, published a short article on Charles Prendergast's carved gesso panels in *Country Life in America* without mentioning Maurice. And although many of the same collectors such as John Quinn, Lillie Bliss, and Albert Barnes bought from both of them, it was Charles who had the closer personal relationship with them. People who knew the brothers in the later teens and twenties got the impression that Charles was the practical one who took care of his hearing-impaired older brother, but the evidence shows that the brothers each took care of his own affairs, offering assistance when needed while maintaining his independence.

In 1921, after Charles had been producing panels for almost ten years, the brothers were paid the compliment of being asked to provide the inaugural exhibition for a new gallery in New York, established by the Frenchman Joseph Brummer. Brummer shared the Prendergasts' interest in mixing modernist and antique art and installed their works in the second floor gallery above a floor of Greek, Egyptian, and Gothic pieces. The juxtaposition of old and new worked very well for the Prendergasts, particularly for Charles whose eight panels were universally admired by critics. Two years later, another old friend, Walter Pach, wrote a profile of Charles in the popular magazine *Shadowland*, which paralleled a similar article he published on Maurice the year before. Pach's tribute confirmed that Charles's decade of participation in the New York art world had brought him a legitimate standing in that elite company and that he had made "a valuable contribution to American achievement."[26]

Only nine months after the Pach article appeared, Maurice Prendergast died, probably from prostate cancer, leaving Charles alone in their New York studio and apartment at 50 Washington Square South. The loss of his closest companion—both personally and professionally—brought Charles to a standstill. Toward the end of 1924, he was persuaded to take a trip to Europe with some friends and in Paris he met a young French woman with whom he discovered an instant rapport. He married Eugénie Van Kemmel in New York in May of 1925. After his marriage he was once more in a loving protected environment, and he began to put his professional life back together again.

After Maurice's death, Charles's standing in the New York art world seemed to increase rather than decrease. Partly this was because he was now the keeper of Maurice's flame, and the numerous memorial exhibitions and tributes to Maurice in the next ten years required his generous participation. He began to associate not only with artists and dealers but with museum directors, curators, and art history writers. As in the past, Maurice's reputation opened doors for him, but Charles established himself on his own. For instance, the Kraushaar Gallery mounted the first memorial exhibition of Maurice's work in 1925 and then became the principal dealer for Charles. The Whitney Museum of American Art held a major retrospective of Maurice Prendergast in 1934 and its director, Juliana Force, became a close friend of Charles and Eugénie. Charles also drew closer to Lillie Bliss, an early collector of Maurice's work who then became devoted to Charles's work. He also came into the orbit of Abby Aldrich Rockefeller who bought Maurice's paintings for the Museum of Modern Art but also collected and commissioned works from Charles. Albert Barnes, who had competed with John Quinn for Maurice's paintings, later became a close friend of Charles and major collector of his work over the years. Even after Charles and Eugénie moved out of the city to Westport, Connecticut, they continued to move in the highest New York art circles.

From the time of Maurice's death until about 1932, Charles's art followed a number of disparate directions. One was the familiar route of continuing the fantasy panels that he had begun in the teens, such as *Hill Town* (fig. 16; CR 2260, Addison Gallery of American Art). Another was to revive his interest in the decorative arts, particularly in making carved and painted chests and small boxes that evoked both Italian Renaissance *cassone* and American folk crafts. He

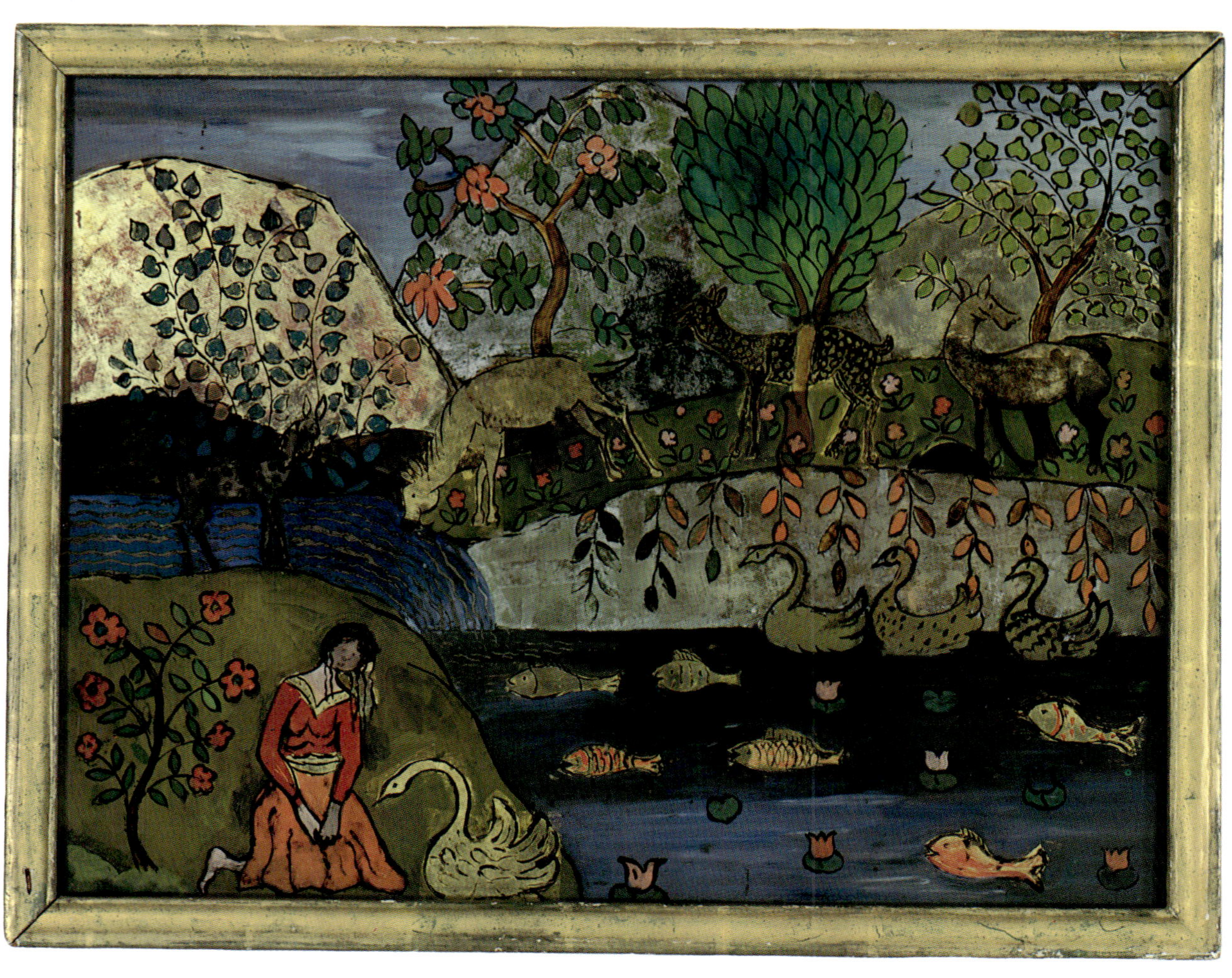

FIGURE 15. Charles Prendergast, *Decoration on Glass*, ca. 1925-30 [?], Collection of Mrs. Charles Prendergast (see p. 72)

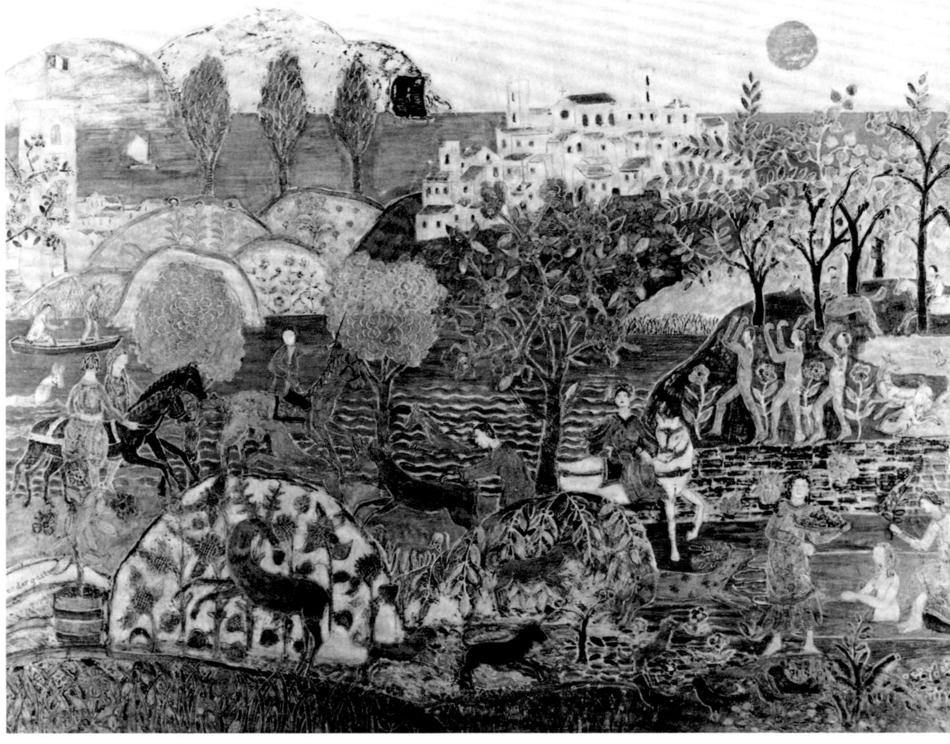

FIGURE 16. Charles Prendergast, *Hill Town*, ca. 1928, incised gesso, tempera, pencil, and gold leaf on panel (38½ x 48½ in.), Bequest of Miss L. P. Bliss, (1931.91) © Addison Gallery of American Art, Phillips Academy, Andover, Massachusetts. All rights reserved

also created a number of painted and gilded pictorial compositions on glass such as *Decoration on Glass* (fig. 15; CR 2233, Collection of Mrs. Charles Prendergast). Finally, he painted a series of watercolors of the hill towns along the southern coast of France after two trips he made with Eugénie in 1927 and 1929.

The hill-town water colors, of which there are twenty-five known examples, are a surprising departure from Charles's earlier pictorial work. Only a handful of drawings and works on paper have survived from the period before 1927, indicating that he did not produce works in this medium for exhibit or sale and that he did not save the cartoons he used for the panels themselves.[27] Furthermore, Charles is not known to have sketched frequently from nature, and only one early travel sketchbook (Italy, 1911 [CR 2409, Museum of Fine Arts, Boston]) exists. But on his trips to France in 1927 and 1929, he was inspired to sketch the patterns of these real-life medieval hill towns as if he suddenly found that such towns existed outside of fairy tales. He tended to simplify forms in a distinctly cubist manner and may have had in mind Cézanne's watercolors of Mont Sainte Victoire, which Maurice had long admired, or even the early cubist works of Picasso and Braque. Charles is not known to have exhibited the hill-town watercolors, but instead kept them as a reference for architectural motifs in future panels. Hill towns can be found in the backgrounds of such panels as *Hill Town*, *The Fountain* (fig. 17; CR 2263, Museum of Fine Arts, Boston), and *Holiday Beach Scene* (fig. 18; CR 2265, WCMA). The hill-town motif came in for special mention in Suzanne LaFollette's tribute to Charles in her influential and early history of American art, *Art in America* (1929): "Here is a little hill town, souvenir of a sojourn in Italy or southern France, and at its foot the blue waters of a Mediterranean bay. If the landscape and the birds and animals are from the sketchbook, however, happily combined into delightful patterns, the people are

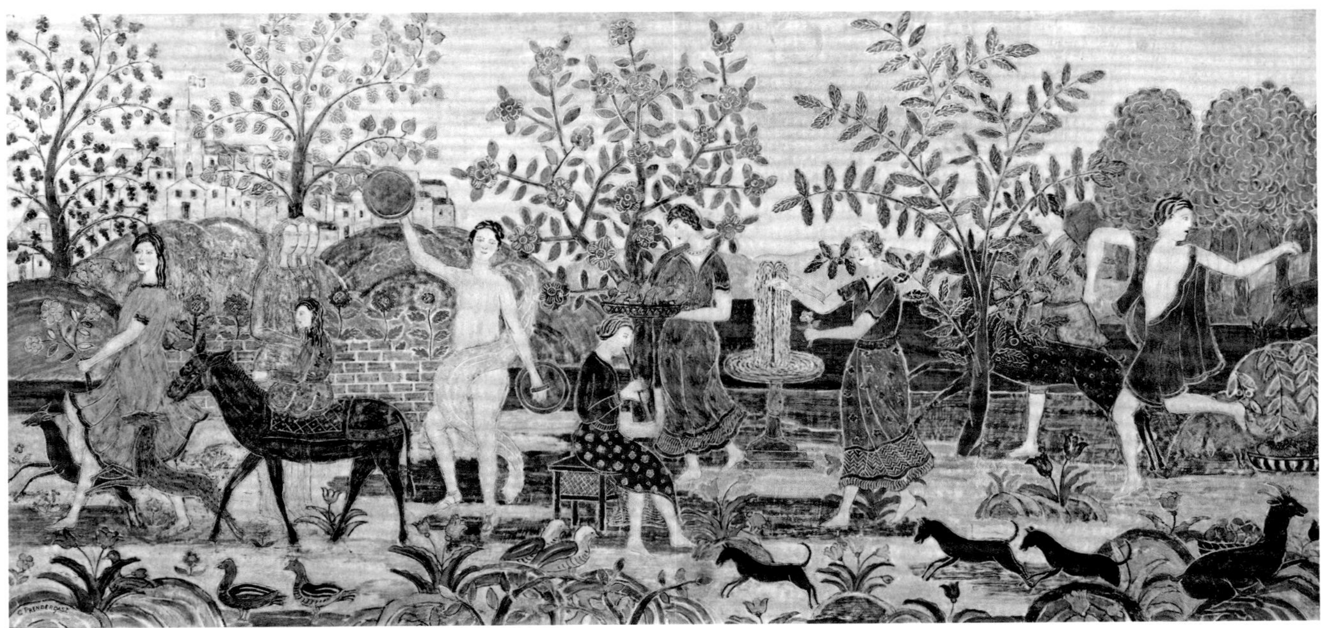

FIGURE 17. Charles Prendergast, *The Fountain*, ca. 1930, incised gesso, watercolor, and gold leaf on panel (31¼ x 61¾ in.), Gift of Mrs. Charles Prendergast, Courtesy Museum of Fine Arts, Boston (62.811)

straight from fairyland, charming and adorable and other-worldly. Mr. Prendergast is a true primitive."[28]

The hill towns, as seen in the watercolors and the panels, were not only a new subject for Prendergast, they signalled a new phase in his art. Critics no longer praised his skill in the evocation of antique or medieval art, they spoke of him as if he *were* an antique or medieval artist—as LaFollette put it, "a true primitive." Prendergast's earlier panels with their rich allusions to the art of other cultures were obviously the product of a learned and clever craftsman; Charles's art from the late 1920s on reduced the number of art historical allusions and stressed instead the artist's own "naive" vision. The distortion of anatomy and natural forms, the flattening of perspective, and the use of simplified outlines could no longer be attributed to a study of this or that exotic art form, but seemed to come from the artist himself. Later in the thirties, Prendergast would marry this approach to scenes of everyday American life and become an identifiable American folk artist; but in the late twenties and early thirties he applied the style to a number of subjects in what he described as his "transition" period.

Charles's new interest in naive or primitive style paralleled the growth of interest among artists and collectors in American folk art in the 1920s and 1930s. The interest became a passion for such collectors as Juliana Force, director of the Whitney Museum of American Art, and Abby Aldrich Rockefeller who would later found her own museum of American folk art in Williamsburg, Virginia. Rockefeller, spurred to many benevolent acts on behalf of artists at the onset of the Depression, commissioned Prendergast to execute a large, mural-sized panel for a residential hall for international college and graduate students in New York, called International House. Prendergast used his new naive style to design a complex composition on the theme of the performing arts titled *Play, International House* (fig. 19; CR 2264, Collection of International House). It was one of many decorations commissioned for the hall over the years (including two by Arthur B. Davies) and should be considered in the context of the large-scale

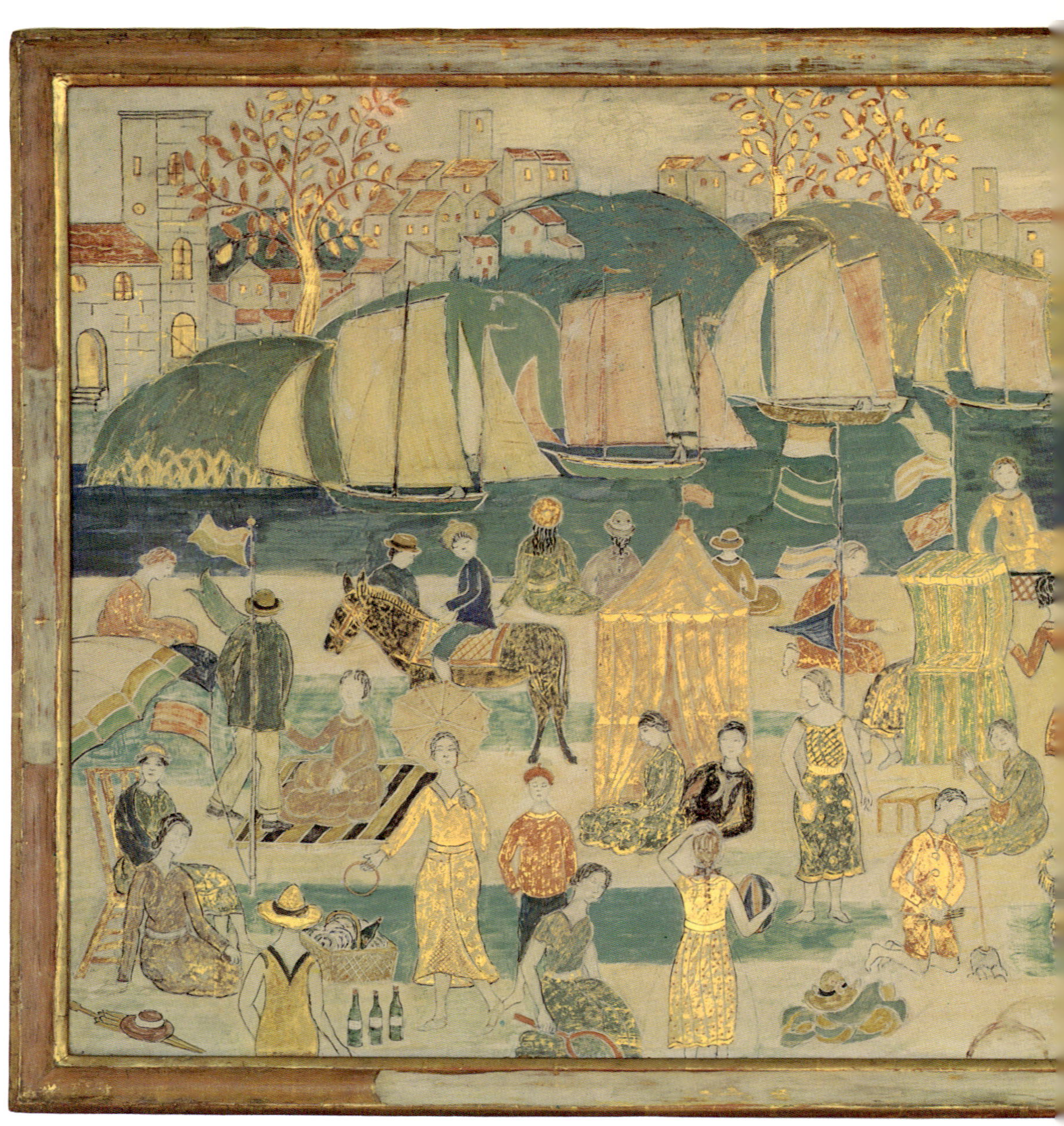

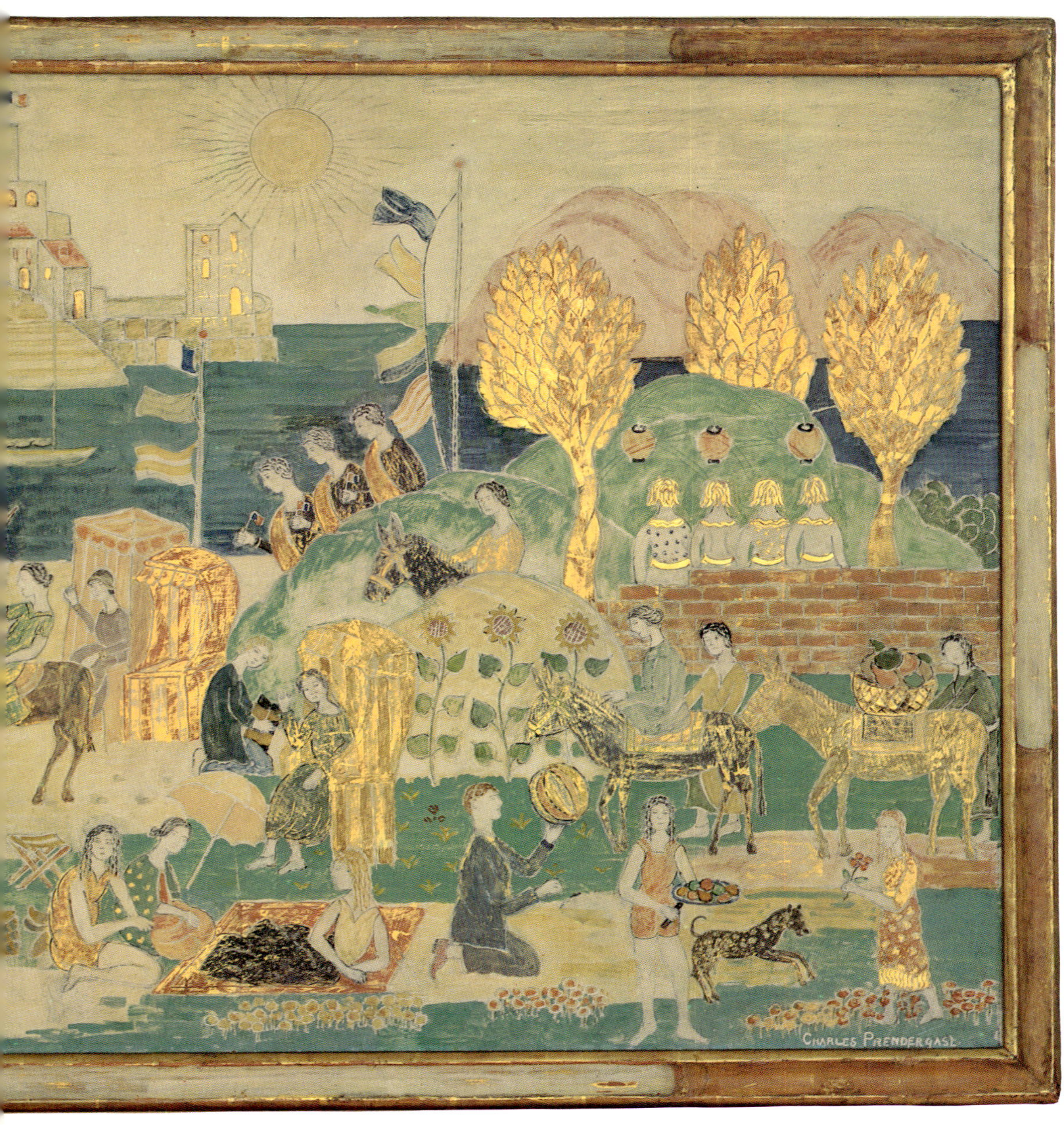

FIGURE 18. Charles Prendergast, *Holiday Beach Scene*, ca. 1931-32, Williams College Museum of Art (see p. 82)

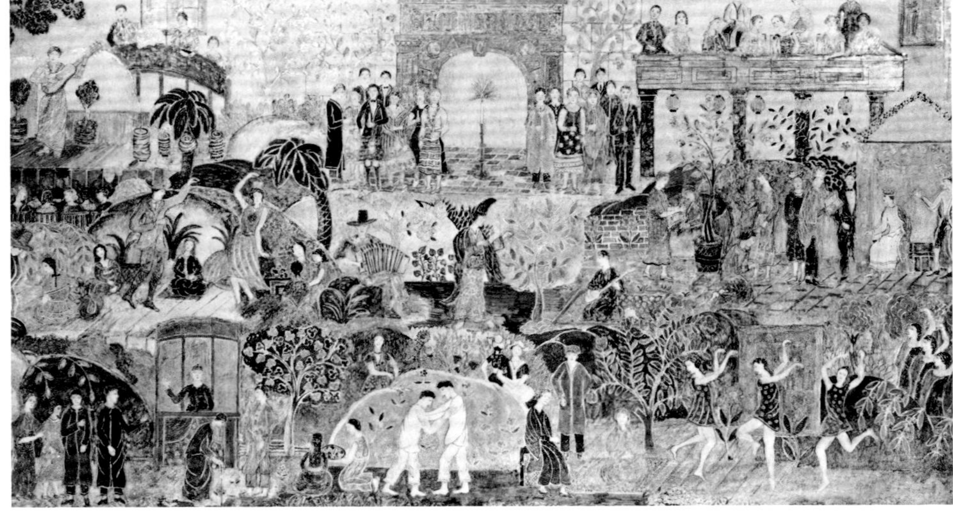

FIGURE 19. Charles Prendergast, *Play, International House*, 1931, incised gesso, tempera, pencil, and gold and silver leaf on panel (44 x 75 in.), International House, New York

FIGURE 20. Thomas Hart Benton, *City Activities with Dance Hall* from *America Today*, 1930, distemper and egg tempera on linen (92 x 134½ in.), Collection of The Equitable Life Assurance Society

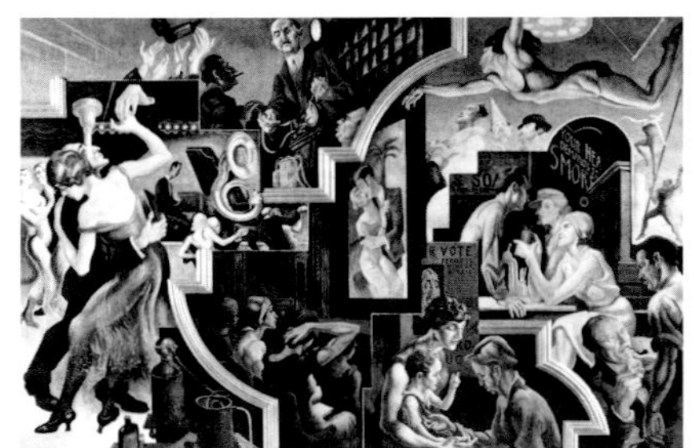

mural movement of the 1930s. Thomas Hart Benton (1889-1975) had recently finished his *America Today* murals for the New School of Social Research (1930) and established a standard for the depiction of such epic themes as Prendergast was grappling with in *Play, International House*. These murals required a composition that would tie together multiple scenes depicting the various aspects of an epic subject. In an example like *City Activities with Dance Hall* from the *America Today* series, Benton resolved the dilemma by dividing up the pictorial surface into irregularly shaped "windows" through which the viewer saw different facets of city life (fig. 20). Prendergast, whose earlier grand compositions like *The Spirit of the Hunt* had woven all the compositional elements into a decorative whole, now divided them up into discrete areas showing the different scenes occurring on the stages of multiple theaters. Thus he showed his naively drawn vignettes of music, dance, and drama from various exotic cultures (based on sketches from actual performances at International House) in three horizontal bands, with the audience in contemporary dress in the background. Although Prendergast never took on another mural project, he did use many of the same compositional devices in panels executed about the same time, such as *Holiday Beach Scene*.

In the 1930s Charles Prendergast found a secure niche in the New York art world, and in 1935, at the age of seventy-two, he was given his first one-person exhibition. Charles's exhibition came on the heels of the major retrospective showing of Maurice's work at the Whitney Museum of American Art in 1934. No doubt the renewed appreciation of his brother, ten years after his death, brought new attention to Charles as well, and when the Kraushaar Gallery engaged to exhibit his work he took the opportunity to show a range of pieces he had done over the years. He included such works from the teens as *The Riders* (fig. 21; CR 2229, WCMA) and *Decoration* (fig. 22; CR 2250, Private Collection) and brought the viewer up to his most recent works such as *Holiday Beach Scene* and *Market Day* (fig. 23; CR 2276, Collection of Mrs. John W. S. Platt). He also included at least two paintings on glass and one painted screen to represent his continuing interest in decorative arts.

The exhibition was well received and led to later exhibitions at Kraushaar in 1937 and 1941, as well as a joint exhibition with Maurice's work at the Addison

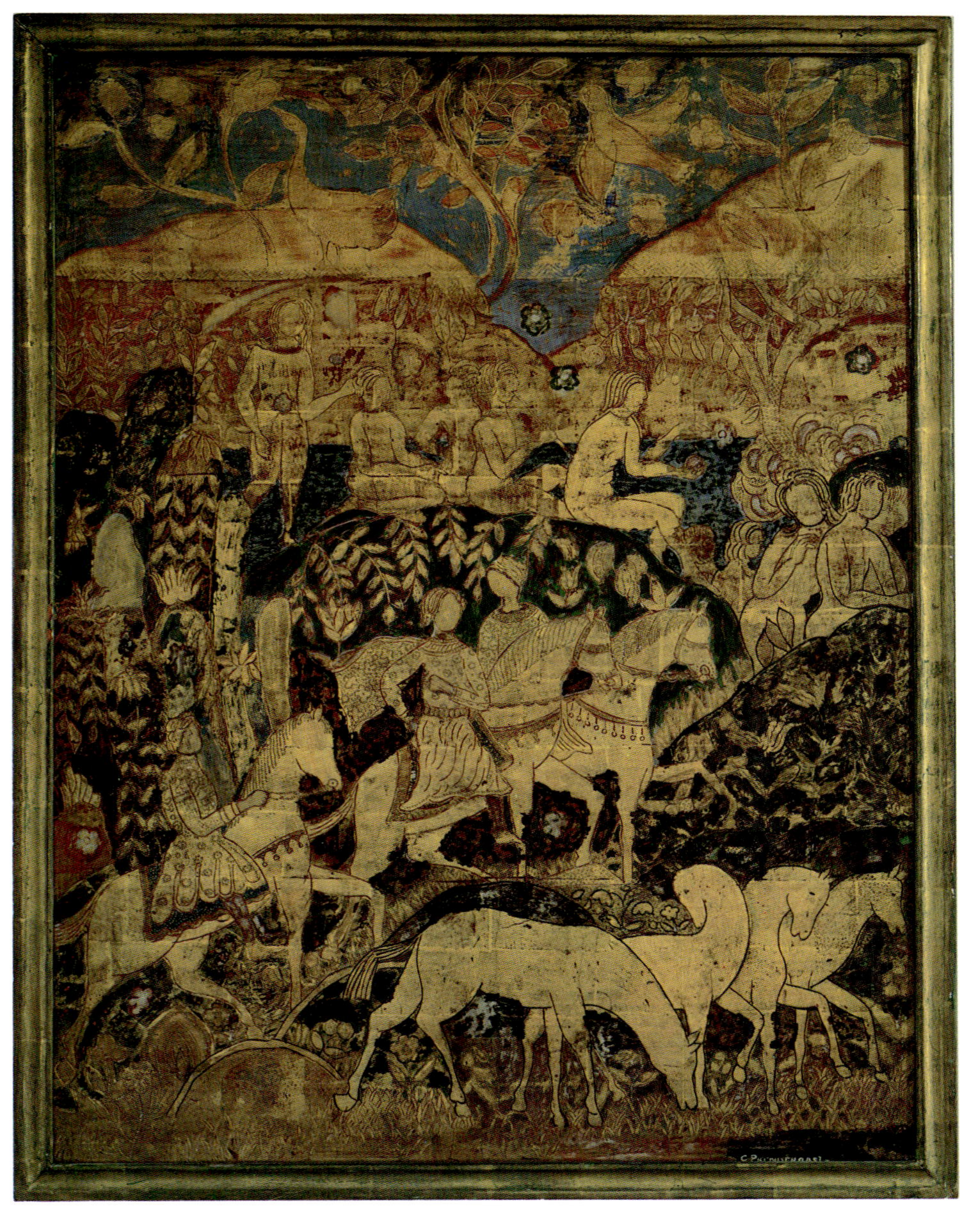

FIGURE 21. Charles Prendergast, *The Riders*, ca. 1915, Williams College Museum of Art (see p. 68)

Gallery of American Art in 1938. Charles no longer held a place in New York avant-garde circles as he had in the teens, nor could he be called "famous" even to the degree that his good friend William Glackens (1870-1938) continued to be, but he was well-respected by the artistic community. Furthermore, he was dearly loved by the wider public that a magazine such as the *New Yorker* represented—educated, refined, and amused by gentle things. Lewis Mumford, writing in the *New Yorker* in 1935, rhapsodized that "each of these pictures is a fresh glimpse of Heaven."[29]

After the 1935 exhibition at Kraushaar, Prendergast increasingly concentrated on the American scene, particularly parks, country fairs, horse and boat races, and special days in small-town life. When he painted animals now, he placed them in familiar settings like circuses, zoos, or bridle paths rather than in exotic forests or prancing in front of medieval castles. He joined the growing ranks of

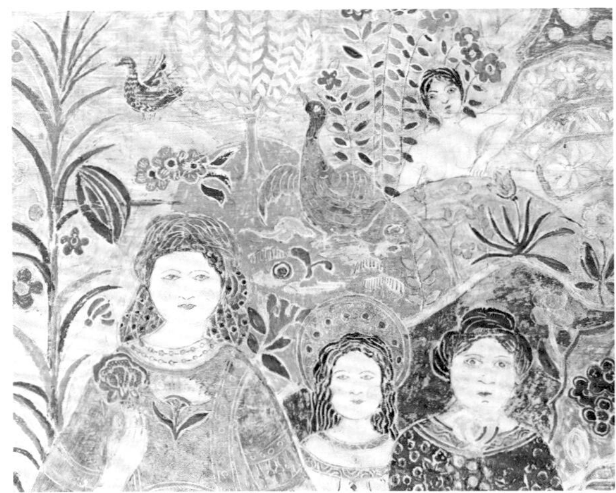

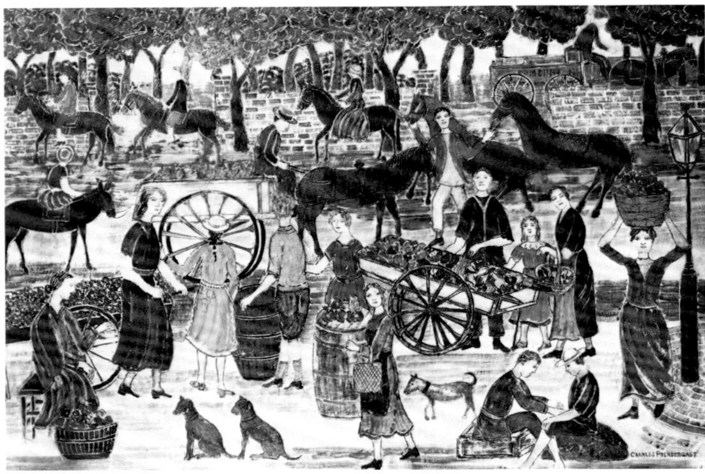

FIGURE 22. (left) Charles Prendergast, *Decoration*, ca. 1916-18, incised gesso, tempera, pencil, and gold and silver leaf on panel (15½ x 18½ in.), Private Collection

FIGURE 23. (right) Charles Prendergast, *Market Day*, ca. 1935, tempera and gold leaf on gessoed panel (23¾ x 32¾ in.), Collection of Mrs. John W. S. Platt

the so-called American folk artists of the 1930s including Grandma Moses (1860-1961), Florine Stettheimer (1871-1944), and Horace Pippin (1888-1946). This naive style was encouraged by high art collectors and museums, particularly the Whitney, which exhibited and acquired works by such artists. American folk artists of this period were generally thought of as having had no academic training, a criterion that Charles barely met. But like many others, Prendergast brought his considerable knowledge and experience to a style that only appears to be naive—lifting the simple technique to a higher, more sophisticated level of expression.

Prendergast's *Circus* (fig. 25; CR 2306, WCMA), for instance, with its animals and performers surrounded by the flat pink of the circus ring, conveys a childlike sentiment through both the technique and the subject matter. His mastery of

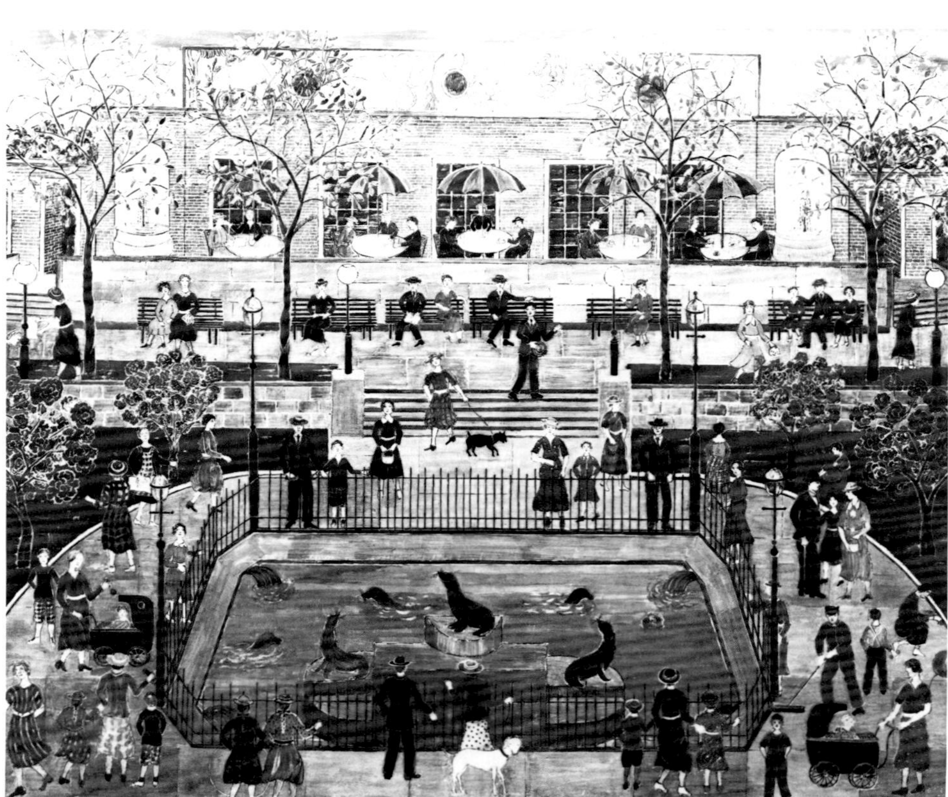

FIGURE 24. Charles Prendergast, *Central Park Zoo*, ca. 1936, incised gesso, tempera, pencil, and gold leaf on panel (41⅛ x 48¼ in.), Private Collection

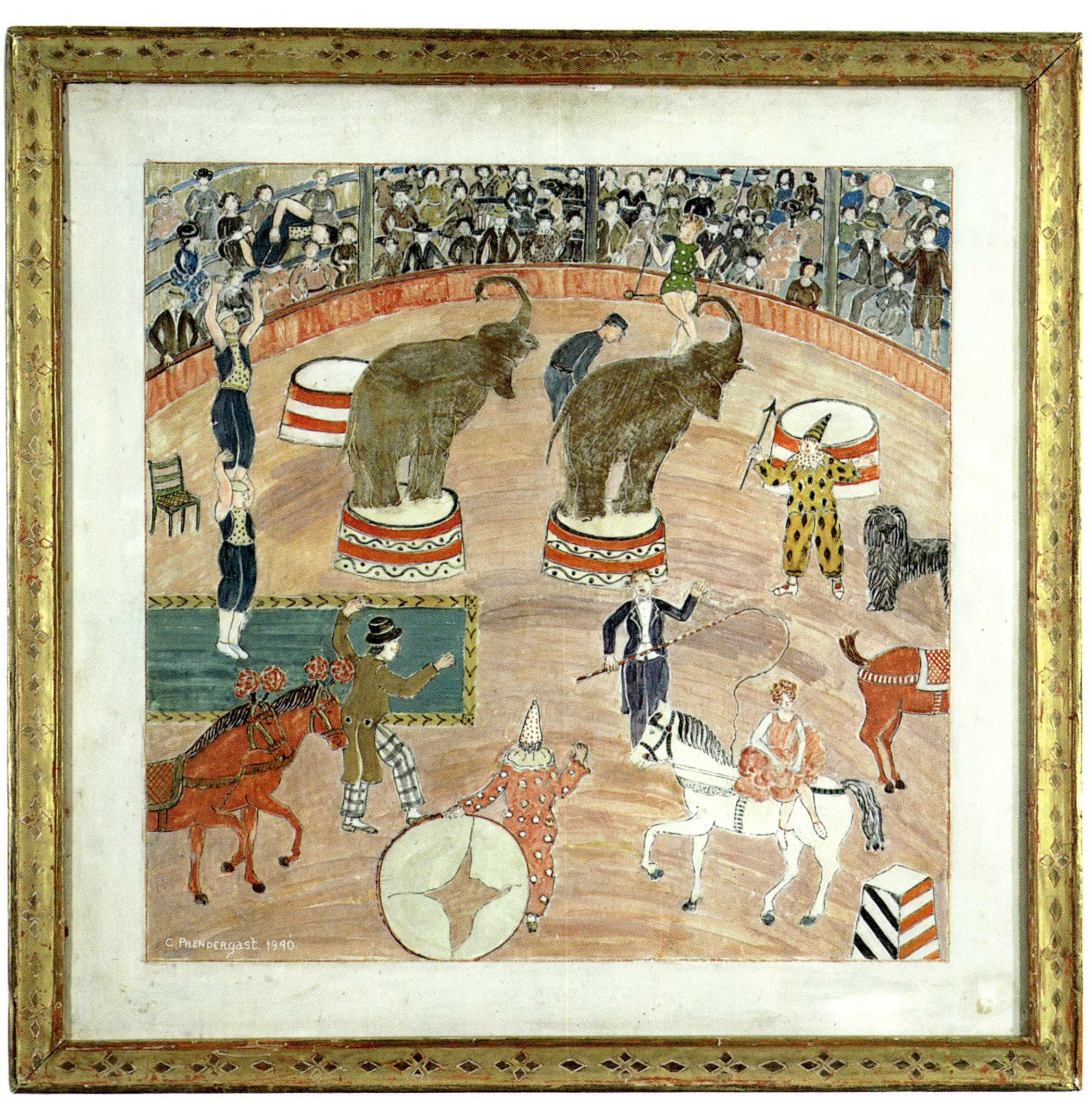

FIGURE 25. Charles Prendergast, *Circus*, 1940, Williams College Museum of Art (see p. 91)

this style was so perfect that viewers were tempted to miss the calculation in it and conclude that Prendergast himself was as innocent as his paintings.[30] While, by all accounts, he was an extremely gentle man, he was at the same time an artist who knew how to manipulate design and color to produce the effect of guilelessness. Prendergast's circus is quiet in color and restrained in movement, and has none of the overtones of sensuality or amorality that have accompanied the theme in the modern period. Charles studied the possible interpretations of the circus in his own artistic circle including his brother, William Glackens, and Everett Shinn (1876-1953). In 1929 he could study the theme in all its variations in Juliana Force's exhibition at the Whitney Studio Galleries (which became the Whitney Museum of American Art in 1930) called "The Circus in Paint," which brought together examples from Watteau to the present. Prendergast was drawn to subjects like the circus because he could bring a lifetime of knowledge to bear on a "childish" experience.

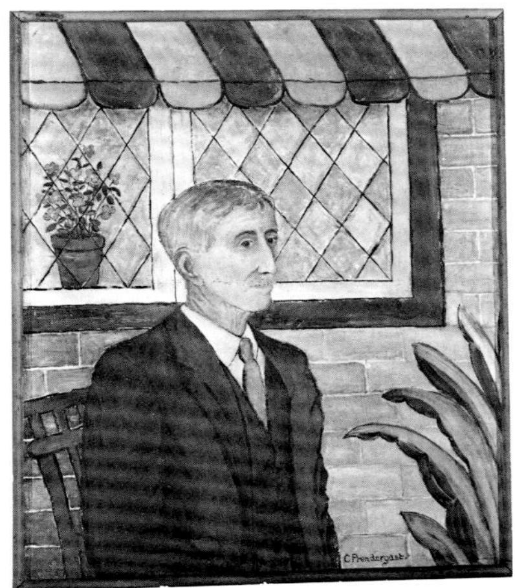

FIGURE 26. Charles Prendergast, Self-Portrait, ca. 1942-43, tempera on gessoed panel (30 x 25 in.), National Academy of Design, New York City.

Charles also juxtaposed sophistication and innocence in his New York panels in which he typically sought out the unspoiled heart of that world-weary city. He applied his naive style to scenes of Central Park and the Central Park Zoo as well as the grand event of 1939, the New York World's Fair. In 1941 he sent *Central Park Zoo* (fig. 24; CR 2286, Private Collection) to an exhibition at the Whitney called "This is Our City," which showed paintings of New York from 1900 to the present. His fond depiction of the zoo's pool of sea lions was very much in keeping with the show's whimsical presentation that featured flower vendors and organ grinders in the galleries.[31]

As Charles Prendergast approached eighty he was honored with another show at the Kraushaar Gallery (1941) and was nominated to associate membership in the National Academy of Design. In accordance with the requirements of the National Academy, Prendergast painted his only known self-portrait (fig. 26; CR 2309, National Academy of Design), indeed his only known portrait of any kind. Painted in the opaque watercolor he referred to as "tempera" on a gessoed panel, the artist depicts himself sitting in a formal black suit outside his Westport home. Every part of the composition has been conquered by a pattern—stripes for the awning, diamond patterning in the window, the rectangles of the bricks and the repeating lines of his suit and vest. All is pattern except his own face, which is smooth and calm with a slightly dubious expression. How could he have imagined when he took the plunge into the fine arts in 1912 that his career would come into full flower thirty years later?

After his completion of the self-portrait in 1943, failing health prevented Prendergast from doing much work for the next three years. In the early months of 1946, however, he and Eugénie took a winter vacation in Florida where he rejoined old artist-friends such as Virginia Keep Clark and was once more inspired to work. Driving around Winter Park and the small towns nearby, he zealously took to his sketchbook to record local scenes. The result was a series of eighteen watercolor sketches that he painted at the time and four gesso panels that he executed when he returned to his studio in Westport and on a subsequent trip to Florida the following winter. This group of works continued his folk-art style of the later 1930s, but was strongly influenced by Haitian folk art that Prendergast was introduced to by an article in an unknown magazine (figs. 28, 29).[32] Prendergast borrowed the Haitian artists' strong coloring and active gestures to paint the black workers in the orange groves of central Florida who he

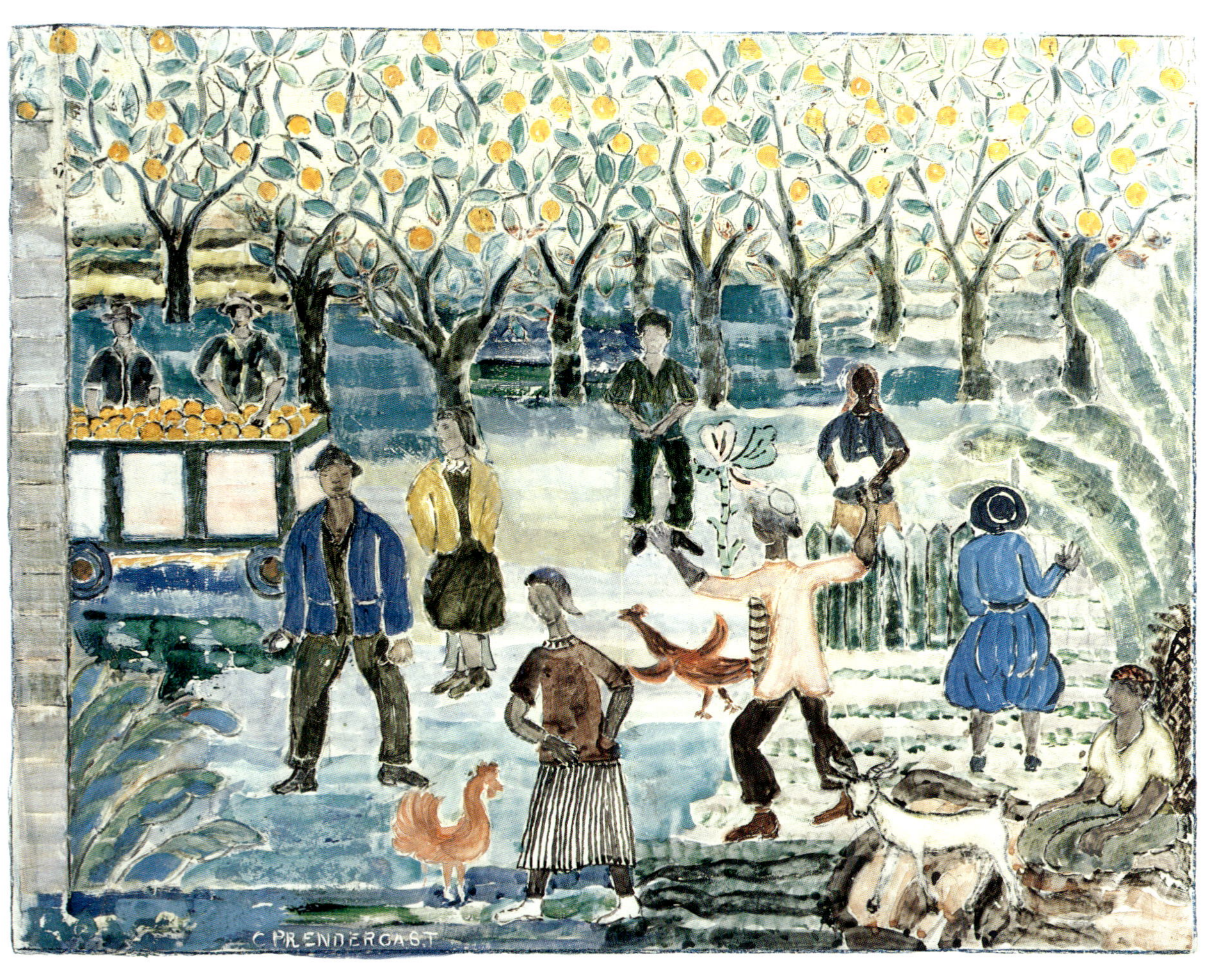

FIGURE 27. Charles Prendergast, *Florida Grove*, ca. 1946-47, Collection of Mrs. Charles Prendergast (see p. 101)

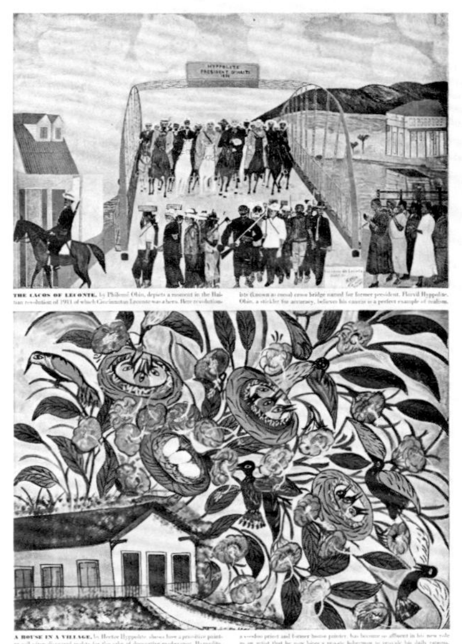

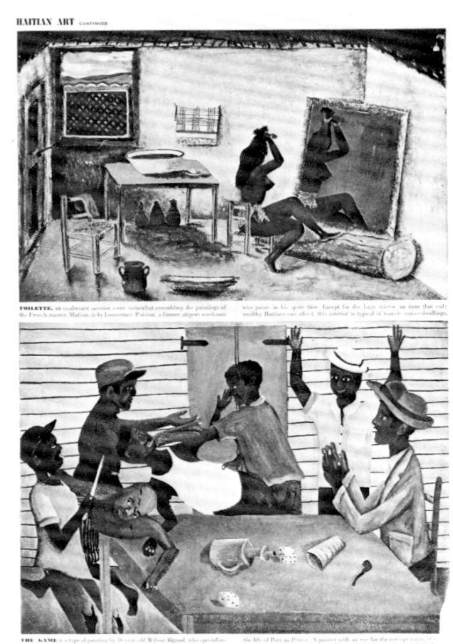

FIGURE 28. (left) Philomé Obin, *The Cacos of Leconte*, and Hector Hyppolite, *A House in a Village*, illustrations from an unknown source, Williams College Museum of Art, Prendergast Archive and Study Center

FIGURE 29. (right) Louverture Poisson, *Toilette*, and Wilson Bigaud, *The Game*, illustrations from an unknown source, Williams College Museum of Art, Prendergast Archive and Study Center

felt had more artistic character than the whites: "The men dress in such a manly way—in real, pure colors. And what material for a sculptor, especially their faces, men and women both! The colors of the women's clothes are wonderful. I got all excited over those Negroes. I even got excited by their roosters."[33]

When Prendergast transformed his watercolor sketches into gessoed panels, he did not borrow directly but used the sketches merely to suggest poses and settings for the finished works.[34] This inventive approach, coupled with a return to more exotic subject matter made the Florida series somewhat reminiscent of his earliest style. These pictures go beyond the naive realism of his 1930s American Scene panels, in which he delicately described scenes of ordinary life, to a more exuberant approach in which forms and gestures are bolder and the world depicted is more colorful than our own. Nor did he forgo the opportunity to celebrate the fruitfulness of the land (symbolized by baskets and crates overflowing with oranges) and his familiar theme of renewal and rebirth, this time against the backdrop of his failing health (fig. 27; *Florida Grove*, CR 2315, Collection of Mrs. Charles Prendergast).

In the Florida series, Prendergast offered yet another application of his beloved primitivism. In his days as a framemaker, he interpreted primitivism to mean a fresh approach to form, an avoidance of over-refined or hackneyed styles. When he first began to work in a pictorial medium, he found his inspiration in historical and non-Western styles that seemed more primitive than those of high art, and thus evocative of a lost golden age. In the thirties, he worked in a folk-art style in which primitivism meant using an untrained hand as a child would to capture the simple pleasures of the everyday world. Finally, in the forties, Prendergast arrived at a primitivism associated with a rural black culture in which he combined a simpler, more expressive style with images of work and repose in an "exotic" culture.

Prendergast's exploration of the many facets of primitivism throughout his career paralleled the ongoing interest in this aesthetic concept among other artists and writers as twentieth-century art evolved. He not only gained the perspective his own art gave him over the years, but he was interested in the theoretical framework debated by the larger art world. A good friend in the late 1930s and 1940s was Robert Goldwater, art historian and critic, whose influential book, *Primitivism in Modern Art*, was first published in 1938. Goldwater's survey of primitivism among twentieth-century European artists stressed the complexity of the aesthetic and its many expressive possibilities. Although Prendergast at the time may have best fit Goldwater's description of "The Child Cult," in which he discusses the work of Paul Klee, he at various other times fell into all the author's categories of romantic, emotional, intellectual, and subconscious primitivism.[35]

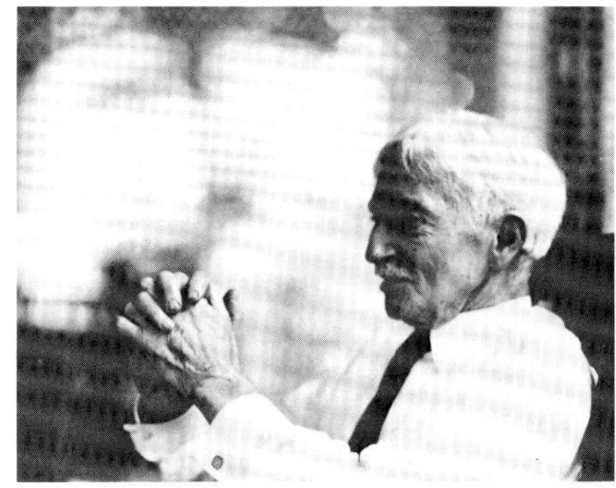

FIGURE 30. Anonymous, *Charles Prendergast*, ca. 1946, photograph (3¾ x 4⅝ in.), Williams College Museum of Art, Prendergast Archive and Study Center

After exhibiting the Florida series at another one-person exhibition at Kraushaar in the spring of 1947, Prendergast's health declined to the extent that he was no longer able to work. He died on August 20, 1948, at the age of eighty-five. Although Charles never achieved the standing among American artists that his brother enjoyed, he had the good fortune to have achieved success in two careers. And, to have begun his work as a pictorial artist at the age one now is considered a senior citizen and to have maintained it for over thirty-five years was an extraordinary accomplishment. Prendergast had the rare pleasure of receiving major tributes until his very last years in the form of exhibitions and glowing publications. He did not live to see his work go out of style because he had long ago bowed out of stylish, avant-garde circles and was content to address his work to a small circle of educated laymen. To a large extent his reputation has been preserved in subsequent generations of this small circle. But with the increasing fragility of his aging gesso panels, frequent exhibitions (as he had in the last years of his life) have become impossible, and thus his admirers have of necessity become an even smaller elite.

Today Charles Prendergast has not been accorded a place in traditional American art history textbooks. He was neither a vastly influential artist nor a pillar of one of the avant-garde movements that have successively given way to one another over the years. Instead, he was an artist who chose his directions carefully so that his own skills and interests would be used to best advantage. As the brother of Maurice Prendergast, he had a guaranteed audience among the most influential dealers, collectors, and museum directors, and so he could afford to be quiet when other artists resorted to being loud. In the end, he used his talent and his circumstances well; he produced an art that exerts an undeniable charm, that is unusually original, and that has the power to last through the generations, celebrating as it does the cycle of rebirth and renewal.

1. See Basso 1946a, p. 28, and Basso 1946b, pp. 28-32: a profile of Charles Prendergast in two installments, based on an interview with the artist.

2. Basso 1946b, p. 28. Basso repeated Charles's anecdote about seeing a drawing of a tulip he had done in grade school still hanging on the classroom wall when he visited forty years later.

3. Boston City Directory

4. Basso 1946b, p. 28. In the account recorded by Basso he went to work of Doll & Richards right out of school and left after three years to sail on a cattle boat to England for the summer. Presumably Charles Prendergast left school at fourteen in 1877, but his trip

to England is not dated before 1886. Therefore, it is difficult to pinpoint the exact years he worked for Doll & Richards.

5. Ibid. Charles told of his days as a traveling salesman, driving "about New England in a buggy taking orders for andirons, candlesticks, brass door knockers, and other examples of the fine arts."

6. Ibid., p. 29.

7. Winter Park Topics 1946, p. 6. In an interview with the Florida newspaper, *Winter Park Topics*, Prendergast related that he had carved frames for the Boston Museum in his early days.

8. The Isabella Stewart Gardner Museum reports a Prendergast frame around John Singer Sargent's Portrait of Charles Martin Loeffler. It is signed and dated "Prendergast/ 1903."

9. Basso 1946a, p. 24.

10. This was an exhibition of monotypes at Hart & Watson in Boston in December of 1897. He showed about twenty works along with other monotypes by Hermann Dudley Murphy and Charles Hopkinson (1869-1862).

11. Prendergast 1909, p. 70.

12. Ibid.

13. Ibid.

14. Ibid.

15. Seaton-Schmidt [1910], p. 291.

16. Ibid.

17. Prendergast 1909, p. 70.

18. Three Lawson frames are mentioned by W. M. Milliken in his memorial article, "Maurice Prendergast: American Artist" (see Milliken 1926, p. 188), but only two are known today.

19. American Art News 1909, p. 6. "An exhibition of picture and mirror frames at the Society of Arts and Crafts a couple of years ago brought out a truly astonishing group of workers in a practically new field." This may refer to an exhibition held in 1905 or, if taken literally ("a couple of years ago"), another in 1907.

20. Ibid.

21. Before 1911 Charles Prendergast's known trips to Europe were in 1886, 1887, and 1891. He apparently did not accompany Maurice on his trips in 1898 and 1907. A trip to Europe for Maurice in 1909 has been mentioned in the literature but has not been documented.

22. For instance, the early panel *Madonna and Child* (CR 2214, WCMA) is based on a reproduction of a book cover in the British Museum that was found in the magazine, *The Art Workers' Quarterly* (April 1902), that Charles had clipped and saved. The page is now in the Prendergast Archive and Study Center, WCMA.

23. This may have been a misprint or a confusion with Maurice who was also listed as a painter, since in every *Who's Who in Art* after 1915, Charles is listed as a sculptor, engraver, and craftsman.

24. Basso 1946a, p. 25.

25. Basso 1946b, p. 30.

26. Pach 1923, p. 172.

27. Prendergast worked out his panel designs on paper first; then he transferred them to the gessoed panels by rubbing the backs with charcoal and tracing over the lines so that

the charcoal rubbed off onto the gesso. For his working method, see Crawford 1919, Basso 1946a and b, and Goethals's essay in this volume.

28. p. 312.

29. Mumford 1935, p. 69.

30. Ibid. Lewis Mumford believed that Prendergast was a primitive because he *felt* that way. "As a painter he is without complications: Life, as he shows it and makes one feel it, is full of joy. . . ."

31. Berman 1990, p. 428.

32. He clipped the article and it is now in the Prendergast Archive and Study Center, WCMA.

33. Basso 1946a, p. 28.

34. None of the existing sketches related directly to the finished panels, which suggests that he worked up his ideas for the panels independently of them. However, it is also possible that in arriving at the final composition, he used certain sketches to transfer designs and in the process destroyed them.

35. Goldwater 1967, p. xxii.

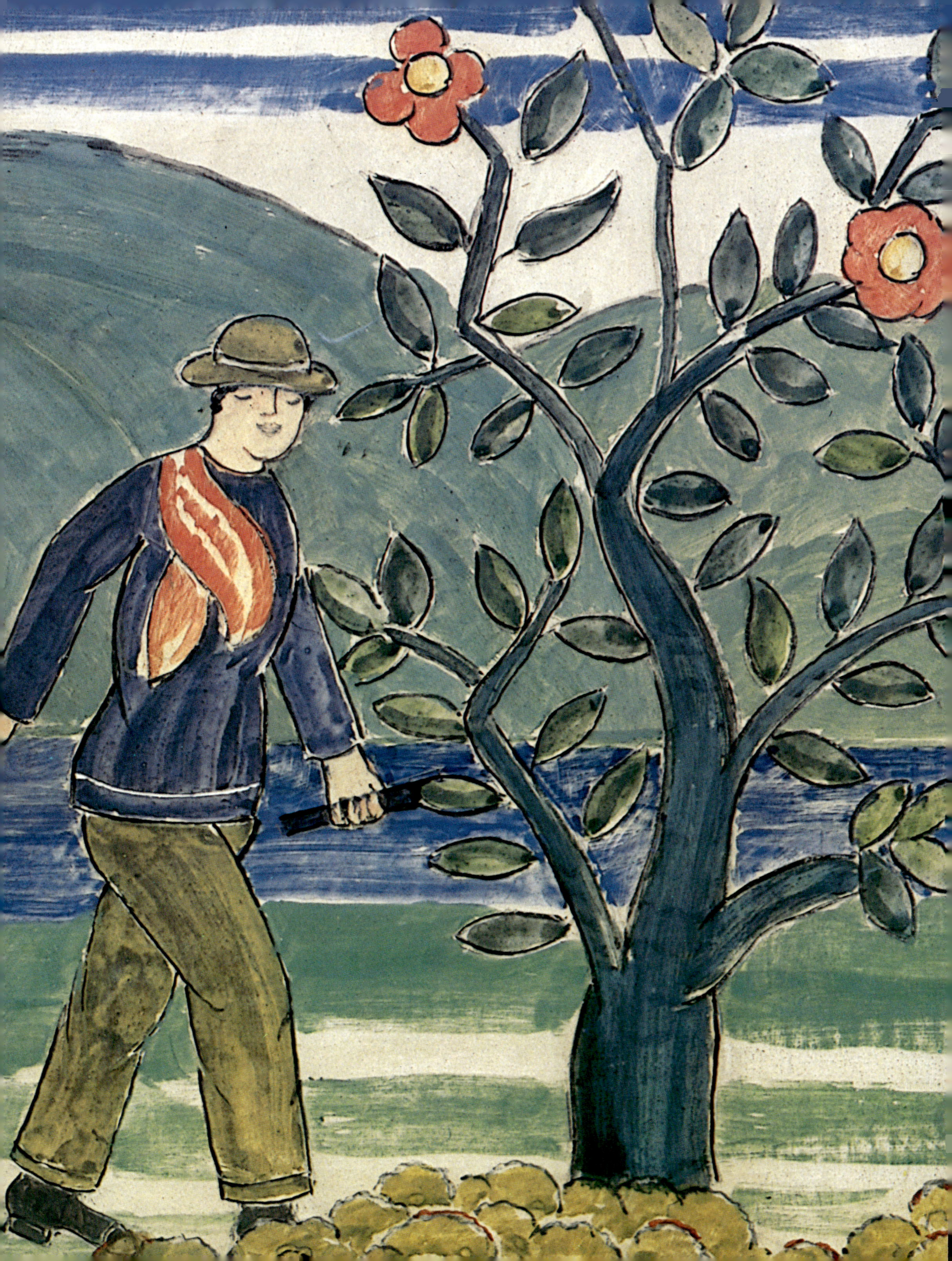

"MY WORK IS DONE IN GESSO THE OLD ITALIAN METHOD. . . ."

Marion M. Goethals

CENTURIES-OLD MATERIALS AND TECHNIQUES were as central to Charles Prendergast's art as the subjects he chose, whether holiday events peculiar to the 1930s, or medieval processions, or folk-art motifs. "My work is done in gesso the old Italian method. I use tempera colors—also gold and silver leaf. . . . I am about the only man in America doing this kind of work. . . ."[1] In drafting this statement in January 1935, more than twenty years after making his first pictorial panel, Charles Prendergast underscored the importance of his chosen medium. Prendergast first was a craftsman of notable picture frames, and then had a remarkable second calling of making objects—scenes in tempera on gesso with gold and silver. By choosing methods and materials from past centuries, and by joining them with sympathetic subjects, his art work is aligned with the craft movements of his times, and distinguishes itself by its primitive qualities. These choices were deliberate and intentional on his part, and because he felt his working method was of great importance, it is necessary to understand how his art was made and how that process changed over time.[2]

In the years before and after the turn of the century, design movements in Europe and, as they took form, in the United States, responded to a need for a new aesthetic for practical objects—an aesthetic that, in its various manifestations, stressed the unity of design, function, and craftsmanship.[3] These movements developed as a counterpoint to the machine age; they fostered an art united with handcrafts as opposed to an art united with industry. Artists embracing these movements welcomed traditional designs and received inspiration from other cultures—Celtic, Islamic, Japanese, Chinese, medieval. Many, including James Abbott McNeill Whistler (1834-1903) in England and Louis Comfort Tiffany (1848-1933) in the United States, sought to blur the distinction between high art and decorative design. In Prendergast's own Boston, Henry Hobson Richardson's (1838-1886) 1870s collaboration with John LaFarge (1835-1910) on Trinity Church and Isabella Stewart Gardner's turn-of-the-century museum nurtured an American artistic renaissance. The Museum of Fine Arts in Boston regularly showed works from the Near and Far East. The journal *Art in America*, particularly in the 1910s, routinely covered subjects of great interest to Prendergast that echo in his own work of the 1910s and 1920s, illustrating Persian rugs with animals, Japanese screens, chests with pictorial panels, and early Renaissance gilded panel paintings.[4] Charles Prendergast came of age in an artistic environment that supported not only a great wealth of crosscultural subjects, but also an interest in traditional materials.

In 1899 Christiana J. Herringham published her translation into English of a copy of the treatise of Cennino Cennini, *The Book of Art*.[5] Cennini's book, written in Northern Italy about 1400, was a technical manual for artists written by an artist. After its reappearance many twentieth-century artists and art schools were influenced by the treatise, and its publication complemented the great interest in Italian panel painting at the time. Cennini's manual or mention of Italian fifteenth-century artisans are referred to repeatedly by contemporary reviewers of Prendergast's work, presumably because of the emphasis the artist himself placed on it.[6] Thomas Hart Benton (1889-1975) used Cennini's manual in experiments during 1925-26 as he studied the special problems of murals.[7] By the 1930s, the Yale University art school had incorporated Cennini's book into its curriculum, and a new translation by Daniel Thompson of the Courtauld Institute, London, had been published.[8] The directions for panel painting and

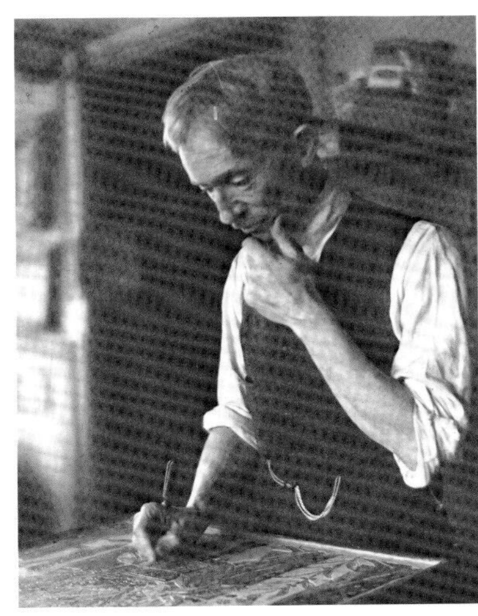

FIGURE 31. Anonymous, *Charles Prendergast*, ca. 1918, photograph (4¾ x 3¾), Williams College Museum of Art, Prendergast Archive and Study Center

gilding in Cennini's book remain essentially the same for techniques revived in the twentieth century. Charles Prendergast knew these techniques from his framemaking, and thus was already a master of the materials and techniques of his new art—wood, gesso, tempera, and gold and silver leaf. It only remained for him to apply the techniques to the making of pictures rather than frames. The writings of Cennini, in conjunction with the accumulated understanding of techniques garnered by artists and art teachers in the craft movements of the late nineteenth and early twentieth centuries, made accessible to Charles Prendergast and others the craft of the "old Italian method."[9]

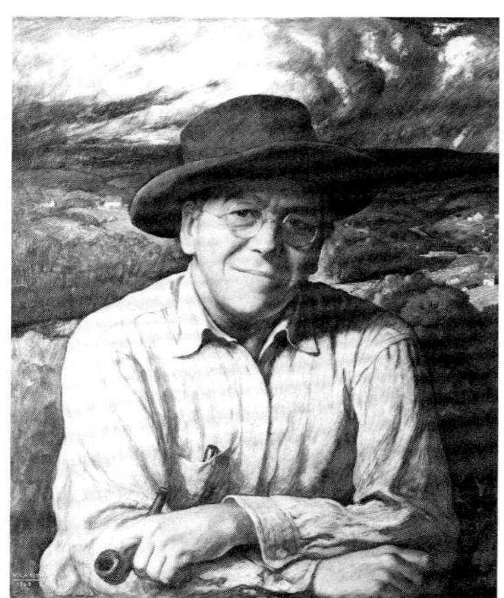

FIGURE 32. N. C. Wyeth, *Self-Portrait*, 1940, tempera on gessoed panel (32½ x 27½), National Academy of Design, New York City

Thomas Hart Benton's influence was considerable during this period, especially because of his teaching position at the Art Students League in New York from 1926-1935, and his mural projects in the city. Benton's *America Today* murals for the New School in New York (see fig. 20, *City Activities with Dance Hall*, p. 28) were painted on gessoed, linen-covered panels and are testimony to Benton's interest in reviving traditional techniques for mural painting.[10] Benton's colleagues—Reginald Marsh (1898-1954), John Steuart Curry (1897-1946), and Denys Wortman (1887-1958)—all took part in the tempera and gesso revival. Many artists came to prefer gesso on panel to similarly primed canvas for its hard brilliance as a pictorial support. Prendergast's self-portrait for the National Academy of Design (see fig. 26, p. 32) was painted in tempera on gesso panel as are those by N. C. Wyeth (1882-1945) (fig. 32), Peter Hurd (b. 1904), and George Tooker (b. 1920). The artists appreciated being able to incorporate the brightness of gesso into the composition or to scrape through the paint to the solid, white ground for a singular highlighting effect.

Interestingly, as experimental approaches to art took hold during the beginning of the twentieth century, many European artists and artistic movements investigated traditional materials. Whereas Charles Prendergast preferred to use his materials in the ways described by Cennini as reenforcement of the primitive aesthetic of his subjects, other artists sought from these unusual materials a liberating vehicle for radical expression. In the collections of his patrons, important collectors John Quinn and Lillie Bliss, were works in tempera and on gesso by Odilon Redon (1840-1916),[11] and exhibited with both Maurice and Charles Prendergast in 1917 was a painted relief sculpture of a rooster by Raymond Duchamp-Villon (1876-1918).[12] Paul Klee (1879-1940) ranged widely in his experimentation with materials and did some works by incising and staining gesso. *Tree Nursery*, 1929 (fig. 33; The Phillips Collection), is such a piece, and it is notable that Duncan Phillips in responding to the material investigations of twentieth-century artists had both this piece and work by Prendergast in his collection.

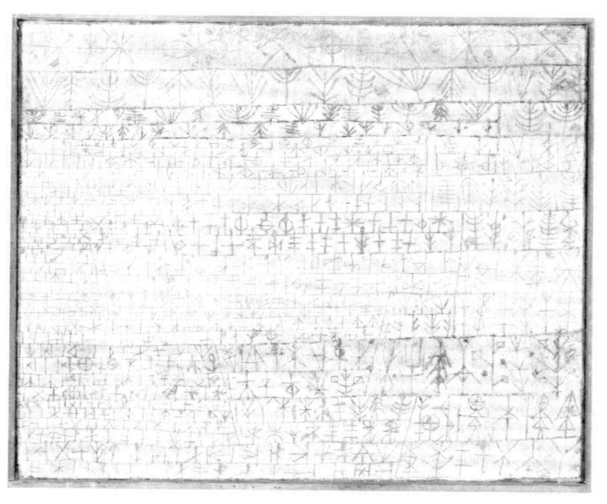

FIGURE 33. Paul Klee, *Tree Nursery*, 1929, oil on incised gesso on canvas (17⅛ x 20⅝ in.), The Phillips Collection, Washington, D.C.

Gold and silver leaf, as Prendergast used them, were unusual as design elements for pictures in the early decades of this century; their use was generally restricted to decorative objects, furniture, and frames. Max Kuehne (1880-1968), a younger friend of the Prendergasts,[13] both created panels, objects, and screens with gold and silver leaf and painted in oil as an American postimpressionist. His work "compares favorably with the similar work executed by Charles Prendergast"[14] according to one observer at the time, and the two men must have enjoyed sharing their common technical problems. Kuehne's work, as in *Decorative Panel: Peacock and Flowers* (fig. 34), despite the similarities to Prendergast's in materials, has a more fashionable sensibility. Where Prendergast's compositions

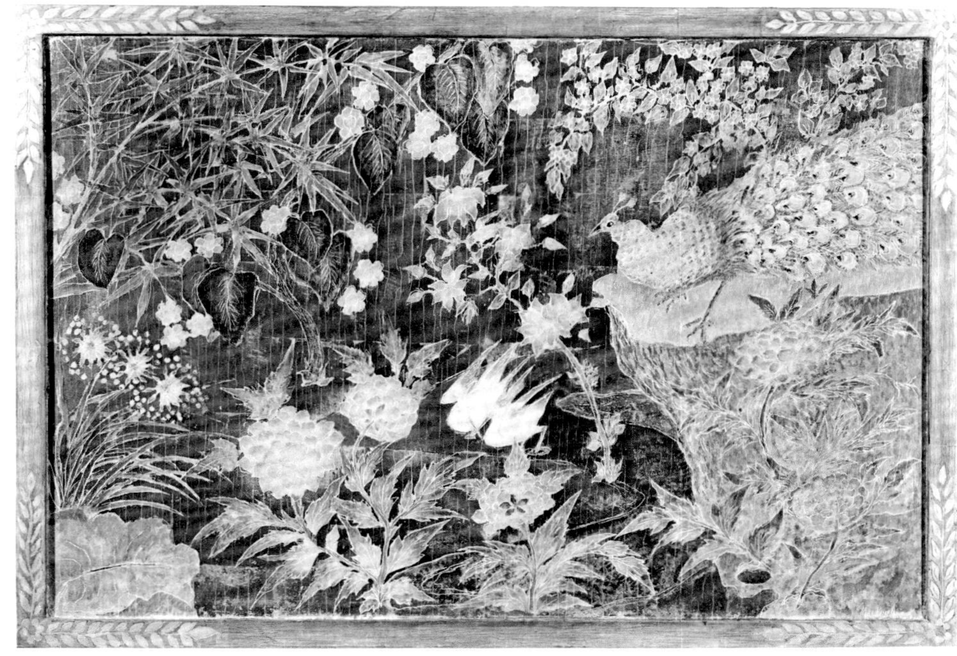

FIGURE 34. Max Kuehne, *Decorative Panel: Peacock and Flowers*, silver and tempera on gessoed panel (27¾ x 41⅝ in.), Collection of Hirschl & Adler Galleries, Inc., New York

are deliberately awkward and archaic, Kuehne's are fluid and bright. Prendergast purposely left his design unprotected to preserve the individual matte qualities of gesso and tempera and the luminosity of the metal leaf. Kuehne, by contrast, in an article explaining the use of gesso, reported that his method was to apply "several coats of lacquer" as the end step, "which seeping through the color sinks into the gesso, making an insoluble whole."[15]

Along with the rediscoveries of materials made by both American and European artists, the decorative craft revivals, and the heightened interest in the art of other cultures, there was in the 1930s a newly found interest in American folk art. Among Prendergast's contacts in New York, both Abby Aldrich Rockefeller and the influential director of the Whitney Museum of American Art, Juliana Force, had notable collections. Mrs. Rockefeller's collection was shown in New York in 1932.[16] There are many references in Prendergast's work of the 1930s and 1940s that allude to the folk idiom of innocence, simplicity, and spareness. His late figurines and reverse paintings on glass may well have been encouraged by the use of these materials by folk artists. Charles Prendergast was an artist alive to his times, who both contributed to and took inspiration from the wealth of artistic creativity around him.

Prendergast painted his scenes in tempera on either carved or incised gessoed panel, and gilded them with gold and/or silver leaf in the manner he described: "The foundation or surface of the Panels are covered with a material call[ed] Gesso. It was used by the Early Italian primatives [sic] when they used a wood panel. I prepare my panels with the same medium. And while the Gesso is still damp, the composition is cut into the surface with a tool. The gold work is prepared seperately [sic]. Layed on Goldsize with water. And finally burnished and toned."[17] (fig. 35). And even though Walter Pach in 1923 and Hamilton Basso in 1946 both hint at Charles Prendergast's "secret" methods, it is possible with the help of Cennini, contemporary and modern accounts, and Prendergast's own notes and supplies to piece together how he made his pictorial panels and objects.[18]

FIGURE 35. Page from Charles Prendergast's "Metropolitan" notebook, no date, Williams College Museum of Art, Prendergast Archive and Study Center

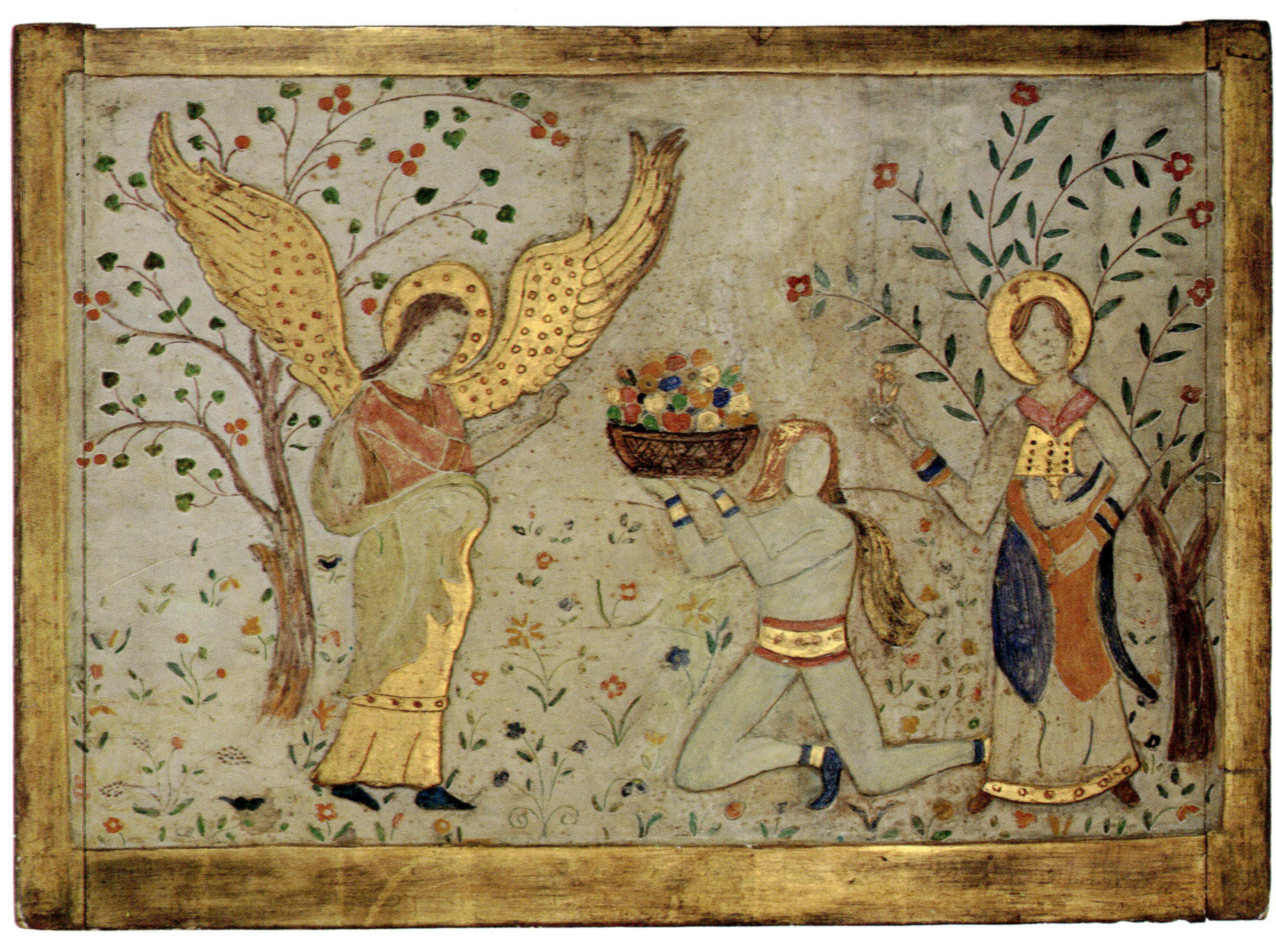

FIGURE 36. Charles Prendergast, *Annunciation*, ca. 1912-15, Williams College Museum of Art (see p. 58)

As a framemaker, Prendergast was accustomed to working in relief with wood and gesso, and he preferred to incorporate a similar sculptural effect in his panels and chests. His first attempts at pictorial works were low-relief sculptural panels carved in wood, then gessoed, painted, and gilded. Each was a unit with a bordering frame conceived and carved as part of the whole. In *Annunciation*, ca. 1912-15 (fig. 36; CR 2215, WCMA) and *Rising Sun*, ca. 1912 (CR 2212, WCMA, p. 56), two of his earliest panels, he chiselled the wood away to expose the figures. The sides of his three chests are similarly carved and decorated (see *Chest*, CR 2398, Collection of Mrs. Charles Prendergast, p. 59).[19]

Prendergast had structural problems with his wood panels, although the adjustments he had to make proved to be beneficial to his still-evolving art form. The decorated wood panels began to warp, he felt, because of the carving.[20] In some of his early work, cracks appeared in the design. In a 1917 letter to John Quinn, Prendergast testified to a recent repair of one of his panels owned by Quinn: "I left the panel at your apartment this afternoon. I finished it according to my original intention. And if you don't like it I will gild it all over. I kept it a little longer . . . to see if the cracks would make their appearance on it again."[21] The warping and cracking of the wood panels must have been a disappointment to Prendergast; his 1909 essay, "Revival of Wood Carving," stressed the importance of restoring a valued handcraft to its preindustrial rank.[22]

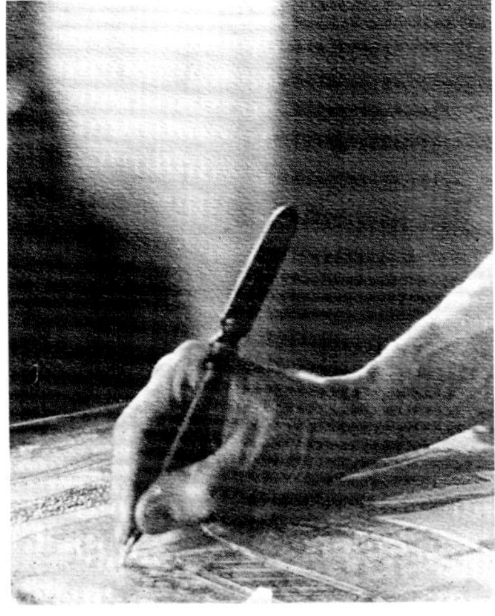

FIGURE 37. Anonymous, *Charles Prendergast's Hand*, ca. 1918, photograph (10 x 8 in.) Williams College Museum of Art, Prendergast Archive and Study Center

According to accounts both at the beginning and at the end of his career, his preferred support panel was white pine.[23] However, during the late 1910s, because of structural problems with the plank panels, Prendergast began using plywood, and later, Masonite, which are not suitable for carving.[24] The loss of the relief surface was a significant one for the artist, but because he had to give up the carved self-frame seen in *Rising Sun* and *Annunciation*, he was free to design separate, more complex frames for his panels. Because of his great genius for designing frames, this adaptation resulted in a more visually interesting object. He thereafter confined his wood sculpting to the large chests of the 1920s, and small figures in the round (see *Eve*, CR 2390; *Angel*, CR 2392; *Man Dancing*, CR 2394; WCMA, pp. 60, 61, 61) that he carved until his death.

Gesso, as Cennini described it, is the element that is common to all Charles Prendergast's work (except most drawings)—sculptures, screens, chests and boxes, and pictorial panels. A panel, whether carved or smooth, pine or manufactured board, was coated with it. Gesso is an exceptionally simple material for creating a smooth, hard, white surface on which to paint and gild. Gesso is made from a whiting powder such as marble dust, which must be suspended in a liquid (usually animal glue and water) to be suitable for spreading on a surface or for use in three-dimensional schemes.

Among Prendergast's tools and supplies in the Prendergast Archive and Study Center are the materials for making gesso (fig. 38). While the materials of the technique were more readily available to Prendergast than to Cennini, the practices remained close to the "old Italian method." Whereas Cennini had to gather scraps of sheep parchment to make his glue, Prendergast bought from H. Behlen & Brothers or other suppliers chips of rabbit-skin glue ready to dissolve. Cennini then combined the glue size with plaster of Paris and water; Prendergast likewise combined Behlen's Ex. Gilder's Whiting and his glue size to make the gesso paste ready for spreading. Prendergast's recipe for gesso is a simple one: "mix 3 ounces of glue to a quart of water. [T]hen mix whiting powder

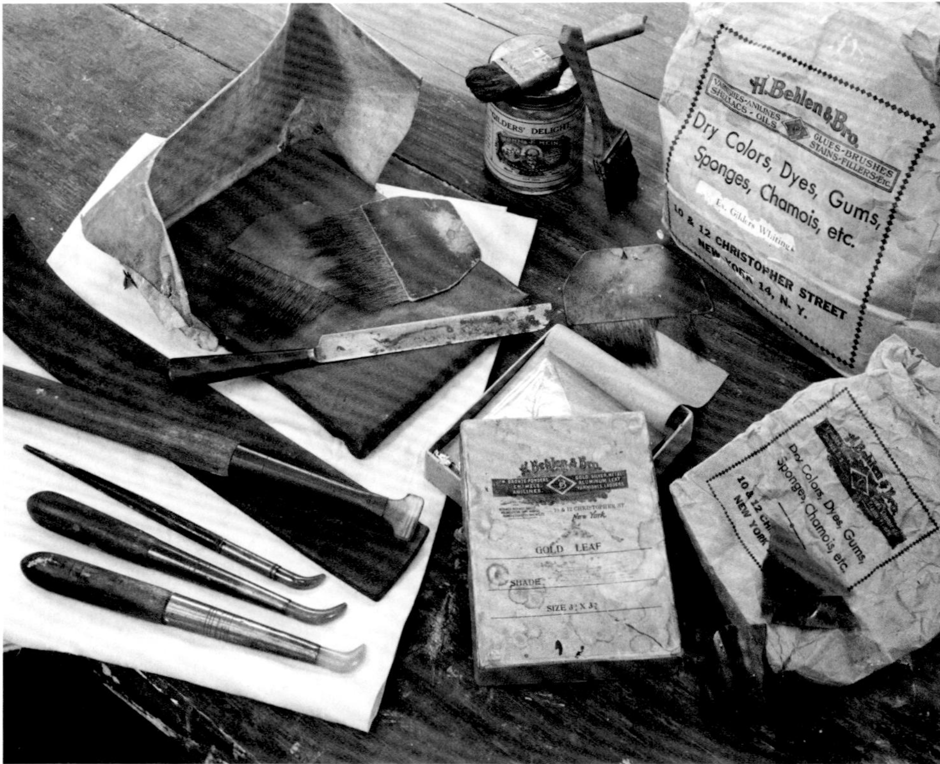

FIGURE 38. Tools and supplies owned by Charles Prendergast, photograph, Williams College Museum of Art, Prendergast Archive and Study Center

until medium thick paste is obtained."[25] Other American artists shared similar recipes for the revived gesso technique.[26]

Prendergast etched lines in the damp gesso following the guide of a preparatory drawing on the panel, thereby giving added importance to the forms by the tactile line, its subtle shadow, and the whiteness of the exposed gesso. By lending a somewhat three-dimensional texture to the forms, incising compensated for the absence of relief carving. The view of *Fairy Story* (fig. 39; CR 2277, WCMA) taken with a strong side light reveals the contribution to the image made by incising the gesso, an effect readily seen in person.

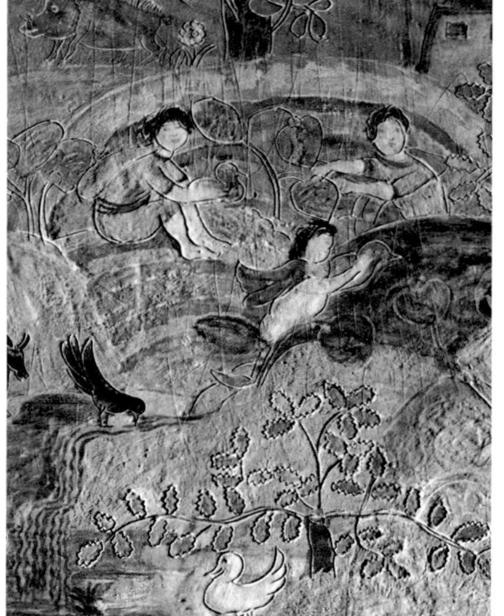

FIGURE 39. Photograph in raking light of a detail of Charles Prendergast's *Fairy Story*, ca. 1922 (reworked ca. 1942-46), Williams College Museum of Art (see p. 70)

The tempera paints that Charles Prendergast preferred adhere securely to any porous surface, but gold leaf used in the manner that Prendergast used it, water-gilded and highly burnished, must be laid on gesso or bole.[27] On the incised gesso, in the areas to be gilded, Prendergast laid the traditional coat of bole, a finely textured suspension of colored clay in size, which rendered the surface of the gesso even smoother. Prendergast used John H. Heins' "Gilders Delight" Gold Size, a red powder that carried the following promise on the label: "Does not spoil after being mixed with Glue, but is rather improved after weeks of mixing. Can gild on it in the hottest weather same as in cold weather. Can also burnish over it with great rapidity and NOT CUT THROUGH."[28] Prendergast's recipe for bole was as basic as his for gesso: "*Gold size*: mix it to a thick paste adding water[,] add glue (guess)[,] 1/2 cup of gold size about 2 table spoon full [sic] of glue."[29] Bole was traditionally a red color, which Prendergast preferred in frames and in panels, but he did gild on other colors of bole, and directly on gesso as well.

Because Prendergast's working method is described in detail in Basso's profile, we know that he followed Cennini's directions for applying gold leaf to gesso with few alterations:

> Cennini: "Prepare a cushion as large as a brick. . . . then on this cushion spread out a piece of gold, and with a flat-edged knife cut the gold into pieces as you want it . . . . and wetting with the lips the handle of the brush, it will be able to take up the little bits of gold and lay them on. . . ."[30]
> Basso: "Now, holding his breath, he picks up his knife with his right hand, slices a piece of gold leaf from the sheet, and deftly lifts it from the cushion with the blade. . . . Keeping one eye on the bit of gold leaf trembling on the knife blade, he runs the hair of the tip across his own hair, then gingerly picks up the bit of gold leaf from the knife blade with the tip, and transfers it to the gesso."[31]

In Prendergast's studio was a box from Behlen & Brothers of gold-leaf sheets 3⅜ x 3⅞ inches; he apparently used both eight- and ten-karat sheets,[32] and, on average, two to three boxes per panel.[33] He used a flat, wide brush called a gilder's tip to move the leaf from cushion to panel. Among the tools from Prendergast's studio specifically accounted for in Cennini's text are a gilder's cushion, gilder's knife, burnishing cloth, and agate burnishers.

Mishandling of the burnishers can very quickly destroy the leaf; Cennini emphasized caution: "Take your burnisher, rub it on your breast . . . . warm it well; then try whether the gold is fit for burnishing. Feel it carefully, always with doubt . . . . moving the stone [burnisher] very softly . . . . When it is properly burnished, the gold will appear almost dark from its own brightness."[34] Charles Prendergast not only mastered the delicate burnishing, but exercised the framemaker's task of "toning down" the gold in his pictorial works. He both painted over and abraded it to reduce its visual strength in the composition. The deliberate muting of the brilliant gold enhanced the antique quality of the picture.

In 1946, as Charles Prendergast reviewed with Hamilton Basso his experiences as a fine artist, he described his own work as falling into three consecutive periods. He labeled them by the predominant subjects of the images: oriental or celestial from 1912 to 1928, transitional from 1928 to 1932, and modern beginning in 1932.[35] Although his choice of materials for art making remained relatively constant during those years, his handling of them evolved as did his pictorial interests.

As has been discussed, Prendergast's first decorated pictorial works were carved reliefs, which he felt were not stable. In having to give up the compositional emphasis of the carved elements, Prendergast lost his primary organizational technique. During the late 1910s and 1920s, he compensated for the loss of sculptural emphasis by attending more carefully to other design elements, such as brilliant gilding and deliberate incising. The clarity of the incised lines—seen, for instance, in *Madonna and Child* (CR 2214, WCMA, p. 105)—and a definite tendency to etch every form in the composition mark his work through the end of the 1920s. The lines are as clearly legible and controlled as if they were sculpted.

To further enhance the effect of the incised line, Prendergast began outlining principal elements in dark tempera. In *The Riders* (CR 2229, WCMA, p. 68) the silhouettes of horses, figures, and middle-ground hills are outlined. Other alternatives to carving may be seen clearly in *Donkey Rider* (CR 2228, WCMA, p. 64), where the foreground is defined in color, the ponies in the middle ground are isolated before hills outlined by gold or color, and the golden background figures and foliage twinkle against the matte gesso sky. Typical of the work in the 1910s and 1920s, virtually every element is incised. The punchwork that Prendergast used in the 1910s, seen in *The Riders*, ceased to appear after the 1920s.

At the end of the 1920s, as his chosen subjects evolved from the ancient Persian/medieval/Byzantine inspirations, Prendergast dramatically loosened his style of preparation. Often he drew his composition directly on the gesso with pencil, skipping the step of the drawing transfer. The lines that Prendergast incised so carefully and deliberately in his earlier panels became more freely

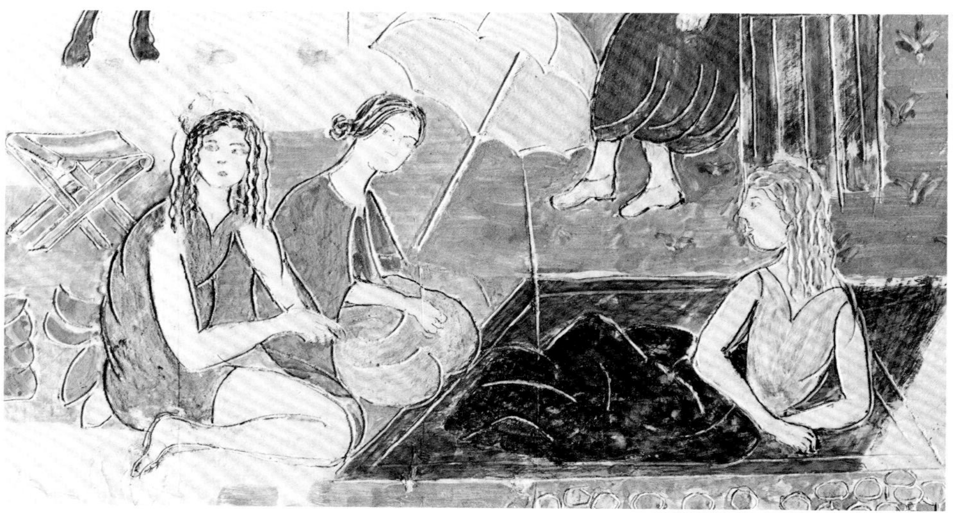

FIGURE 40. Detail of Charles Prendergast's *Holiday Beach Scene*, ca. 1931-32, Williams College Museum of Art (see p. 82)

incised, and on occasion were etched directly in the damp gesso without benefit of either pencil or transfer drawing. Some later panels, such as *Holiday Beach Scene* (CR 2265, WCMA, p. 82), show evidence of all three approaches at once: transfer drawing, sketch in pencil, and freehand incising.

Even after the incising on a panel was done, Prendergast felt free to disregard the lines. In the illustrated detail from *Holiday Beach Scene* (fig. 40), both the blanket and the kneeling figure have been altered from the original scheme. The blanket was changed simply by painting it a different shape. The hair of the figure appears to have been reduced by a late addition of a gesso patch. Changes may often be detected in works from the late 1920s on, and they indicate a greater freedom on the part of the artist to adapt the composition as it developed. This represents a major change from the complete etching of all design elements seen in *Madonna and Child* and other panels of the 1910s and 1920s.

During the later 1930s and 1940s, Prendergast seemed to return to the more controlled, static compositions of his carved panels;[36] these compositions reflect a folk-art aesthetic. He greatly reduced the amount of gold leaf he used, and only partially incised the compositions— elements he had originally added to replace the sculpture of the early panels. His strategies for pictorial design emphasized simplicity and relied on form: silhouetting the subjects with simple fields of color and eliminating the rich interplay of gesso and gold. Elements in *Donkey Rider #2* (fig. 41; CR 2282, WCMA) are as much defined by color as by incising; etched lines are restricted to the principal figural elements. Here, gold leaf plays a supporting, rather than a dominant, role.

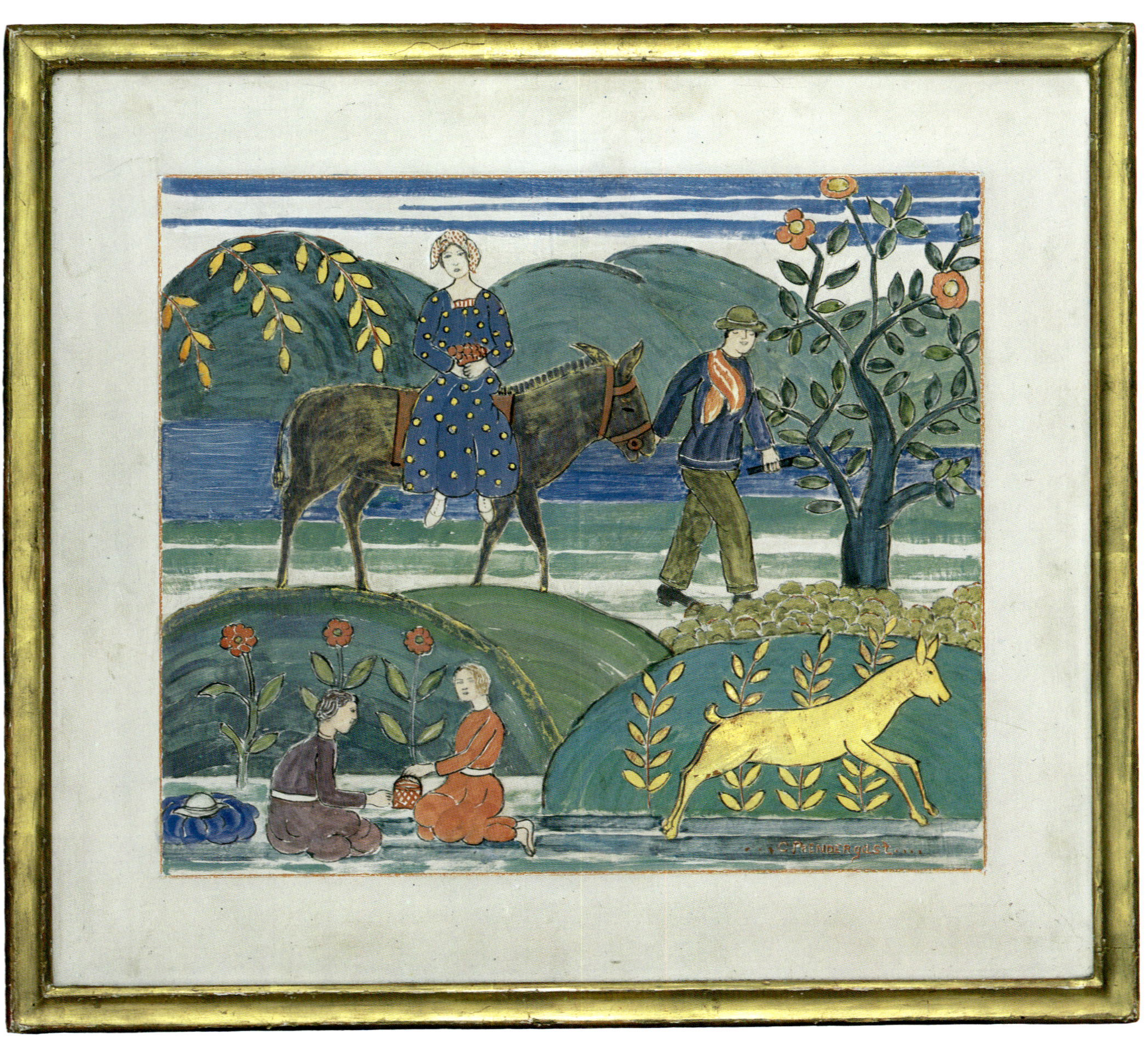

FIGURE 41. Charles Prendergast, *Donkey Rider #2*, ca. 1936, Williams College Museum of Art (see p. 87)

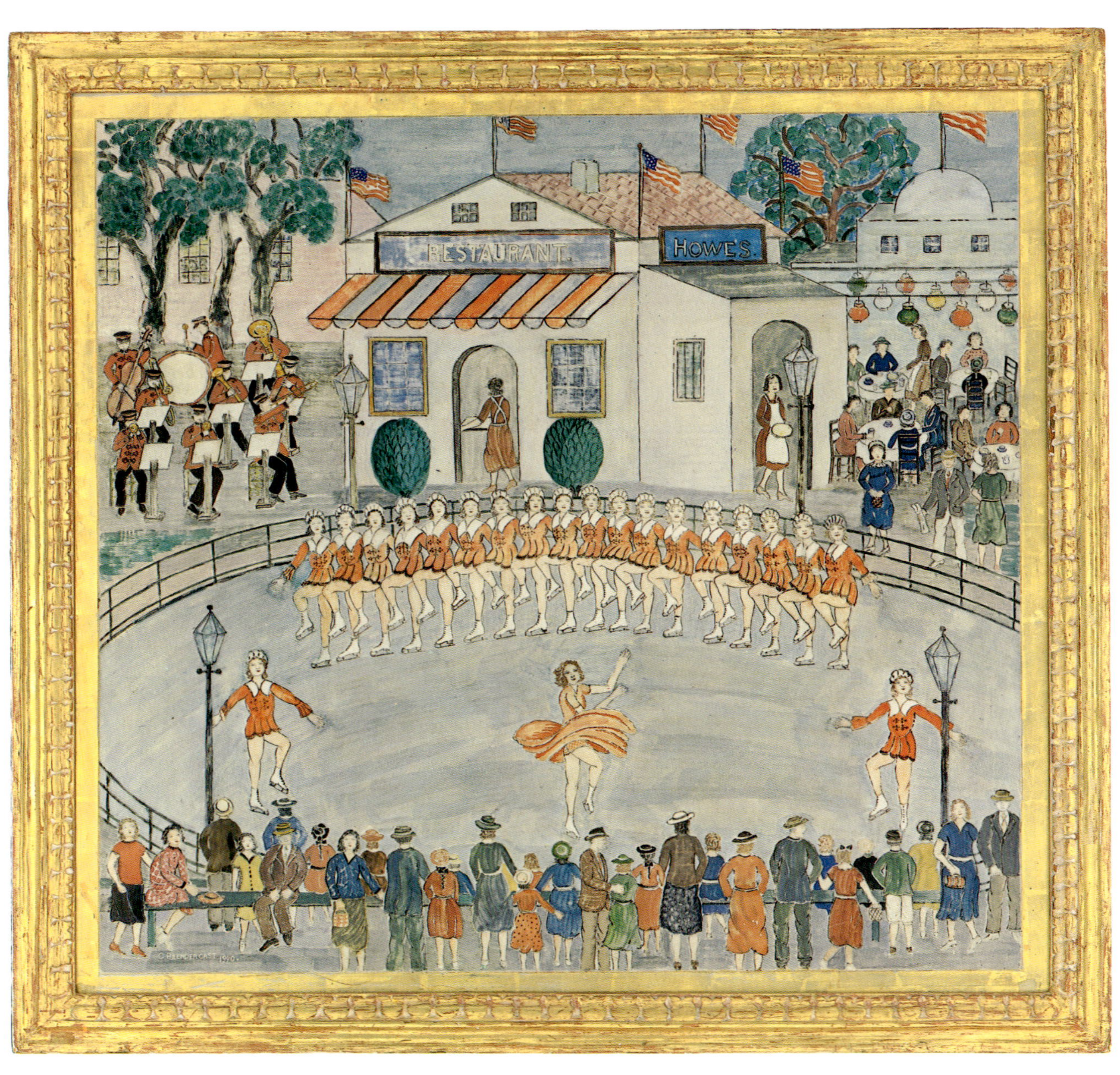

FIGURE 42. Charles Prendergast, *Skaters at the World's Fair*, 1940, Williams College Museum of Art (see p. 90)

As he reduced the quantity of gold leaf on his panels in the 1930s and 1940s, Prendergast took heightened interest in manipulating the visual effects of the tempera. In *Skaters at the World's Fair* (fig. 42; CR 2302, WCMA) Prendergast burnished the tempera into the gesso to create the shiny surface of the ice rink, and similarly burnished two sides of the restaurant building, leaving the third, shadowed side matte. Close observation of many of the late panels reveals similar burnishing for expressive effect; in *Bathers Under the Trees* (CR 2300, WCMA, p. 89) he created a subtle interplay of toned-down metal leaf foliage and matte blue tempera background with the polished arms and legs of the bathers.

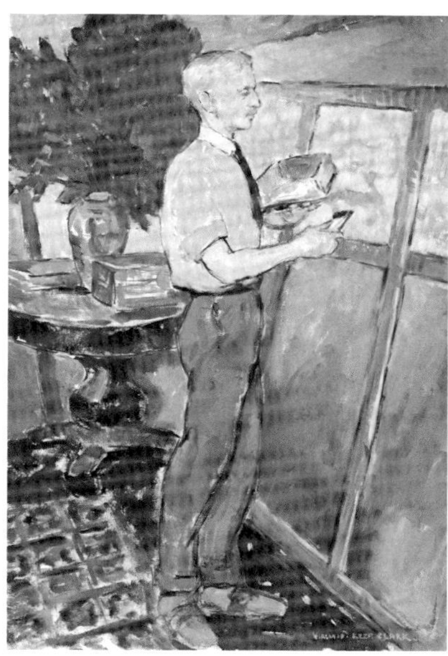

FIGURE 43. Virginia Keep Clark, *Portrait of Charles Prendergast*, 1923, oil on canvas (30⅛ x 20 in.), Gift of Mrs. Charles Prendergast, Courtesy Museum of Fine Arts, Boston (1974.605)

An innovation first seen in his flower vase panels of the 1930s is the inclusion of a self-mat in the composition of the panel. In both *Bathers Under the Trees* and in *Donkey Rider #2*, the composition is centered in the gessoed panel leaving a wide, white border; this device is effective in setting off both the image and the design of Prendergast's frame surrounding the whole. Occasionally, he gilded the self-mat as in *Skaters at the World's Fair* or *Fruit in a Silver Bowl* (CR 2285, Private Collection).

Charles Prendergast's panels evolved from the awkwardly carved decorations of the early 1910s to the simply painted, genre scenes and still lifes of the later 1930s and 1940s with their uptilted compositions. In between, he created ornately gilded and richly etched works through the 1920s and actively "drawn" scenes at the decade's turn. As much as his work was adapted and evolved from the old Italian "primitives," still it remained graced with his golden touch.

Charles Prendergast's work with these materials illuminates a relatively unexplored facet of twentieth-century art. In part, his art is characterized by explorations of the visual heritage of many cultures and historic eras, but it also shows an interest in techniques and methods pulled from the periphery— from the non-academic, decorative realms of art making. In this sense, Prendergast joined in the search of many twentieth-century artists to find new means of expression; in his case he chose wood, tempera, gesso, and gold to give material form to his unique vision.

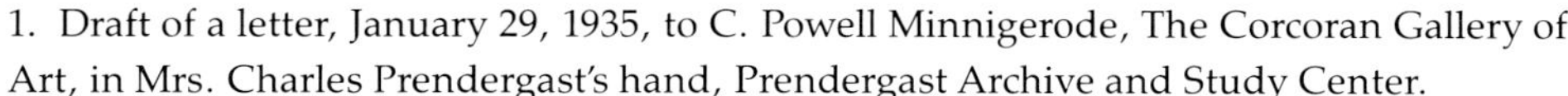

1. Draft of a letter, January 29, 1935, to C. Powell Minnigerode, The Corcoran Gallery of Art, in Mrs. Charles Prendergast's hand, Prendergast Archive and Study Center.

2. This essay could not have been written without the resources of the Prendergast Archive and Study Center and those who contributed to it—especially Mrs. Charles Prendergast; Nancy Mowll Mathews, Prendergast Curator; Carol Clark; Carol Derby; and Ann Greenwood; also Mike Heslip and Hugh Glover at the Williamstown Regional Art Conservation Laboratory; M. P. Naud, Hirschl & Adler Gallery; Anne Havinga, Jerry Ward, and Linda Foss at the Museum of Fine Arts, Boston; and Erika Passantino, The Phillips Collection, Washington, D.C.

3. See Johnson 1979 for a thorough presentation of these movements.

4. For example, Meyer-Riefstahl 1916, pp. 147-61; Wetzel 1915, pp. 284-99; Binyon 1916, pp. 328-39; Mather 1920, pp. 148-59.

5. Cennini 1899.

6. Prendergast 1909, p. 70; Christian Science Monitor 1913; Crawford 1919, p. 47; Pach 1923, p. 11.

7. Benton 1969, pp. 57-58.

8. See York 1933, pp. 105-6; or Thompson's tribute to York and other teachers in Thompson 1962, intro.

9. Other treatises on methods of making similar objects were to a more or less degree available to Prendergast such as *Treatise of Japanning and Varnishing*, Stalker and Parker, 1688, described in some detail in Comstock 1935, p. 283; or Crane 1893, pp. 45- 48.

10. See Benton 1969, pp. 3-4, 42 for early interest in tempera, and p. 64 for materials of *America Today* murals. See also Braun 1985 for documentation of the most recent restoration of the murals.

11. *Etruscan Vase*, tempera, ex-Quinn collection, Metropolitan Museum of Art, New York; *Silence*, oil on gesso, ex-Bliss collection, Museum of Modern Art, New York.

12. *Rooster*, The Phillips Collection, Washington, D.C. Exhibited 1917, Society of Independent Artists, New York. Cf. *Unfinished figure of a rooster* by Charles Prendergast, WCMA, p. 107.

13. Interview with the artist's son by Carol Clark, June 2, 1984, Prendergast Archive and Study Center.

14. A.E. Gallatin, quoted in Hirschl & Adler 1972.

15. Kuehne 1932, p. 61.

16. "American Folk Art: The Art of the Common Man," at The Museum of Modern Art, New York, 1932.

17. Notebook belonging to Charles Prendergast, "Metropolitan," not microfilmed, Prendergast Archive and Study Center.

18. Thompson 1956 proved enormously helpful in understanding all aspects of making panel pictures, but especially in understanding the nature of gold leaf.

19. The artist had a fine collection of woodworking tools by such makers as S. J. Addis, London; H. Taylor, Sheffield; Peugot Frères; and Buck Brothers. Prendergast Archive and Study Center.

20. On some of these early works, Charles appended strips of wood to opposite ends of the panel, which are carved and treated as part of the pictorial surface, as in *Annunciation* (fig. 36; CR 2215). They were intended to prevent warping, but were not successful. Regarding Charles's belief that carving caused warping, see citation of an interview with Mrs. Charles Prendergast in 1977 by Ross C. Anderson, in his unpublished paper, "The Panels of Charles Prendergast: Stylistic and Iconographic Sources," Prendergast Archive and Study Center.

21. Letter from Charles Prendergast to John Quinn, April 5, 1917. Copy in Prendergast Archive and Study Center.

22. Prendergast 1909, p. 70.

23. Crawford 1919, p. 47; Basso 1946a, p. 24.

24. The verso of *Donkey Rider #2* (fig. 41), which is a plywood panel, shows some figures in relief as if the artist were testing this support material for the possibility of carving.

25. Loose note from Charles Prendergast to the owner, after 1938, private collection. Copy at Prendergast Archive and Study Center.

26. In Kuehne 1932, p. 61, Kuehne calls for "sheet glue and whiting." In American Artist 1941, p. 4, John S. de Martelly calls for one part rabbit-skin glue, sixteen parts water, and seven to ten parts whiting.

27. Mayer 1981, p. 542.

28. These tools and supplies were in Charles Prendergast's studio when he died; it is not certain whether they represent the materials he used throughout his career or only at the end.

29. Note from Charles Prendergast to the owner, after 1938, private collection. Copy at Prendergast Archive and Study Center.

30. Cennini 1899, pp. 110-111.

31. Basso 1946a, p. 30.

32. Basso 1946a, p. 30.

33. Notation "2 1/2 Books a panel" in Charles Prendergast, "Sketchbook C," The Museum of Fine Arts, Boston, 1972.1167.

34. Cennini 1899, p. 114.

35. Basso 1946b, pp. 30-34.

36. It is important to note that about the time of his "transitional" period—1928-1932—the artist completed an extraordinary amount of work: six sides of a tall three-panel screen (CR 2258) and four of his largest panels (CR 2260, 2263, 2264, 2265). The shifts either in medium (reverse painting on glass, see CR 2233, Collection of Mrs. Charles Prendergast, p. 72) or to the radically simplified compositions of his flower panels seem to be explained by a desire to steer a new course.

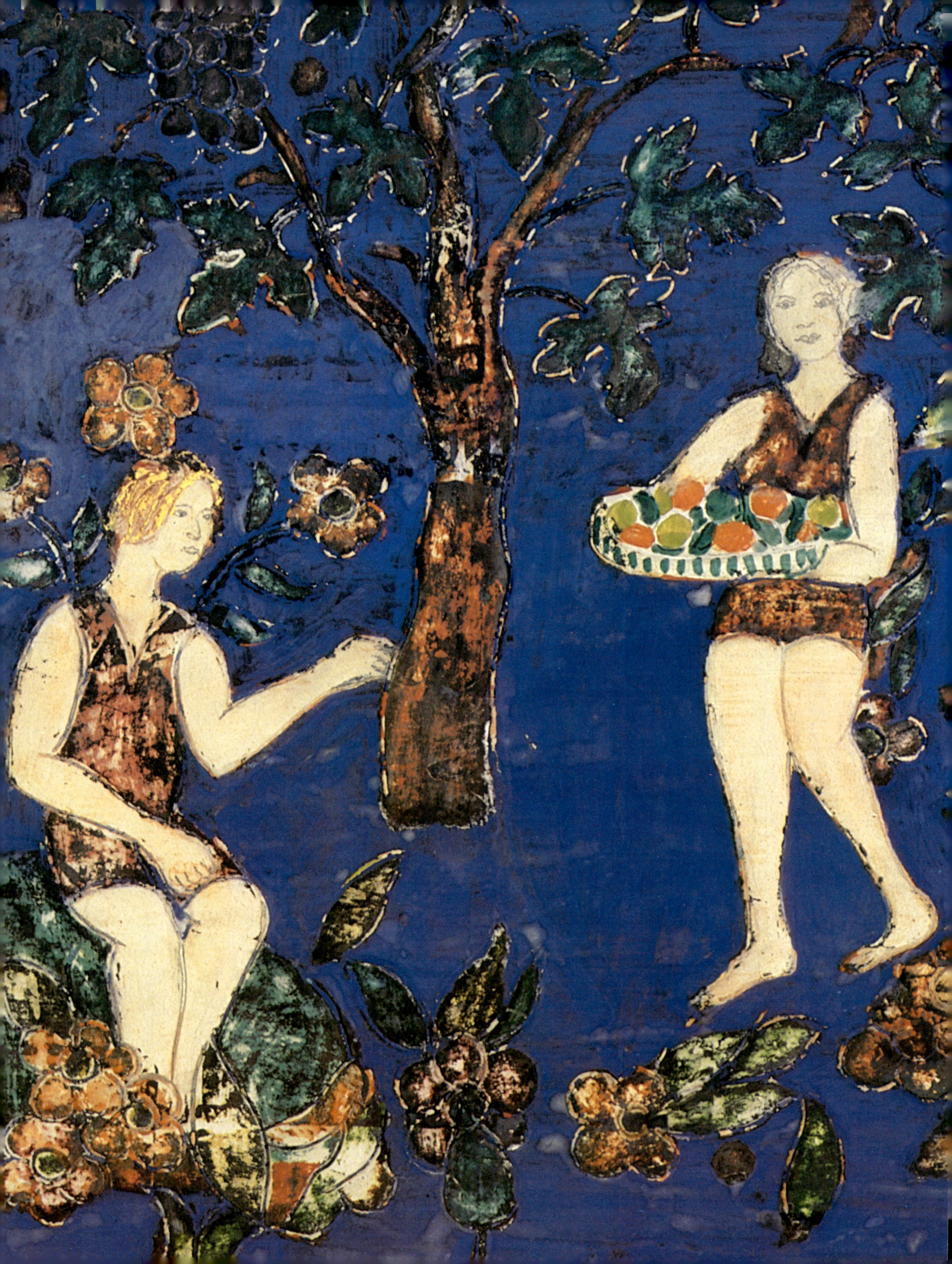

INTRODUCTION TO THE CATALOGUE

THE WORKS INCLUDED in the following catalogue are in the collections of the Williams College Museum of Art and Mrs. Charles Prendergast.[1] Together they represent approximately one-quarter of Charles Prendergast's known work, including the entire range of his media and every phase of his career. The entries have been arranged chronologically with closely-related works from the same period of Prendergast's art often discussed in a single entry.

The basic information in each catalogue entry has been drawn from the Prendergast catalogue raisonné,[2] abbreviated "CR," which was published by the Williams College Museum of Art in 1990 after seven years of research by a team of scholars led by Carol Clark, Nancy Mathews, and Gwendolyn Owens. The catalogue raisonné information has been supplemented by the object's exhibition history at the Williams College Museum of Art, technical notes about the object, and by an essay examining and interpreting the object in depth. Many authors have contributed to the catalogue including Molly Donovan, Anne Dowling, Susan Imbriani, Rachel B. H. Petrik, Linda Reynolds, and Stefanie Spray, students in the Williams College Graduate Program in the History of Art; and Marion M. Goethals, Vivian Patterson, Ann Ugast Greenwood, and Claudia Hill, members of the Williams College Museum of Art staff. Their names will appear after their entries; all unsigned entries have been written by Nancy Mowll Mathews, Prendergast Curator.

The dating of Charles Prendergast's art is very difficult in light of the scanty documentary evidence available and his tendency to repeat motifs, often at intervals of several years. The dates proposed for works in this catalogue sometimes diverge from those offered in the catalogue raisonné and represent another step toward a firm chronology, but they are still under examination.

Prendergast's materials and working methods are also difficult to identify. The information presented here has been gathered by close examination and by consultation with the conservators at the Williamstown Regional Art Conservation Laboratory—Leslie Paisley, Michael Heslip, Hugh Glover, and Ingrid Neuman. Since this aspect is also the subject of ongoing research, some of the conclusions about materials may differ from the information found in the catalogue raisonné. For the most part, this information is found under "technical notes." Technical notes have been eliminated for works on paper that do not involve any unusual aspects of Prendergast's materials or methods.

This catalogue does not attempt to provide information about all the frames by Charles Prendergast currently in the two collections under review. A more extensive project to research Prendergast's frames is underway at the Prendergast Archive and Study Center at the Williams College Museum of Art and will document the frames at a later date. The three frames included in this catalogue are those that have entered the Williams College Museum of Art collection as frames, and not as part of a work of fine art by Maurice or Charles Prendergast.

1. The works by Charles Prendergast in the collection of his widow, Eugénie Prendergast, have been designated as promised gifts to the Williams College Museum of Art.

2. Clark, Mathews, Owens 1990.

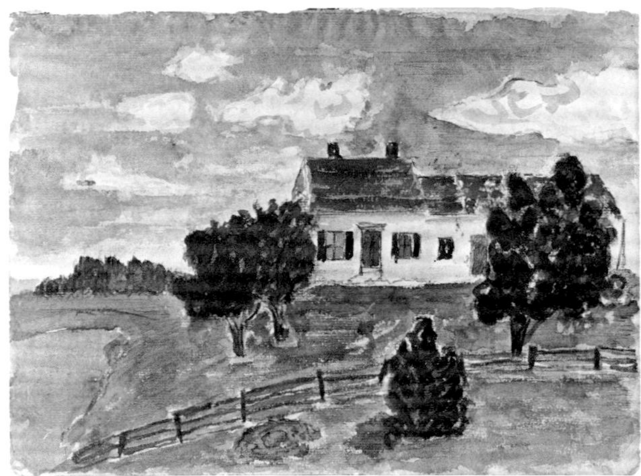

Study of a House, before 1890 [?]
CR 2319
Watercolor and pencil on paper (9 x 12 in.; 22.9 x 30.5 cm)
Williams College Museum of Art, Gift of Mrs. Charles Prendergast (87.5.14)

INSCRIPTIONS
verso, u.l.: my first watercolor-/ CP

PROVENANCE
The artist; to Mrs. Charles Prendergast, 1948; to present collection, 1987

EXHIBITIONS
1988a Williams College (no #)

TECHNICAL NOTES
The application of the watercolor has left some areas of opaque color and others of puddled pigment. The laid paper used has yellowed due to its high acidic content.

PRENDERGAST'S INSCRIPTION, "my first watercolor" (found on the verso), helps to explain the surprisingly amateurish quality of this work. It is distinctly less accomplished than Prendergast's other early pictorial work such as his first carved panel, *Rising Sun*, 1912 (CR 2212, WCMA, p. 56), or his earliest known drawings found in "Sketchbook D," 1911 (CR 2409, Museum of Fine Arts, Boston). Although it has been assumed that *Study of a House* dates from this same period (1911-15), it is perhaps useful to see it as much earlier, even dating to the early 1880s before he received any formal training.

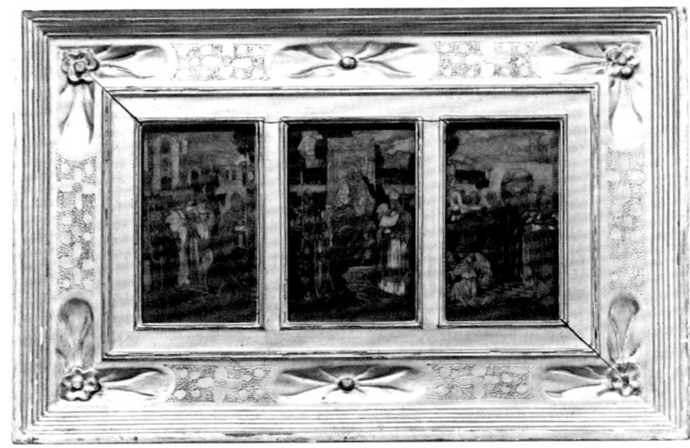

Frame for "Study of Altarpiece" by George Hallowell, 1902
not catalogued
Gold leaf with punchwork on gessoed, carved wood (11 x 16⅛ in.; 27.9 x 41 cm)
Williams College Museum of Art, Gift of Mrs. Charles Prendergast (85.10.1)

INSCRIPTIONS
verso, burned into wood: Prendergast/ 1902

PROVENANCE
(William Postar); to (Lewis Shepard); to present collection, 1985

BIBLIOGRAPHY
Gengarelly 1989 (p. 30; ill.)

EXHIBITIONS
1988b Williams College (#50); 1989b Williams College (#54); 1990 Williams College (no #)

TECHNICAL NOTES
The molding is so wide that this frame is actually larger than the watercolor it encircles. The carved designs have been coated with a thick layer of gesso and then gilded to produce a satiny surface.

THIS FRAME IS REPRESENTATIVE of the type of work Prendergast was engaged in during his close association with Hermann Dudley Murphy in the Boston suburb of Winchester. The elaborate decoration of the frame, featuring punchwork designs and Art Nouveau corner motifs, shows his mastery of both traditional and contemporary design elements. The frame was commissioned by the artist George Hallowell for his watercolor studies of an important altarpiece Hallowell executed for the All Saints Church on Ashmont Street in Boston. This and four other studies for the altarpiece were exhibited at the St. Botolph Club in 1903 and the New York Watercolor Club exhibition in London in 1905.[1]

1. See Derby 1989, p. 29.

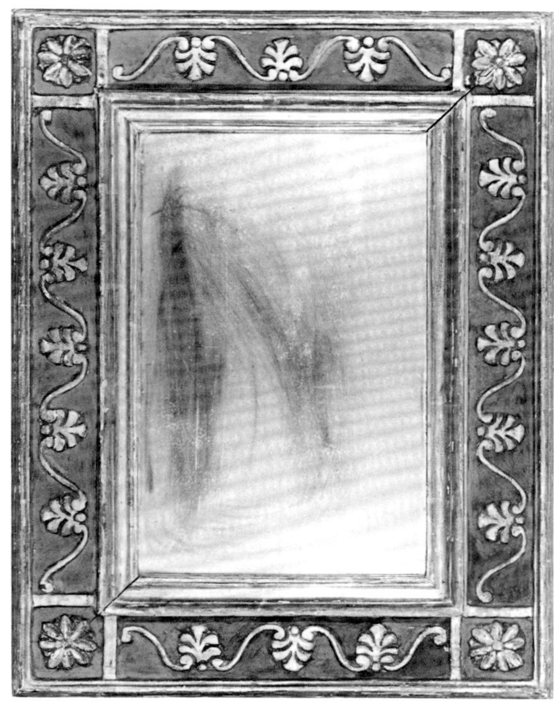

Mirror Frame – Blue and Gold, ca. 1907-12
not catalogued
Tempera and gold leaf on gessoed, carved wood
(22 x 17 in.; 55.9 x 43.2 cm)
Williams College Museum of Art, Gift of Mrs. Charles Prendergast (86.18.16)

INSCRIPTIONS
Unsigned

PROVENANCE
Mrs. Charles Prendergast; to present collection, 1986

BIBLIOGRAPHY
Gengarelly 1989 (p. 38; ill.)

EXHIBITIONS
1968 Rutgers University (#77, ill. p. 114); 1984 Williams College (#19); 1988b Williams College (#60); 1990 Williams College (no #)

TECHNICAL NOTES
The shallow carving design on the front of the four pieces of mitered, wood molding is made up of anthemion leaves placed in contrary positions, connected by yin-yang spirals with classical rosette-like ornaments in each corner. After carving, the molding was glued and nailed together, then the entire frame was gessoed, and afterwards given a coat of red bole and finally gilded. Bright blue tempera was painted in the lower, recessed areas surrounding the design on the top face of the molding. The silver-backed mirror, which fits into the mirror frame, has corroded on the proper right side.

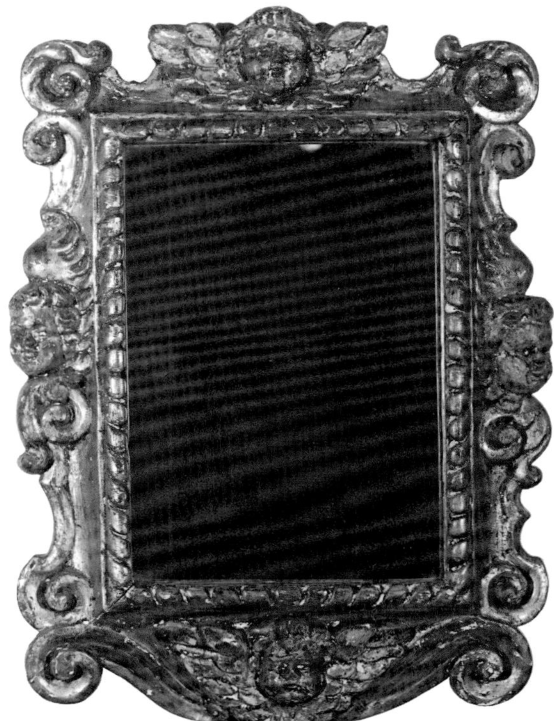

Mirror Frame with Four Angels' Heads, ca. 1912
not catalogued
Gold leaf on gessoed, carved wood (22 x 16 in.; 55.9 x 40.6 cm)
Williams College Museum of Art, Gift of Mrs. Charles Prendergast (86.18.15)

INSCRIPTIONS
Unsigned

PROVENANCE
Mrs. Charles Prendergast; to present collection, 1986

BIBLIOGRAPHY
Gengarelly 1989 (p. 39)

EXHIBITIONS
1968 Rutgers University (#75, ill. p. 112); 1969 Hirschl & Adler (#58); 1984 Williams College (#18); 1988b Williams College (#68)

TECHNICAL NOTES
Four pieces of thick and wide wood molding are mitered to make a rectangular form. Each piece has a carved, three-quarter-turned cherub head, surrounded by wings in high relief. Curvilinear, spiral motifs link the heads together, and there is a rope motif, for the bead molding, along the inner lip of the frame. After the molding was glued and nailed together, a thin gesso layer was applied to the front surface of the frame, followed by a thin coat of red bole and then gold leaf. A silver-backed mirror was then inserted from the reverse, and held in place by large nails.

 THE ANTHEMIONS AND ROSETTES from the *Mirror Frame – Blue and Gold* are classical motifs, while the winged angel heads linked together with large scrolls on the *Mirror Frame with Four Angels' Heads* are Renaissance motifs. The anthemion is classified as a palmette band and an ornament belonging to antiquity.[1] It resembles the fingers of an outspread hand, with the center leaf as the largest finger. The rosette also derives from antiquity, though this motif is used throughout the ages. The highly decorative carving on *Mirror Frame with Four Angels' Heads* brings to mind strap-work frames. Strap-work frames have interlaced and curling bands adorned with fantastic shapes such as animal and cherub heads, festoons, foliage, and fruit. This type of frame, like leathern straps, was frequently used in the Renaissance to surround empty spaces for decorative purposes in architecture, cabinet-making, coins, decoration on books, epitaphs, heraldry, jewelry, medals, and sepulchral monuments.[2]

These Classical and Renaissance motifs appear in architectural door, wall, and window moldings of American Art Nouveau architects Henry H. Richardson, John Wellborn Root, and Louis H. Sullivan.[3] Sullivan, in particular, sought to fuse function and ornament in his architecture, establishing a mixture of building utility with geometric and naturalistic decoration. The motifs are also found in the typographical ornament of periodical and poster designs of the same date. Curvilinear bands and scrolls inhabit Art Nouveau illustrations by Aubrey Beardsley, and anthemion leaves frame a late nineteenth-century poster by Will H. Bradley.[4]

The same ornamentation appears on four of Charles Prendergast's frames, and also in Maurice Prendergast's sketchbooks. At the top of Charles's *Mirror Frame with Birds on a Blue Ground* (Collection of Mrs. Charles Prendergast) is an angel head, flanked by wings, that is carved and gilded. A drawing of a head and an anthemion decorate a frame edge in one of Maurice's sketchbooks.[5] Charles Prendergast carved anthemion leaves and corner rosettes and employed a blue/gold color scheme in the frame for Maurice's *Clock Tower, St. Mark's Square* (CR 1011, Stanford University Museum of Art), his own *Decorated Mirror with Two Figures* (CR 2231, WCMA, p. 66), and the frame for Maurice's *Splash of Sunshine and Rain* (CR 674, Collection of Alice M. Kaplan). Charles could also have copied the anthemion design from one of his brother's studies for frames.[6]

Claudia Hill

1. Meyer 1957, p. 145.
2. Ibid., pp. 468-9.
3. Examples of the Classical and Renaissance ornament discussed are used on buildings by Henry H. Richardson (1838-1886) such as the second-floor panels of cut brick decoration of rosettes and leaf designs on the Rectory for Trinity Church, Boston, 1879-80, as well as on the fireplace in the reading room of Oliver Ames Free Library, 1877-79 (although the architect and framemaker, Stanford White, is credited with its design). Those ornaments found in the architecture of John Wellborn Root (1850-1891) are the flora designs on the arched entrance to the Rand-McNally Building, Chicago, 1888-90, and the stylized anthemion leaves framing the arched entryway of the Rookery, West Vestibule, Chicago, 1885-88. These same motifs appear in Louis H. Sullivan's (1856-1924) plans for the strap-work facade of Carson, Pirie, Scott Store, Chicago, 1903-04, and over the entrance to the Equitable Building, Atlanta, 1890-1892. The stylized anthemion leaf was used on Sullivan's frieze from the facade on the Rothschild Store, Chicago, 1880-81.
4. I am referring to illustrations by Aubrey Beardsley (1872-1898) in Pope 1902, a book in the Prendergasts' library. The poster with the anthemion border by Will H. Bradley (1868-1962) is *The Kiss*. This woodcut was used as the poster for *Bradley: His Book*, Vol. II, No. 1, November 1896.
5. Maurice Prendergast, "Sketchbook #74," ca. 1911-12 (CR 1499, Museum of Fine Arts, Boston, Gift of Mrs. Charles Prendergast [1972.1164]); AAA Roll # 3587, frame #282.
6. Maurice Prendergast's "Sketchbook for Frame Studies," ca. 1898-1903 (CR 1481, WCMA, Gift of Mrs. Charles Prendergast [85.23.9]); AAA Roll #3583, frames #221-3. See Derby 1989, pp. 37-38, and Derby 1990, p. 102.

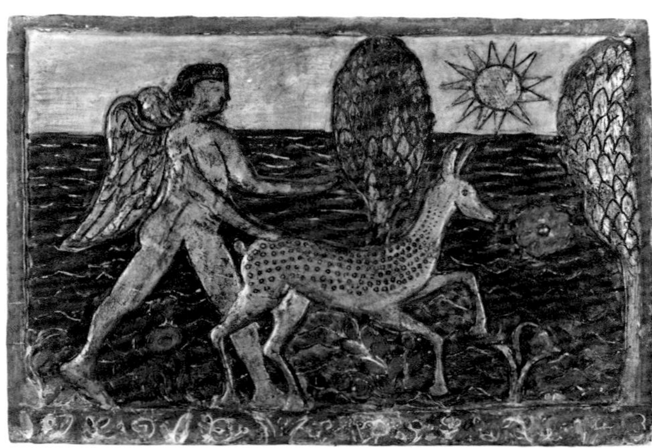

Rising Sun, ca. 1912
CR 2212
Color illustration, p. 14
Frame by the artist
Tempera and gold leaf on incised, carved, and gessoed panel (12 x 17¾ in.; 30.5 x 45.1 cm)
Williams College Museum of Art, Gift of Mrs. Charles

Prendergast (91.28.15)

INSCRIPTIONS

l.r. incised: CP

PROVENANCE

The artist; to Mrs. Charles Prendergast, 1948; to present collection, 1991

BIBLIOGRAPHY

Crawford 1919 (pp. 47-49; ill.); Hudson 1919 (pp. 86-89; ill.); LeBrun 1968a (p. 26); Wattenmaker 1968 (pp. 12, 25, 30); Taylor 1984 (B:3; ill.)

EXHIBITIONS

1954 Kraushaar (#1, ill.); 1968 Rutgers University (#1, ill. p. 8); 1969 Hirschl & Adler (#1); 1984a Williams College (#1); 1988b Williams College (#65); 1989b Williams College (#25); 1990 Williams College (no #)

TECHNICAL NOTES

Gold leaf has been applied to the angel, deer, trees, and sun, but the "false frame" has been painted with yellow ochre in imitation of gold. The bottom edge of the panel has been incised and painted in a floral design; a patch of punchwork unrelated to the design is found to the right of center. The reverse of the panel is coated with gesso and has numerous pencil marks and test swatches of gold. The panel is warped, but in good condition because of treatment in 1989.

ALTHOUGH CHARLES PRENDERGAST did not inscribe the date on this panel,[1] he identified it to writers such as Morris Crawford as his earliest panel, and he later told Hamilton Basso[2] that it was done in 1912. It has many features that are characteristic of his early carved panels, such as the use of a rather thick (one inch) board of sugar pine, which allowed him to carve a design in high-relief but which also warped very badly. By the end of the teens, he had switched to plywood supports, which solved the problem of warping but in turn only allowed Prendergast to make shallow incisions in the surface. *Rising Sun* also has a "false frame"—a ridge carved along the outside edge in the shape of a frame. The result is a close integration of pictorial and frame design that is appropriate for Prendergast's transition from frame-making to picture-making.

The image of a figure alongside a deer is one that Prendergast would use many times in the future. As in *Rising Sun*, the figure in *Bounding Deer* (which belonged to Morris Crawford [CR 2223, Collection of Mr. and Mrs. Meyer P. Potamkin]) is male and is running as if to suggest a hunting scene. In other versions, the figure is female (such as in *Fantasy* [CR 2234, The Fuller Collection]) and embraces the deer (or sometimes goat) as if it were a pet. Prendergast no doubt took the original design from a source in ancient art because a sketch of the same composition is found in a Maurice Prendergast sketchbook ("Sketchbook #56," CR 1504, Museum of Fine Arts, Boston) in which Maurice copied many other designs from antique art.[3] The composition suggests an image of Apollo who was often depicted as if he were running with his horses (rather than in the usual chariot) to bring the rising sun.[4] Apollo's twin sister, Artemis, was a hunter but was also known to protect herds from the attacks of wild animals,[5] and thus Prendergast may have used the female version of this motif in such works as *Fantasy*.

A further variation of the theme might be found in *Sunset* (CR 2219, WCMA, p. 63), which shows three men alongside a bull. In Prendergast's *Manual of Mythology*,[6] the Near Eastern god Mithras was discussed as a darker variant of Apollo, symbolizing the absence of light ("Sunset") and represented by a man strangling or plunging a knife into the neck of a bull. But even if Prendergast used such a violent mythological precedent, he transformed the image into a peaceful one, and his interest in Apollo-related themes (rising sun, springtime, rebirth, and resurrection) would continue throughout his career.

1. It was reproduced in Crawford 1919, p. 49, with the caption: "This is the first panel that Mr. Prendergast made, and it is interesting for comparison with his later work." Morris Crawford—photographer, historian of design, and writer on contemporary fashion—was a close friend of the Prendergast brothers.

2. Basso 1946b, p. 30.

3. Inscribed in this sketchbook is "Cesnola Collection," a reference to the collection of ancient Cypriot art donated to the Metropolitan Museum by its first director Luigi Palma di Cesnola. Unfortunately a handbook of the collection published in 1914 does not include any illustrations from which Prendergast might have gotten the design for *Rising Sun*. The discovery of the sketch related to *Rising Sun* in Maurice Prendergast's sketchbook was made by Elizabeth Durkin, and discussed in Durkin 1989.

4. Such an image is reproduced in Prendergast's copy of Murray 1895 as Figure 22, captioned: "Helios, or Apollo. Relief. (From Troy)."

5. Ibid., p. 136.

6. Ibid., pp. 131-2

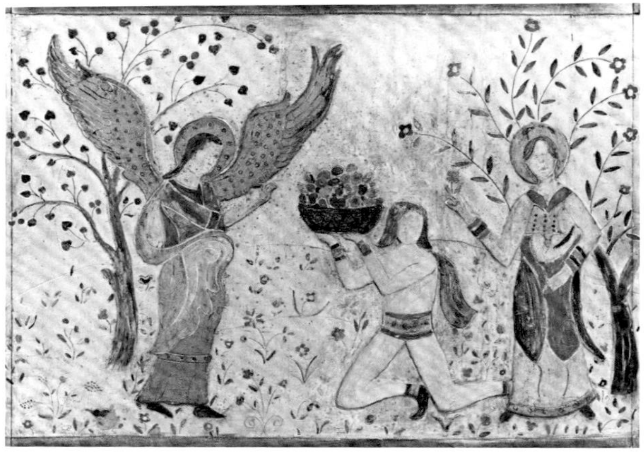

Annunciation, ca. 1912-15
Offering of the Material to the Spiritual
CR 2215
Color illustration, p. 42
Frame by the artist
Tempera and gold leaf on incised, carved, and gessoed panel (20 x 27 in.; 51.4 x 68.6 cm)
Williams College Museum of Art, Gift of Mrs. Charles Prendergast (86.18.11)

INSCRIPTIONS
l.l. incised: CP

PROVENANCE
The artist; to Mrs. Charles Prendergast, 1948; to present collection, 1986

BIBLIOGRAPHY
Crawford 1919 (pp. 48; ill.); Antiques Arts Weekly 1986 (p. 113); New England Monthly 1986 (p. 96); Lauzon 1990 (p. 28)

EXHIBITIONS
1935 Kraushaar (#16); 1969 Hirschl & Adler (#2); 1970b Society of Four Arts (#30); 1983a Williams College (#27); 1984a Williams College (#2, ill.); 1985 Williams College (no #); 1986 High Museum (no #, p. 145, ill.); 1986 Williams College (no #); 1988b Williams College (#66); 1989a Williams College (no #); 1989b Williams College (#32); 1990 Williams College (no #); 1992 Williams College (no #)

TECHNICAL NOTES
The figures, offering basket, and trunks and branches of the trees are all carved in ca. 1/8-inch relief. The flowers in the foreground and the contours of the garments have been incised. The panel may be unfinished as Prendergast did not paint over or gild the white gesso of the background. The panel appears to be made from an old drawing board.

ONE OF CHARLES PRENDERGAST'S earliest panels, *Annunciation* depicts a traditional Christian theme. Prendergast, who was not particularly religious, did not intend to convey a conventional Christian message, as evidenced by the Persian derivation of certain elements of the composition. The tree seen on the left side, for example, with its curved, upsweeping branches, each sparsely capped with a spade-shaped leaf, is nearly identical to a tree found on a fourteenth-century Persian polychrome plate that Prendergast knew through an illustration in *Les Arts* that he had torn out of the magazine and saved.[1] The other tree, with its long branches culminating in bright flowers, seems to be a playful variation of this motif. Dotting the foreground are an abundance of tiny plants, each producing a single, colorful bloom; these have their precedent in the numerous Persian miniatures in the Museum of Fine Arts in Boston that had greatly impressed Prendergast[2] such as "Dara Receiving the Crown," a sixteenth-century illustration of an episode from the epic *Shah-nama*.[3] Even the attire of the Angel Gabriel, with a gently flared hemline and pointed shoes shown in profile, both of which are conventions in Persian painting, indicate Prendergast's familiarity with and appreciation of the Museum of Fine Art's Islamic holdings.[4]

Rarely limited to a single source, Prendergast may have also been drawing upon the Byzantine mosaics found in Ravenna, Italy. Although it is unclear if Prendergast visited Ravenna during his Italian sojourn, he was familiar with its rich mosaics at least through an illustrated book that he owned.[5] Like many of these mosaics, the foreground of *Annunciation* is barely distinguishable from the background; only a gentle, curving incision in the gesso and the confinement of the flowers to the lower area define the space. The central, kneeling figure bearing an offering, a cloth flowing down his back, may have been inspired in dress and posture by the Three Magi at S. Apollinare Nuovo.[6] Likewise, the very frontal figure of Mary on the far right, whose arms are sharply bent at the elbows, resembles numerous similarly posed figures seen in Ravenna mosaics. Although the Persian and Byzantine sources for Prendergast's *Annunciation* are quite recognizable, he fully reinterpreted his borrowings by conflating and modifying them, thus creating an image that is uniquely his own.

Stefanie Spray

1. Migeon 1910, p. 21.
2. Basso 1946a, p. 25.

3. Museum of Fine Arts, Boston, 14.503.

4. The Museum of Fine Arts exhibited Persian and Indian manuscripts, drawings, and paintings from the collection of Denman W. Ross from January 23 through June 9, 1914; and Persian and Indian paintings from the Goloubew Collection, a major gift to the museum in 1914, were shown from February 6 through April 5, 1915.

5. Ricci 1911.

6. Ibid., plate 55.

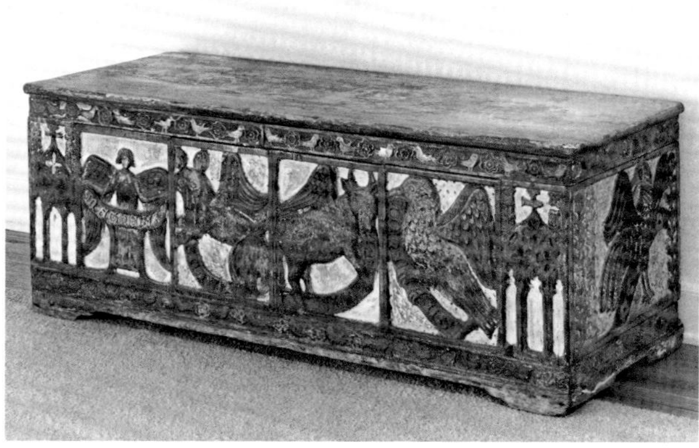

Chest, ca. 1915
CR 2398
Tempera and gold leaf on carved, incised, and gessoed wood (18½ x 49½ x 18½ in.; 46.9 x 125.7 x 46.9 cm)
Collection of Mrs. Charles Prendergast

INSCRIPTIONS
Unsigned

PROVENANCE
The artist; to present collection, 1948

TECHNICAL NOTES
This is a six-board wooden chest with overhanging lid to which eight gessoed, carved, incised, and polychromed panels and eight similarly fashioned moldings have been applied. The original chest is dove-tail joined; Prendergast's decorated panels have been applied to the front and sides with machine-cut nails. Opening the lid reveals a deep well; the chest has no interior storage till (see Anderson 1990, p. 88; Butler 1989, p. 66). The original chest's lock and accompanying front escutcheon have been removed, and a wooden block has been inserted in the lid where the top of the latch mechanism once existed. Three (brass) metal butt hinges secure the lid to the body of the chest. The chest has a simple skirt or apron and modest molded base legs.

The primary and secondary woods of the original chest are undetermined; Prendergast's applied panels are probably sugar or white pine coated in gesso. Each of the 1/2-inch-thick panels and separate pieces of molding exhibit deeply carved and heavily polychromed gesso decoration, especially in the rendering of generalized shapes of figures, flowers, and birds. Prendergast employed shallow incised lines for finer detailing and for textural effect. Vivid tempera colors have been used overall, on sculpted forms, and in the foliate design of the background; there is evidence of applied gold leaf. The lid and back of the chest have been left untouched.

ANTHROPOMORPHIC SYMBOLS of the four evangelists—the angel of Saint Matthew, the lion of Saint Mark, the ox of Saint Luke, and the eagle of Saint John—adorn the front of the chest.[1] Each of the figures has wings and holds a scroll bearing its name: "Mathew," "Marcus," "Lucus," and "Iohannus." The symbols are separated from each other by decorative, vertical bands that, in combination with top and bottom borders displaying birds and rosettes, anchor the main figures within an elaborate arcade. The group of evangelists is flanked left and right by two additional panels. Each panel depicts a small temple structure comprised of four pillars supporting a domed roof topped by a cross and is, in style, evocative of the Byzantine East.

The side panel to the left of Saint Matthew's angel depicts a monstrous fish framed by fronds of laurel and the bird-rosette motif. The second side panel depicts a large colorful bird, facing left, with wings outstretched. This creature is similarly framed, save for the addition of a second laurel branch to its left.

The artist's thoughtful arrangement of the central, side, and border panels suggest an iconographic program on the theme of rebirth and resurrection. This is established mainly by the omnipresent symbols of the evangelists and, secondarily, by the presumed symbols on the end panels of a large fish or whale and a bird of prey or phoenix.

The fish was an early Christian symbol, connected from the second century on with baptism and eventually associated with the acrostic "Jesus Christ, Son of God, Saviour." The Bible describes the creature that swallowed the prophet Jonah as a "great fish." Early artists were generally unfamiliar with the appearance of a whale; and in primitive

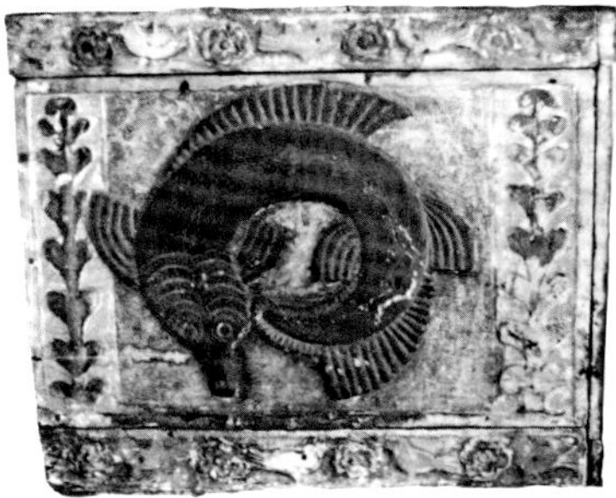

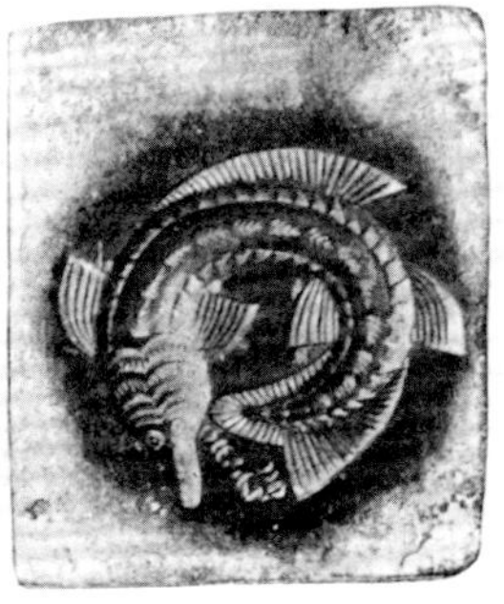

Left, detail of *Chest*. Right, carved wooden cake mold illustrated (no. 245) in *Peasant Art in Russia*, edited by Charles Holme, 1912, Williams College Museum of Art, Prendergast Archive and Study Center

Christian art, where the theme of Jonah is chiefly found, the fish is represented as a kind of sea-dragon or occasionally as a dolphin. The story of Jonah was referred to by Christ himself (Matt. 12:40) as a prefiguration of his own death and resurrection.[2]

Prendergast's source for the design of the "fish" emerges from his own library: a 1912 edition of Charles Holme's *Peasant Art in Russia* in which wooden molds used for gingerbread decoration are described[3] (see illustration). Such carvings were popular from the sixteenth through the eighteenth centuries, used to fashion confections appropriate to birth, wedding, funeral, and major religious feasts. Plate 245 depicts a mold of a monstrous, curled fish, presumably a design for cookies popular at Eastertide. The design proves identical to the creature on the side panel of Prendergast's decorated chest.

The colorful bird on the second side panel (a far more malevolent creature than St. John's eagle on the face of the chest) could well be another eagle; however, in all likelihood, and maintaining the symbolism of resurrection, it is a fabulous phoenix —the bird that having lived to a ripe old age, burned itself to ashes on an altar fire, from which a new, young phoenix arose. Sources for Prendergast's second side panel design may as well be found in Holme's treatise on Russian folk art.[4] Presumably, it was never Prendergast's intent to effect a rigorous or esoteric treatment of traditional religious symbols. Rather, he adapted enough from his general reading and visual repertoire to master basic ideas and then combined them according to the dictates of his own whimsy and overriding aesthetic sense. His program was more the generalized use of time-honored motifs suggesting rebirth and resurrection, but seeking to convey such concepts in layman's terms.

The chest exhibits the hallmarks of the artist's carving techniques from the early teens, especially in the reliance on deeply carved lines to define the outer contours of forms. A comparison with *Rising Sun* (CR 2212, WCMA, p. 56) from 1912, Prendergast's first effort carving gessoed wood panels, reveals distinct similarities in technique and treatment of the frame or surround of each panel.[5] The piece does share similar images with his 1927 chest now in the collection of the Museum of Fine Art, Boston (CR 2401): an angel on the front and a rampant lion on the back panel. Nonetheless, the overall construction, the greater reliance upon incising in lieu of deep carving, and the use of gold leaf with tempera on the Boston chest signal it as a much later, more mature effort by the artist. Another decorated chest (CR 2395, Daniel J. Terra Collection, Terra Museum of American Art, Chicago), dated 1920, exhibits deep carving in the main figures on the front, but general construction —no applied panels—the prevalence of incising and the heavy use of gold polychroming again testify to the more deft handling of the medium.

Vivian Patterson

1. Such symbolic representations of the four saints are based on the words of Saint John in the Apocalypse (Rev. 4:6-8) or on those of Ezekiel (1:5-14).
2. Hall 1974.
3. Holme 1912, p. 10, plate 245.
4. Ibid., plate 246.
5. Derby 1989, p. 38. The frame or surround of each panel is simply the reserve edge of the same piece of wood in which the picture is carved. Rising slightly above the surface of the picture, each frame is pictorially related to the composition of the four main panels, the lower member becoming the ground upon which the four saintly attributes stand.

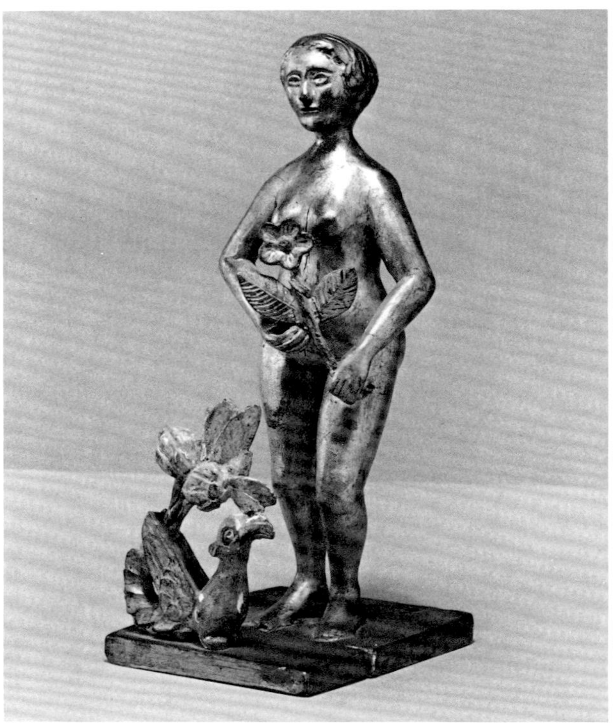

Eve, ca. 1912-14
CR 2390
Gold leaf on wood with gilded base (12⅜ x 4⅝ x 5½ in.; 31.4 x 11.7 x 14.0 cm)
Williams College Museum of Art, Gift of Mrs. Charles Prendergast (86.18.20)

INSCRIPTIONS
Unsigned

PROVENANCE
The artist; to Mrs. Charles Prendergast, 1948; to present collection, 1986

BIBLIOGRAPHY
Wattenmaker 1968 (p. 28); Komanecky 1984 (p. 193)

Exhibitions

1954 Kraushaar (#38); 1963b Davis Galleries (#34); 1968 Rutgers University (#57, ill. p. 94); 1969 Hirschl & Adler (#41); 1984a Williams College (#24); 1986 Williams College (no #); 1988b Williams College (# 87); 1989b Williams College (#51); 1990 Williams College (no #); 1992 Williams College (no #)

Technical Notes

The sculpture is carved from an unknown wood that is very light in weight. It has been gilded overall, but in various places abrasions in the gold allow the red bole to show through. The flower Eve holds has been carved separately and attached to her left hand. The fanciful bird in the foreground is on a separate base that has been joined to the front of the base Eve is on.

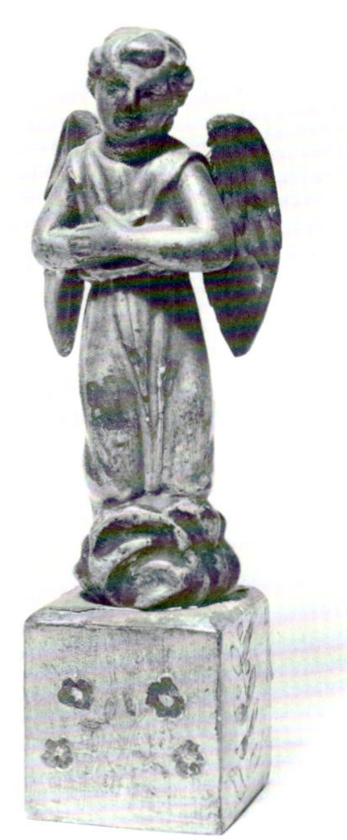

Angel, ca. 1915
CR 2392
Watercolor and gold leaf on wood with incised and painted base (9⅝ x 3¼ x 2⅛ in.; 24.4 x 8.3 x 5.4 cm)
Williams College Museum of Art, Gift of Mrs. Charles Prendergast (86.18.22)

Inscriptions

Unsigned

Provenance

The artist; to Mrs. Charles Prendergast, 1948; to present collection, 1986

Bibliography

Wattenmaker 1968 (p. 30); Komanecky 1984 (p. 193)

Exhibitions

1954 Kraushaar (#37); 1968 Rutgers University (#58, ill. p. 95); 1969 Hirschl & Adler (#42); 1984a Williams College (#25); 1986 Williams College (no #); 1988b Williams College (# 88); 1989b Williams College (#48); 1990 Williams College (no #); 1992 Williams College (no #)

Technical Notes

The gilding of the angel is darker than that of the base and is discolored in many places. Both wings have been reattached with glue and the lower one-third of the right wing appears to have been replaced. The replacement is carved with less definition and is gilded in a brighter gold.

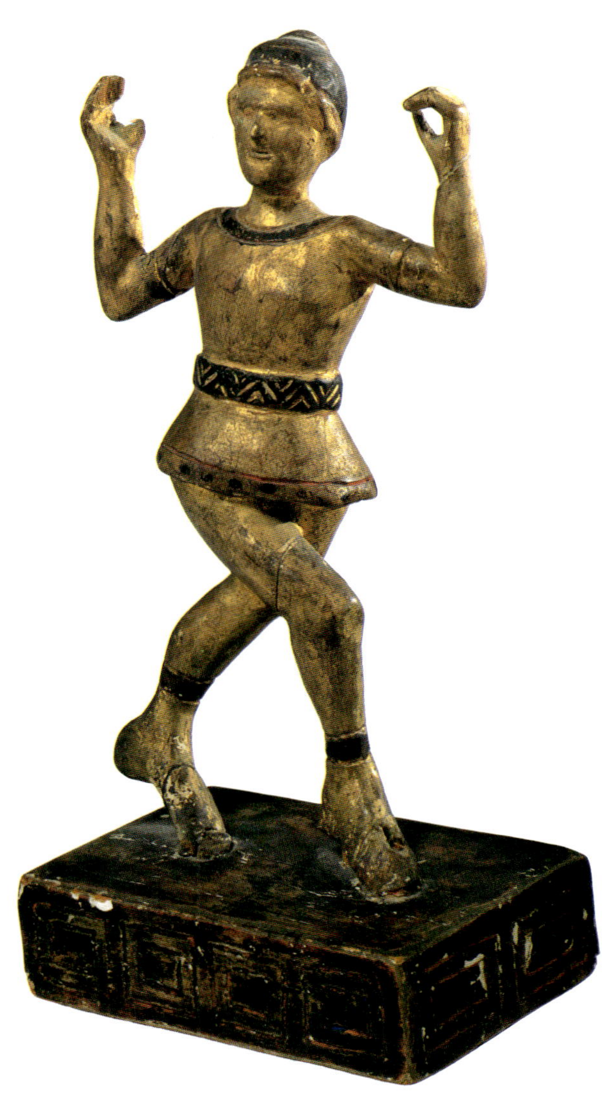

Man Dancing, ca. 1917-24
CR 2394
Figure
Watercolor and gold leaf on wood with incised and painted base (8 x 3⅞ x 2½ in.; 20.3 x 9.8 x 6.4 cm)
Williams College Museum of Art, Gift of Mrs. Charles Prendergast (86.18.23)

Inscriptions

Unsigned

Provenance

The artist; to Mrs. Charles Prendergast, 1948; to present collection, 1986

Bibliography

Wattenmaker 1968 (p. 30)

Exhibitions

?1941 Kraushaar (no #, *Figure*); 1954 Kraushaar (#39); 1968 Rutgers University (#60, ill. p. 98); 1969 Hirschl & Adler (#43); 1984a Williams College (#26); 1986 Williams College (no #); 1988b Williams College (#89); 1989b Williams College (#52); 1990 Williams College (no #); 1992 Williams College (no #)

Technical Notes

After this sculpture was gilded, it was painted with tempera to produce a polychrome effect. Touches of blue, red, and brown can be found on the hair, neckline, belt, hem, and anklets of the dancing man. The entire base has been toned with dark brown enlivened with touches of red and blue.

Prendergast's carved, gilded sculptures are some of his simplest and most attractive works. Five are believed to date from the teens when he is known to have included at least one in an exhibition in New York.[1]

Eve, depicted as a stolid, archaic woman, holds a long-stemmed flower very much like the one held by Mary in Prendergast's panel, *Madonna and Child* (CR 2214, WCMA, p. 105), suggesting that Prendergast had adopted the traditional association of Eve and Mary and saw both as harbingers of spring, fruitfulness, and rebirth.

The figurine called *Angel* is as smooth and graceful as *Eve* is angular and awkward. The possibility exists that Prendergast did not execute this figure, but acquired it in Italy and subsequently mounted it on a base of his own design.[2] Even if this is true, the *Angel's* place in Prendergast's work is important as illustrating his version of the "found object" and as the probable inspiration for his own gilded figurines.

Man Dancing undoubtedly was inspired by an ancient work of art and conveys in three-dimensional form a pre-Renaissance compression of space. Prendergast often borrowed the poses of dancing figures from Etruscan tomb paintings, and *Man Dancing* may be derived from a figure dressed in a short tunic with both arms raised that was illustrated in Prendergast's copy of Fritz Weege's *Etruskische Malerei* of 1921.[3]

1. 1918 Penguin. Item #19, *Figure Composition* (Sculpture), is believed to be *Two Nudes* (CR 2393, The Barnes Foundation).
2. A handwritten inventory of the Prendergasts' Westport house in the 1930s lists an "Angel carved in wood—Italian." The other works in the inventory are identified by artist, including several statues "carved in wood by CEP."
3. Weege 1921, p. 32.

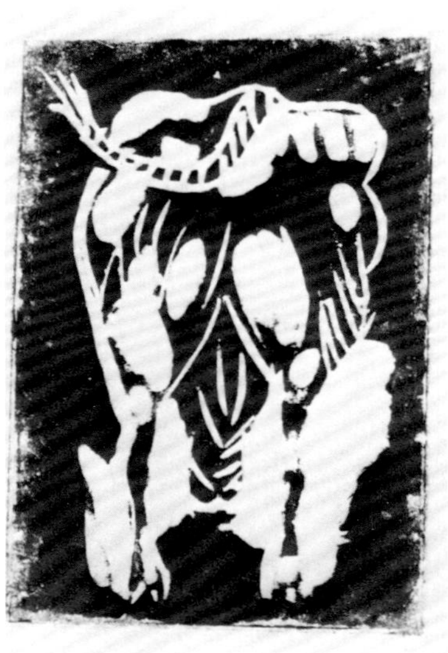

Cow, 1977
CR 2246
Woodcut in black ink [posthumously printed from the verso of *Four Figures and Donkey with Basket of Flowers*, Daniel J. Terra Collection, Terra Museum of American Art, Chicago] on thin Japanese tissue (10¾ x 8⅞ in.; 27.3 x 22.5 cm)
Williams College Museum of Art, Gift of Roy and Cecily Langdale Davis (86.1)

The versos of some of Prendergast's panels have been partially carved. In the case of *Donkey Rider #2* (CR 2282, WCMA, p. 87) the carving appears to be an abandoned composition. In the case of *Four Figures and Donkey with Basket of Flowers*, ca. 1915-17 (CR 2246, Daniel J. Terra Collection, Terra Museum of American Art, Chicago), an image of the rear end of a cow has been carved into the verso as a whimsical sketch. This relief carving was inked and printed in an edition of ten by Davis & Long Company in 1977.

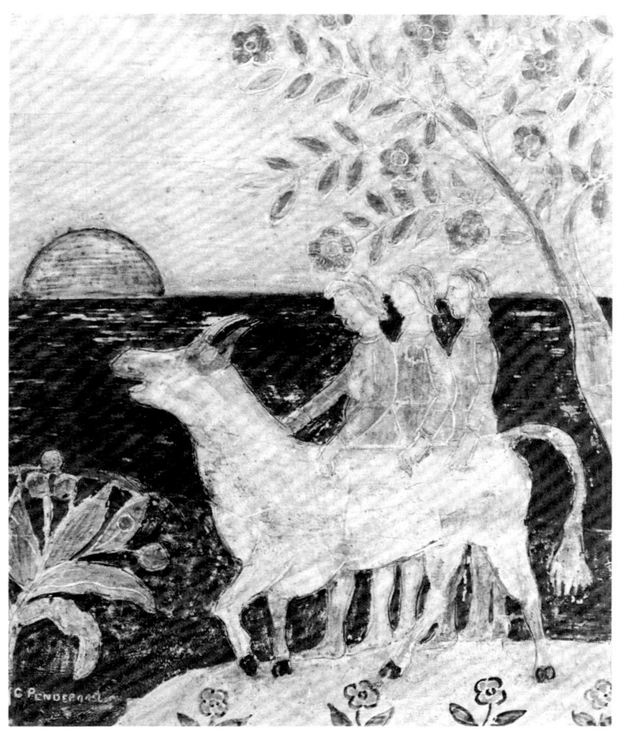

Sunset, ca. 1914-16
CR 2219
Incised gesso, tempera, and gold leaf on panel (16½ x 13¾ in.; 41.9 x 34.9 cm)
Williams College Museum of Art, Gift of Mrs. Charles Prendergast (86.18.25)

INSCRIPTIONS
l.l. incised: C Pendergast

PROVENANCE
The artist; to Mrs. Charles Prendergast, 1948; to present collection, 1986

EXHIBITIONS
1968 Rutgers University (#10, ill. p. 50); 1969 Hirschl & Adler (#8); 1970b Society of Four Arts (#45, ill.); 1984a Williams College (#4); 1985 Williams College (no #); 1989a Williams College (no #); 1989b Williams College (#27); 1990 Williams College (no #); 1992 Williams College (no #)

TECHNICAL NOTES
The panel is constructed of three-ply pinewood (two thin plys and one thick one with horizontal grain), which is heavily gessoed, incised, painted, and gilded. There is no surface coating on the face of the work, and the panel reverse is unsealed. The frame is carved, gessoed wood with red ground gilded and abraded. It appears to have been adjusted to fit the size of the panel, a conclusion reached primarily because of design variances in the corner areas of the frame. Using the gold leaf like paint, the artist covered the sky area, then removed most of the gilt, leaving an impression of a balanced gold, yellow, and white sky. The sun contains no gold leaf, yet the yellow and red paints create the illusion of a glowingly gold sun. The sea area, done primarily in blue tempera, together with the green portion behind the golden knoll, form the background for the primary figures and foliage, all done in varying tones of gold over red, with the exception of the bull's black hooves and tiny foreground flowers, which are painted over gold.

THERE IS A FETCHING INNOCENCE about this panel, one of Charles Prendergast's earliest,[1] that derives not only from the simple clarity of its two-dimensional figures, but also from its subject matter, which imparts both an Edenic and mythic feel, speaking to us of an ancient, more hopeful time where youthful men, strong beasts, and luxuriant flora all dwelt together comfortably, and all paid natural and harmonious homage to the great life source—the sun.

Sunset should be compared with Prendergast's first panel, done about 1912, entitled *Rising Sun* (CR 2212, WCMA, p. 56). Despite the marked improvement in smoothness of execution and composition evident in *Sunset*, and the passage of some years, the two are clearly related. Both evoke that same sense of ancient innocence and, compositionally, they are mirror images of each other due to the opposite positions of the suns, with the figures facing toward the sun, their hands gently lying on the backs of the animals.

Prendergast lived in or near Boston until 1914 when he and his brother Maurice moved to New York, and Boston's Museum of Fine Arts boasted extensive Oriental, Near Eastern, and Egyptian collections, as the museum's bulletins from the early 1900s attest. These bulletins are filled with descriptions of the latest consignments from Egypt sent back by members of the Harvard/Museum of Fine Arts Egyptian Expedition beginning in 1906, which were set up in the Mastaba Gallery when the Museum of Fine Arts moved to its grand new building in November of 1909. The bulletins also note the museum's holdings of more than 5,000 Chinese and Japanese paintings[2] in 1911 and contained frequent references to, and descriptions of, Persian and Indian artifacts and miniatures prior to 1915. That year's bulletin proudly announces its acquisition of an important group of Persian and Indian paintings known as the Goloubew Collection.[3]

Sunset has much of the Near East in it. Though many of his Oriental-period panels have a distinctly Persian/Indian feel, *Sunset* takes only its foliage from that tradition. A comparison of his flowering tree and his foreground flowers with Persian/Indian paintings reveals an almost direct borrowing.[4]

However, the subject matter, composition, and particularly the figures and the bull appear to have been influenced by Egyptian art. Among Prendergast's library books was Maspero's volume, *Art in Egypt*, published by Scribner in 1912. The book contains extensive evidence of Charles having examined it thoroughly: many pages are turned down, he marked certain plates with Xs, and he made handwritten notes in the back of the book—marking down plates on certain pages with notations such as "good" or "fig. good" or "animals good." Maspero's description of several of the plates marked and noted by Charles in the Memphite art section could well be a description of *Sunset*: "Men or beasts, they present themselves in profile against the background, their faces turned to the point of common interest or attraction . . . when it was impossible to bring all the figures to the front without destroying the unity . . . the artist planted them one against the other."[5]

The composition, too, is more open, less filled-in with figures and plants than that of the Persian miniatures or Oriental art and, as such, it is closer to the Egyptian tradition. The emphasis on the sun as central to life is, of course, common to many myths and civilizations including the Persian-originated Mithraic religion, but was also central to Egyptian religion.

Anne Dowling

1. Dated in Clark, Mathews, Owens 1990 as 1914-16, the same work was dated 1916-17 for the 1968 Rutgers University Charles Prendergast exhibition. See Wattenmaker 1968.
2. Boston MFA 1911, p. 48.
3. Boston MFA 1915, pp. 1-16.
4. See plates 22, 27, 37a, and 115 in Coomaraswamy 1929.
5. Maspero 1912.

Donkey Rider, ca. 1915-17 or ca. 1925-26

CR 2228
Frame by the artist
Incised gesso, tempera, pencil, and gold and silver leaf on panel (22⅝ x 20⅝ in.; 57.5 x 52.5 cm; framed)
Williams College Museum of Art, Gift of Mrs. Charles Prendergast (86.18.81)

INSCRIPTIONS
l.r. incised: C. Prendergast

PROVENANCE
The artist; to Mrs. Charles Prendergast, 1948; to present collection, 1986

BIBLIOGRAPHY
Wattenmaker 1968 (p. 25)

EXHIBITIONS
?1935 Kraushaar (#4); 1954 Kraushaar (#13); 1968 Rutgers University (#19, ill. p. 58); 1969 Hirschl & Adler (#11); 1986 Williams College (no #); 1988a Williams College (no #); 1989a Williams College (no #); 1989b Williams College (#39); 1990 Williams College (no #)

TECHNICAL NOTES
The plywood panel has a slight side to side convex warp. The donkey bearing the basket of fruit and one of the horses were gilded and then covered with an overlay of another type of metal leaf, likely to have had a silver component. The silver leaf was not sealed and is now tarnished and irretrievable. A small area just left of the center of the picture appears to have been rubbed or erased.

The frame, by the artist, is molded, carved, and water-gilded using red bole with recut gesso on the edges.

PRENDERGAST'S SYMMETRICAL PATTERNING of gold and silver leaf is the dominant feature of *Donkey Rider*. The figure of the donkey rider, clothed in gold, is balanced by the second gold- and silver-leafed donkey who precedes her. The three gilded female figures greeting the donkey rider are matched by the three gold- and silver-leafed horses that disappear into the sea. Even the gentle arcs of the gold-banded hills are echoed in the arabesques formed by the branches of the gilded trees. This balanced golden patterning is continued to the edge of the panel in the gilded trefoil leaves that decorate the entire sky.

Although *Donkey Rider's* imagery seems secondary to these symmetrical patterns of gold, Prendergast remains consistent by borrowing from both the early Renaissance and Persian traditions for this work. The trefoil leaves have an identifiable source in a fragment of a Persian painting found in a photograph belonging to the Prendergasts.[1] The

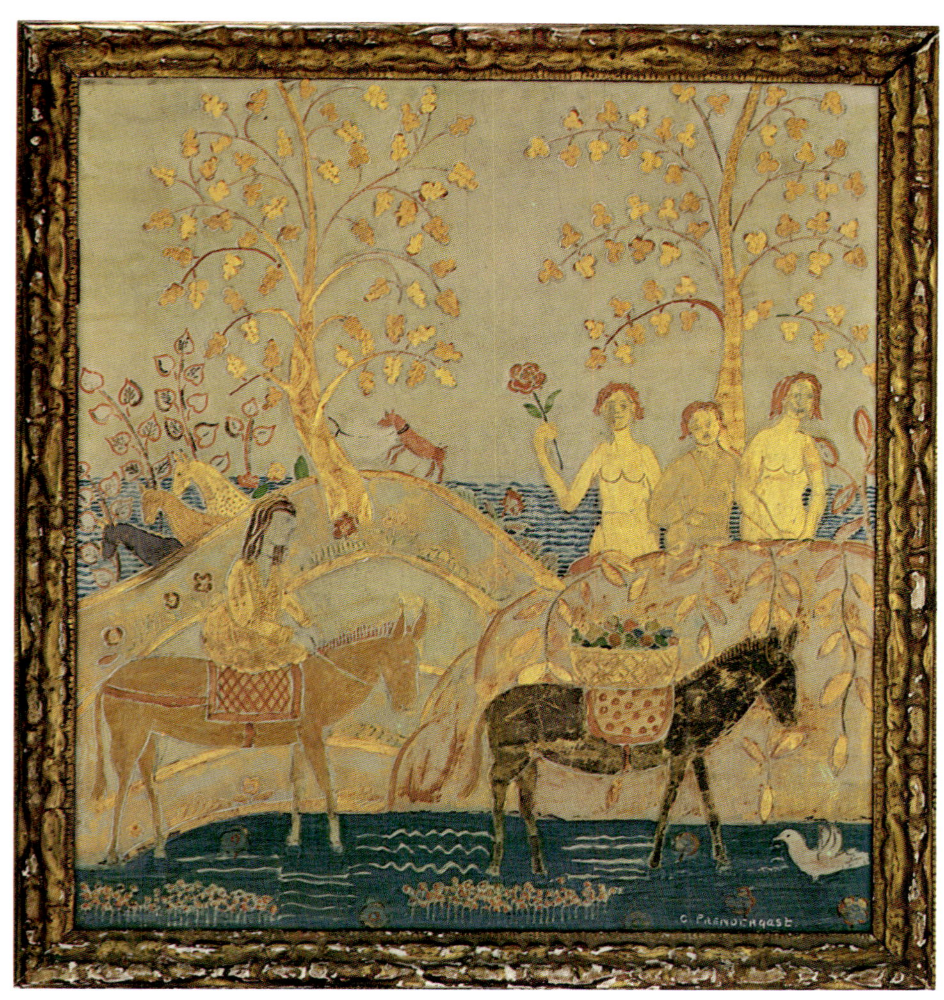
C. PRENDERGAST

 border of flowers, with tiny stems that dot the foreground, has a medieval source. An illustration from one of Prendergast's books, *Ravenna*, depicts a mosaic from S. Apollinare Nuovo with a similarly naive border of tiny-stemmed flowers at the feet of a procession of saints.[2] The donkey rider of the title bears a resemblance to the Madonna in Giotto's painting, *The Flight to Egypt*, in the Arena Chapel in Padua.[3] A photograph of this fresco was found among Prendergast's personal collection of photographs.

The images of the rider, the donkey, the three female figures, the golden vines, and the basket of fruit are motifs that are repeated in Prendergast's panels throughout his oeuvre. Various combinations of these motifs as well as the use of gold and silver leaf are found in both *Flight of the Birds* (CR 2225, Addison Gallery of American Art), ca. 1915, and *Fantasy* (CR 2234, The Fuller Collection), ca. 1915-17.

The composition as a whole, however, is most closely repeated in the end panel of one of Prendergast's carved, painted and decorated chests (CR 2401, Museum of Fine Arts, Boston), 1926-27. This compositional relationship might suggest that the *Donkey Rider* panel was a preliminary or preparatory "sketch" for the chest, which is inscribed "Made by Charles Prendergast 1926-27" on the underside. This relationship could also provide the donkey-rider image with a religious significance. Two of the six carved surfaces of the chest have an identifiable religious symbolism. The rear panel of the chest depicts three of the four evangelical symbols, while one of the scenes in the front panel of the chest is titled "Annunciation." Given the religious symbolism of the chest images, the donkey rider in both the panel and the chest could represent Prendergast's own version of the Madonna, inspired by the imagery of Giotto's Arena Chapel fresco, *The Flight to Egypt*.

Although *Donkey Rider* is dated ca. 1915-17 because of its subject matter, there is evidence to support a later date, closer to ca. 1925-26. The original backing of the framed panel has a handwritten date of 1925, which is the date assigned to the work in the 1954 Kraushaar exhibition catalogue, possibly the source of this 1925 notation. Also, the close compositional relationship with the 1926-27 chest supports the later date, as does the use of a signature rather than the monogram found on most of his early panels.

Although the date and symbolism of *Donkey Rider* remain in question, there is no doubt that the donkey rider was one of Prendergast's favorite images. The rider-figure is repeated over and over, well into his work of the 1930s and 1940s where the rider is no longer a quasi-religious figure, but a representation of "everyman" wandering through the artist's narrative panels.

Ann Ugast Greenwood

1. Prendergast Archive and Study Center, WCMA.
2. Ricci 1907, plate 55.
3. Prendergast Archive and Study Center, WCMA.

Decorated Mirror with Two Figures, ca. 1915-17

CR 2231

Frame by the artist

Reverse painting in oil with gold leaf on glass in carved, painted, and gilded wooden frame (18¼ x 31 in.; 46.4 x 78.7 cm)

Williams College Museum of Art, Gift of Mrs. Charles Prendergast (86.18.28)

INSCRIPTIONS

Unsigned

PROVENANCE

The artist; to Mrs. Charles Prendergast, 1948; to present collection, 1986

BIBLIOGRAPHY

Gengarelly 1989 (p. 40; ill.)

EXHIBITIONS

1968 Rutgers University (#54, ill. p. 90); 1984a Williams College (#22); 1985 Williams College (no #); 1986 Williams College (no #); 1988b Williams College (#72); 1990 Williams College (no #)

TECHNICAL NOTES

The rectilinear frame, which contains a central mirror and two flanking pieces of reverse painting on glass, has been roughly constructed. The posterior rebate has been chiselled by hand, but the channels to hold the vertical separations were made by a tenoner saw. The corners are mitered, but since the two lateral pieces are narrower than the top and bottom pieces, the lateral pieces are dog-legged at the juncture to maintain a 45 degree angle.

The mirror has an approximately 1-1/4 inch square patch on the lower central area and a large central horizontal line indicating that the atmosphere was prevented from direct contact. The lower edge of the mirror is irregular, instead of a straight edge. The mirror is made of a tin and mercury amalgam that was common in 1850 but not manufactured by 1900.

The sash of the figure on the left has an area of loss of gold leaf, incorrectly repaired, that may be due to dam-

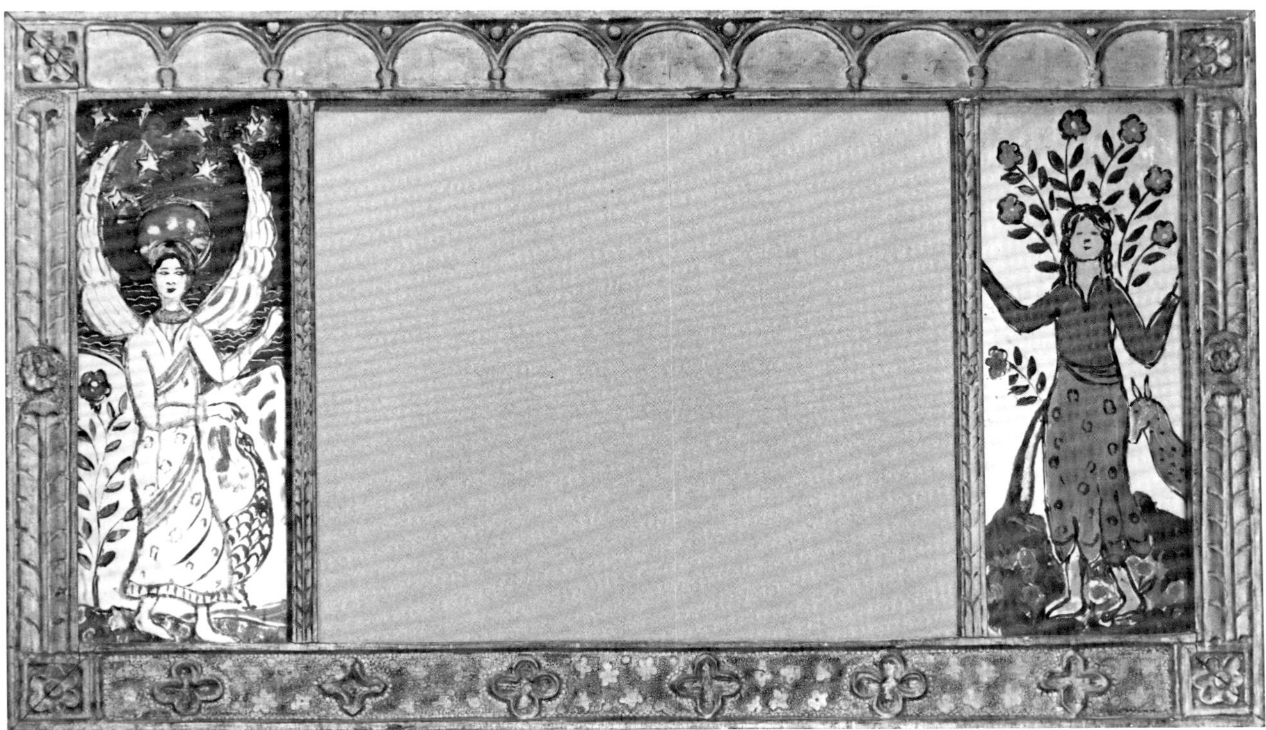

age as the build-up of dirt in the rebate would indicate that it was unbacked and exposed.

PRENDERGAST'S *Decorated Mirror with Two Figures* was executed in the technique of reverse painting on glass, in which the paint is applied to the back of transparent glass in reverse order; first, the foreground highlights are applied and, last, the background.[1] Having reached a high point of popularity in the early eighteenth century in Switzerland and the Netherlands, this technique enjoyed a minor revival with the Arts and Crafts Movement as well as with certain modernist painters; Marsden Hartley was inspired directly by Wassily Kandinsky's inclusion of one of his reverse paintings on glass published in *Der Blaue Reiter*.[2] Theirs was a response not only to the primitive and spiritual qualities of folk art observed in the Hintermalerei of rural Bavaria, but an esteem of genuineness that contributed to the incorporation of folk art into the concept of fine art, taking hold in the early decades of the twentieth century.[3] Prendergast was well acquainted with modernist art, and, in fact, Hartley had visited Charles and his brother in Boston in 1909 and received a letter of introduction from Maurice to Robert Henri and William Glackens.[4]

Prendergast's efforts in reverse painting on glass, although sharing this same concept of genuineness, are more in keeping with the Arts and Crafts Movement, as he has combined the art and technique within an object of practicality. Both the roughness of handling of the frame and the simplicity and naiveté of the figures reflect English originator John Ruskin's praise of asymmetry and irregularity. Prendergast's use of an old mirror and possible adaptation of an older frame[5] are compatible with this aesthetic.

The design elements of the frame, both decorative and architectural, demonstrate Prendergast's original combinative style and collaboration with his brother. Both brothers sketched versions of this frame: Charles's sketches of the feather motif and band of quatrefoils relate to elevation and profile views that Maurice had sketched.[6] Sources of these designs may have included a magazine clipping in their study collection of an illustration of a Hindu carved doorway.[7] The Romanesque architectural motif could have been inspired directly by Prendergast's exposure to Renaissance architecture during the brothers' trip to Italy in 1911.

Prendergast repeated both individual decorative elements as well as overall frame design. An earlier frame (WCMA 85.10.1, p. 54) designed for George

 Hallowell's presentation sketch for an altarpiece is also tripartite and intersperses punchwork among the decorative elements. The "Crawford Frame,"[8] tripartite and containing three mirrors, also has architectural elements on top with decorative elements on the sides and bottom. The "Heraldic Frame,"[9] carved for artist George Linden Smith, also has Romanesque arches on the top, with feather and rosettes on the sides and alternating shields and quatrefoils on the bottom.

Comparisons with screens, decorated chests, and panels again reveal Prendergast's manner of repeating favorite motifs. *Screen* of 1916-17 (CR 2235, Collection of Mr. and Mrs. Laughlin Phillips, Washington, D.C.), shares the mirror's tripartite overall design and its figures. Both on the recto and, monumentally, on the verso, are angelic figures similar to the angel of the left side of the decorated mirror. The angel on the verso shares the upward pointing wings and halo with a band of circles; and the one on the recto shares the dress details, foot position, and surround of stars with a celestial blue background.

Several of Prendergast's objects contain angelic figures, and demonstrate iconic borrowings and mixings. The figure on the left appears to be a conflation of an angel, the Virgin Mary, and the Woman of the Apocalypse. Related to Prendergast's panel, *Madonna and Child* of ca. 1915-20 (CR 2214, WCMA, p. 105), with attributes of Mary's red rose and specific halo[10] and the Apocalyptic Woman's stars, crescent moon, and brilliant light from behind, this design was based on a tooled-leather book cover reproduced as an illustration in a magazine kept by Prendergast.[11]

Although no specific source or exact borrowing can be found for the right-hand figure, her simplified dress is similar to that of two women on the central panel of *Screen*, 1916-17. The two figures are charmingly related through gesture and balanced by contrasting backgrounds (a device Charles would again use in the divided panel of *Flowers* of 1919 [CR 2253, Last known in the Collection of Mrs. Thomas Spencer]). The figures' feet and the animals point towards each other, and the open arms of the woman receive the gaze and gesture of her partner.

Ten years later, Prendergast would again execute an equally small number (three) of reverse paintings on glass, notable in that each singular painting is also in combination with a mirror (*Animals in a Wood* [CR 2259, Collection of Mimi and Sanford Feld], *The Zoo* [CR 2261, Collection of Margot Newman Stickley], and *Animal Decoration on Glass, with mirror* [CR 2262, Collection of Mrs. Charles Prendergast, p. 83]), but complex composition and increased detail indicate a more mature handling of the medium.

Linda Reynolds

1. Corning 1992, p. 35.
2. Luddington 1992, p. 84.
3. Guggenheim 1966, p. 8.
4. Luddington 1992, p. 56.
5. Conversation with conservator Hugh Glover of the Williamstown Regional Art Conservation Laboratory following receipt of conservation report, December 16, 1992.
6. Derby 1990, p. 104.
7. Ibid.
8. A photographic reproduction of this frame is in the Prendergast Archive and Study Center, WCMA.
9. Derby 1990, p. 104.
10. Weber 1927, p. 58.
11. Art Workers' Quarterly 1902.

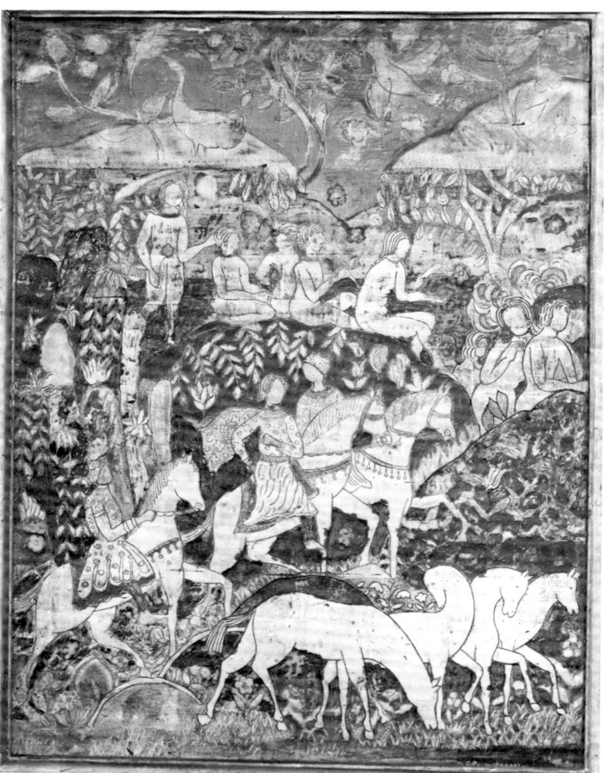

The Riders, ca. 1915
Decorative Panel
CR 2229

Color illustration, p. 29
Frame by the artist
Incised gesso, tempera, and silver and gold leaf on panel (32¾ x 25¼ in.; 83.2 x 64.1 cm; framed)
Williams College Museum of Art, Gift of Mrs. Charles Prendergast, in honor of Dr. Francis Oakley, President of Williams College (86.18.12)

Inscriptions
l.r. incised: C. Prendergast

Provenance
The artist; to Mrs. Stanley Resor; to (Parke-Bernet), 1966; to Mrs. Charles Prendergast, 1966; to present collection, 1986

Bibliography
Chanin 1954 (p. 20); Parke-Bernet 1966b (#77); Wattenmaker 1968 (pp. 25-26, 30); Komanecky 1984 (p. 192; ill.); Antiques Arts Weekly 1986 (p. 113)

Exhibitions
1938 Addison (#2); 1954 Kraushaar (#3); 1968 Rutgers University (#7, ill. p. 46); 1969 Hirschl & Adler (#6); 1983a Williams College (# 28); 1984a Williams College (#4); 1986 Williams College (no #); 1989a Williams College (no #); 1989b Williams College (#47); 1990 Williams College (no #); 1992 Williams College (no #)

Technical Notes
The plywood panel was prepared with gesso and gold and silver leaf; tempera was then applied over the leaf in certain areas. Darkened areas may have been caused by tarnishing silver leaf. Punchwork was simulated by lightly hammering a dull nail into the leaf; both a square and a round nail were used. The slight difference in paint strokes and color in the top fifth of the panel suggests that this area was painted later than the main body of the composition.

While the impact of Persian painting is seen in a number of Charles Prendergast's panels, it reached an apogee in *The Riders*. By composing a landscape of mound-like hills where the imagery rises toward the top of the panel to a high horizon, Prendergast organized his pictorial elements in a manner typical of Persian painting. Within this landscape copiously filled with flowers, foliage, and undulating trees, three mounted figures amble through the picture space. Like the figures and horses surrounding them, these horsemen are strongly outlined, recalling a fluid, almost calligraphic, line (often seen in both Persian painting and Islamic ceramics) that contains a flat area of color or pattern. At the lower right corner, three horses walking in step, their gracefully arched necks held high, strongly suggest that Prendergast had admired a sixteenth-century illustration of an episode of the epic *Shah-nama*, "The Meeting of Jacob and Joseph," where maneless horses of similar contours can be seen.[1]

No mere copyist, Prendergast enjoyed finding inspiration and technical ideas from disparate sources that he would then conflate to create works uniquely his own. During his 1911 trip to Italy, he must have been impressed with the numerous gilded panels, many enlivened with punchwork, that filled churches and museums. The use of gold leaf in *The Riders* suggests such sources, yet Prendergast generously used the gold not only for the background, but also for the majority of the surface. The three horsemen, clad in sumptuous garb and accompanied by figures playing music or bearing offerings, suggest the Three Magi; perhaps Prendergast saw Benozzo Gozzoli's lavish display of pageantry in his *Procession of the Magi* (Uffizi, 1459) when he was in Florence.

Two larger versions of this composition are known, both of which are contained in three-panel screens (*Screen*, ca. 1916-17 [CR 2235, Collection of Mr. and Mrs. Laughlin Phillips, Washington, D.C.]; and *Screen*, ca. 1928-32 [CR 2258, Private Collection]). In the Phillips screen, the horsemen are seen heading toward a seated female figure suggesting that *The Riders* is intended to be a similar scene of homage or adoration.

Stefanie Spray

1. Museum of Fine Arts, Boston, 14.625.

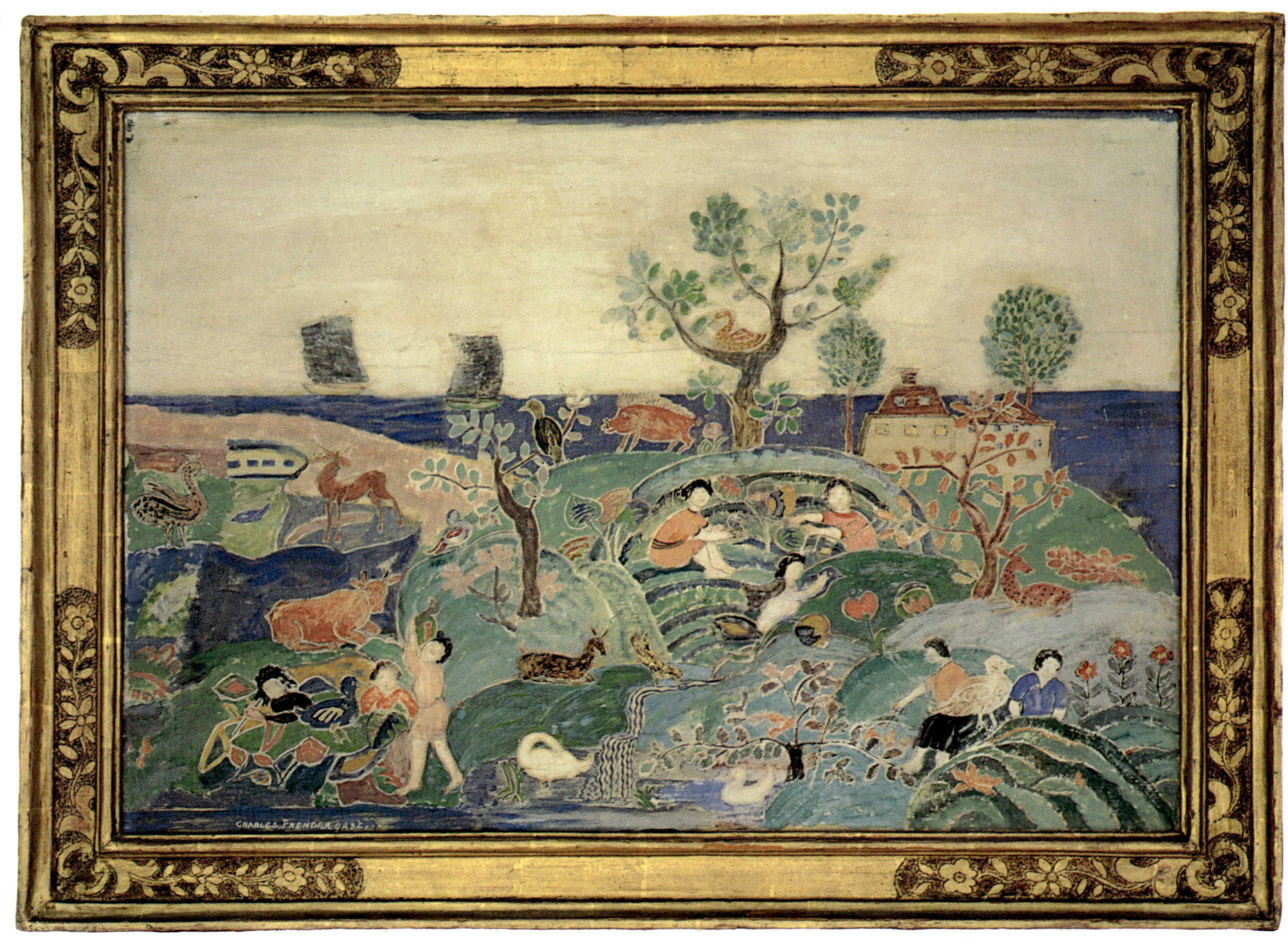

Fairy Story, ca. 1922 (reworked ca. 1942-46)
Enchanted Island
CR 2277
Frame by the artist
Incised gesso, tempera, pencil, and gold leaf on panel (22 x 31 in.; 55.9 x 78.7 cm)
Williams College Museum of Art, Gift of Mrs. Charles Prendergast (86.18.26)

INSCRIPTIONS
l.l. incised: Charles Prendergast
l.r. incised: C Prendergast

PROVENANCE
The artist; to William Glackens; to the artist, ca. 1942; to Mrs. Charles Prendergast, 1948; to present collection, 1986

BIBLIOGRAPHY
Breuning 1947 (p. 18); Wattenmaker 1968 (p. 25); Antiques Arts Weekly 1986 (p. 113)

EXHIBITIONS
1938 Addison (#5, as *Enchanted Island*); 1947 Kraushaar (#2, ill.); 1954 Kraushaar (#31); 1968 Rutgers University (#18, ill. p. 24); 1969 Hirschl & Adler (#10); 1984a Williams College (#6); 1986 Williams College (no #); 1988a Williams College (no #); 1988b Williams College (#80); 1989a Williams College (no #); 1989b Williams College (#35); 1990 Williams College (no #)

TECHNICAL NOTES
Thin washes of tempera paint were applied over multiple layers of gesso on a plywood panel of approximately 3/8-inch thick. Small areas of gold leaf are apparent within the image, although most of the gold leaf was overpainted. In 1986 the panel was treated for the pronounced horizontal cracking in association with panel movement, particularly in the sky area. The lifting cracks in the sky were set down and inpainted. Beneath the frame, in the lower right corner of the panel, is a second

signature incised within what remains of a thin gold border. It appears that the panel was trimmed in order to fit the frame, and, in the process cut off the bottom half of the signature in the lower right corner.

THE ADDISON GALLERY of American Art at Phillips Academy exhibited this work as *Enchanted Island* in its 1938 exhibition, "The Prendergasts." By comparing the work to one of the photographs of the Addison Gallery installation, we can document that changes were made to *Fairy Story* after this 1938 exhibition, between the time the panel was returned to the artist in 1942 and its March 1947 exhibition at the Kraushaar Galleries (where it was featured on the cover of their brochure). Unfortunately the black-and-white Addison Gallery photograph depicts only three quarters of the panel. But aided by conservation notes, a comparison of this photograph with the present-day panel reveals several alterations to the image. The major areas where changes can be ascertained are in the lower right where the positions of the figures, particularly the arms, have been changed and overpainted, and in the hillside just above these figures, which appears to have been scraped and overpainted. The pink dress of the figure in the center was originally dark trousers and shirt, and the sky has been dramatically altered. The upper left of the photograph shows a large orb, presumably the sun, next to a fairly dark arabesque line, possibly a rainbow or hillside, both of which have been overpainted with multiple layers of white gesso. It also appears that there may have been clouds in the upper right of the image. Since the photograph is black-and-white, it is impossible to determine if there was substantially more gilding within the image than that which remains today.

The remaining imagery is as complex as the pentimenti. Banded, pastel hills suggesting terraced Oriental gardens are dotted with whimsical birds and animals, interspersed with small groups of primitive figures tending the exotic flora and fauna. Many of these elements reappear in his later works, particularly in the composition *Hill Town*, ca. 1928 (CR 2260, Addison Gallery of American Art), and in the animal motifs of his three decorated mirrors dated 1928-32 (*Animals in a Wood* [CR 2259, Collection of Mimi and Sanford Feld]; *The Zoo* [CR 2261, Collection of Margot Newman Stickley], and *Animal Decoration on Glass, with mirror* [CR 2262, Collection of Mrs. Charles Prendergast, p. 83]). The boar, the little swans, and the deer are repeated in each of these mirrors.

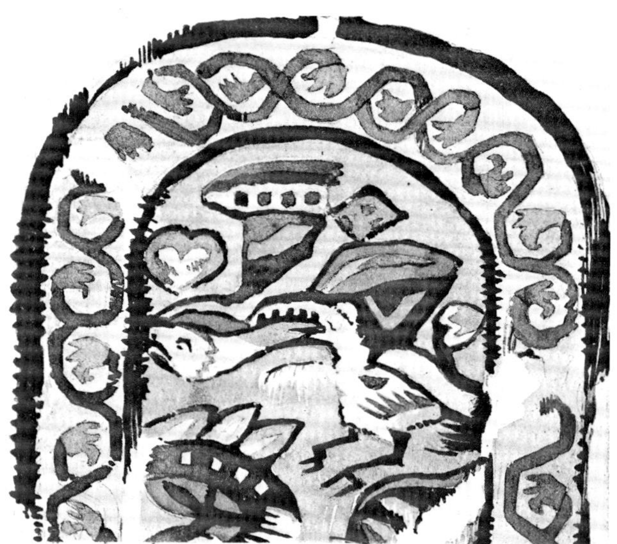

Fragment of design, illustrated (plate 9) in *Étoffes Byzantines Coptes, Romaines, etc. du IV au X siècle*, edited by Armand Guérinet, [1922], Williams College Museum of Art, Prendergast Archive and Study Center

It appears that several of the *Fairy Story* images were taken directly from an illustrated book owned by the Prendergast brothers, now in the Prendergast Archive and Study Center. The book, *Étoffes Byzantines, Coptes, Romaines, etc. du IV au X siècle*, 1922,[1] consists of sixteen colored and partially colored plates of fragments of Byzantine and Coptic textiles. The cryptic image of a white and blue band with small blue "windows" at the left of the picture was taken directly from an image depicted on plate 9 of this book (see illustration). The little figures, whose hands seem to blend with the birds within their grasp, and the heart-shaped leaves, found nowhere else in his oeuvre, can be found on plates 2, 5, and 10. Several of the versos of the plates have small painted sketches by either Charles or his brother Maurice.

Ann Ugast Greenwood

1. Guérinet 1922, plates 2, 5, 9, and 10. This portfolio-sized book was part of the series, *Matériaux et Documents d'Art Décoratif*, published in Paris between 1890 and 1925 by the Librairie d'Architecture & d'Art Décoratif. Dumbarton Oaks Bibliographies (1973-77), vol. 2, p. 315, assigns a date of 1922 to this work.

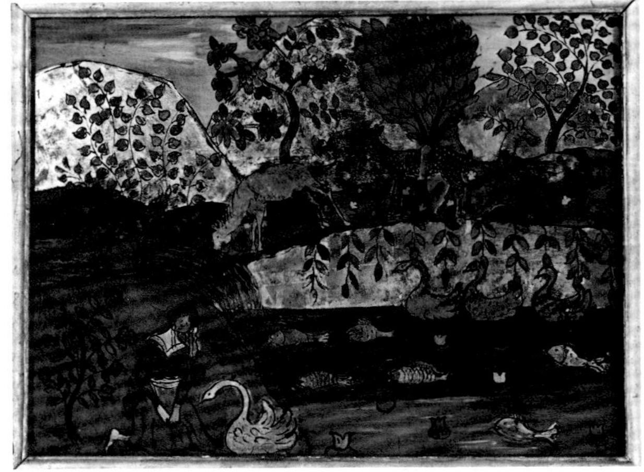

Decoration on Glass, ca. 1925-30 [?]
Girl with Swan
CR 2233
Color illustration, p. 23
Frame by the artist
Reverse painting with silver and gold leaf on glass (22 x 27¾ in.; 55.9 x 70.5 cm)
Collection of Mrs. Charles Prendergast

INSCRIPTIONS
Unsigned

PROVENANCE
The artist; to present collection, 1948

EXHIBITIONS
1935 Kraushaar (#2 as *Girl with Swan*); 1954 Kraushaar (#15); 1968 Rutgers University (#55, ill. p. 92); 1969 Hirschl & Adler (#40); 1983a Williams College (#29); 1984a Williams College (not on checklist)

TECHNICAL NOTES
Prendergast used a reverse painting technique to build up the colors, and deftly laid on squares of gold leaf to decorate the deer, the swans, and the fish. He miscalculated the order of the layers in the trunk of the central tree in the background, which should have had a layer of brown paint before he put on the final square of gold leaf. The ripples in the water are not gold leaf, but applied in gold paint.

THIS IS PRENDERGAST'S largest reverse painting on glass and draws on traditional American folk painting and embroidery for its imagery. In this regard it differs from Prendergast's typical "celestial" period imagery, and thus probably dates from after 1925, rather than the mid-teens as formerly believed. Prendergast's interest in American folk art parallels that of many artists, curators, and collectors in Prendergast's circle including Juliana Force and Abby Aldrich Rockefeller.

An elegiac mood is established by the forlorn, kneeling woman and the leafy boughs trailing over the hills in the manner of a willow tree. These elements were borrowed from traditional mourning pictures executed in watercolor on paper or velvet, or in embroidery from the late eighteenth century to the late nineteenth century and were eagerly collected by those interested in Americana. Prendergast inserts a personal note in the form of the swans, which were a favorite motif of his brother Maurice, and may be a reference to his brother's death in 1924.

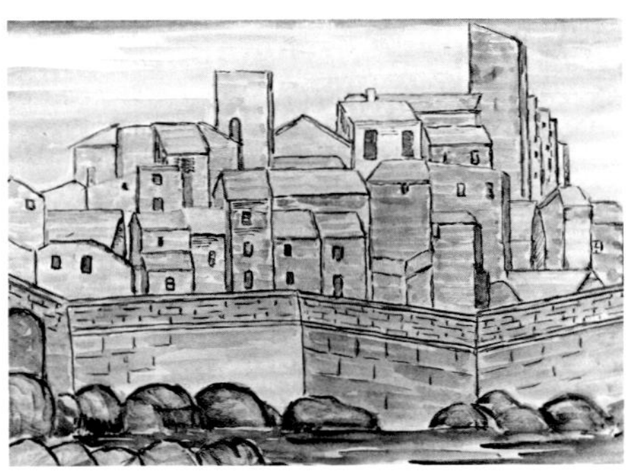

Antibes, South of France, ca. 1927-29
CR 2322
Watercolor and pencil on paper (9⅞ x 13 in.; 25.1 x 33.0 cm)
Collection of Mrs. Charles Prendergast

PROVENANCE
The artist; to present collection, 1948

INSCRIPTIONS
Unsigned

EXHIBITIONS
?1963b Davis Galleries (#1); 1969 Hirschl & Adler (#53)

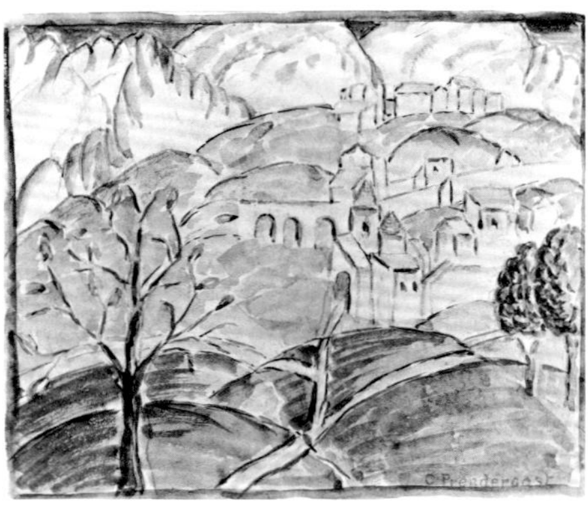

Aqueduct, Vence, ca. 1927-29
CR 2346

Watercolor and pencil on paper (7 x 8¾ in.; 17.8 x 21.3 cm)
Collection of Mrs. Charles Prendergast

INSCRIPTIONS
l.r. in red: C Prendergast

PROVENANCE
The artist; to present collection, 1948

EXHIBITIONS
1963b Davis Galleries (#9); 1970b Society of Four Arts (#31)

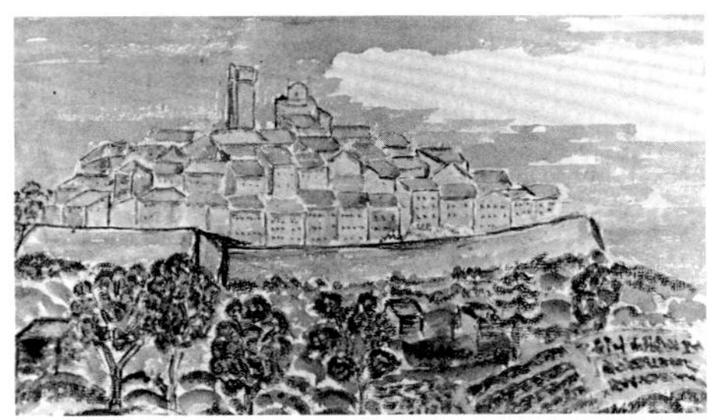

St. Paul de Vence, ca. 1927-29
CR 2349
Watercolor and pencil on paper (7 x 11½ in.; 17.8 x 29.2 cm)
Collection of Mrs. Charles Prendergast

INSCRIPTIONS
Unsigned

PROVENANCE
The artist; to present collection, 1948

EXHIBITIONS
1968 Rutgers University (#67, ill.); 1969 Hirschl & Adler (#50)

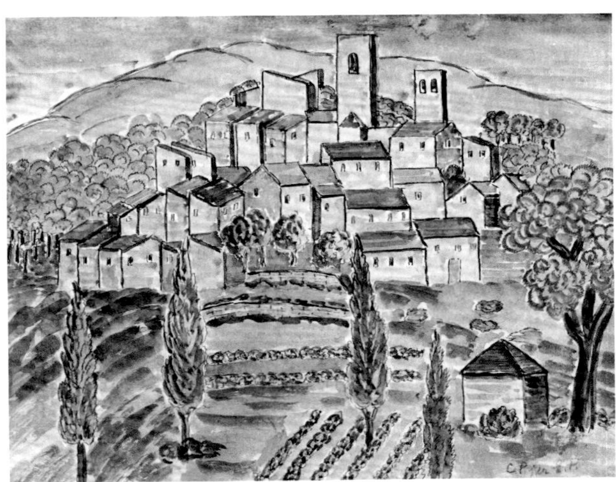

Hill Town, ca. 1927-29
CR 2321
Watercolor, ink, and pencil on paper with perforated left edge (10⅛ x 13⅜ in.; 25.7 x 34.0 cm)
Williams College Museum of Art, Gift of Mrs. Charles Prendergast (87.1.1)

INSCRIPTIONS
l.r. (in Eugénie Prendergast's hand): CP per EP

PROVENANCE
The artist; to to Mrs. Charles Prendergast, 1948; to present collection, 1987

EXHIBITIONS
1988 Williams College (no #); 1989b Williams College (#28); 1990 Williams College (no #); 1992 Williams College (no #)

ASIDE FROM THE TENTATIVE *Study of a House* (CR 2319, WCMA, p. 54) and a few sketches in Prendergast's 1911 Italian sketchbook ("Sketchbook D," CR 2409, Museum of Fine Arts, Boston), there is no precedent for the extensive series of architectural studies that Prendergast produced in conjunction with his two trips to France in 1927 and 1929. Notes in his travel diary of 1927 (Prendergast Archive and Study Center) indicate that in October he began to sketch views of Cannes where he and his wife were staying for about a month. On side trips to neighboring towns on the Riviera he no doubt produced such sketches as *Antibes, South of France*.

In 1929 the Prendergasts took an eastern route through France, stopping at small towns in the Alps between Chamonix, Grenoble, Briançon, Barcelonette, and, finally, Nice. Prendergast was fascinated by the configurations made by the clustered geometric shapes perched on top of mountains and sketched such hill towns as Biot, Briançon, and St. Paul. It is to this second trip that *Aqueduct, Vence* and *St. Paul de Vence* probably belong. The more finished watercolor, called simply *Hill Town*, may have been done upon Prendergast's return to Westport.

In all, Prendergast painted twenty-six known views of French towns in this series. In addition, he incorporated architectural motifs based on these sketches into two major gesso panels, *Hill Town* (CR 2260, Addison Gallery of American Art) and *Holiday Beach Scene* (CR 2265, WCMA, p. 82) as well as into two finished watercolors, *Beach Scene with Prancing Goats* (CR 2362, WCMA, p. 78) and *Allegory* (CR 2363, The Metropolitan Museum of Art, Robert Lehman Collection). The interest he had in the geometrical designs made by the simple architecture of these towns may have stemmed from his background as a craftsman/ designer in combination with his reverence for the proto-cubist work of Cézanne, whose studio he visited in Aix in 1929. From this time on, Prendergast often based his compositions on the geometric patterns of curious architectural sites such as theatrical stage sets (*Play, International House*, CR 2264, Collection of International House), country fairs, race tracks, circuses, the Central Park Zoo, and the 1939 New York World's Fair.

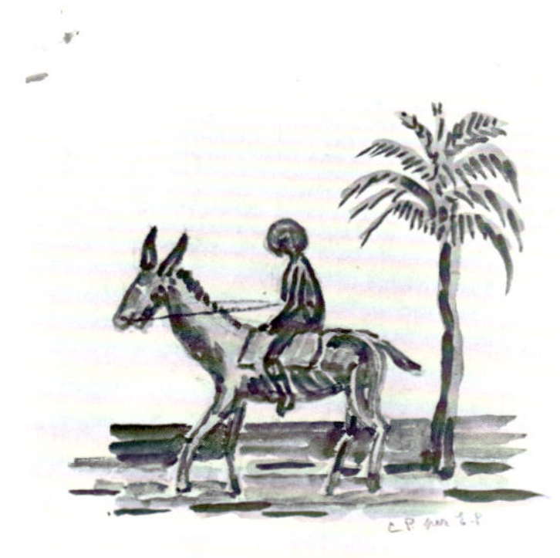

Donkey Rider, Cannes, ca. 1927-29
CR 2330
Watercolor and pencil on paper (6⅞ x 5⅞ in.; 17.5 x 14.9 cm)
Collection of Mrs. Charles Prendergast
INSCRIPTIONS
l.r. (in Eugénie Prendergast's hand): C.P. per E.P.
PROVENANCE
The artist; to present collection, 1948

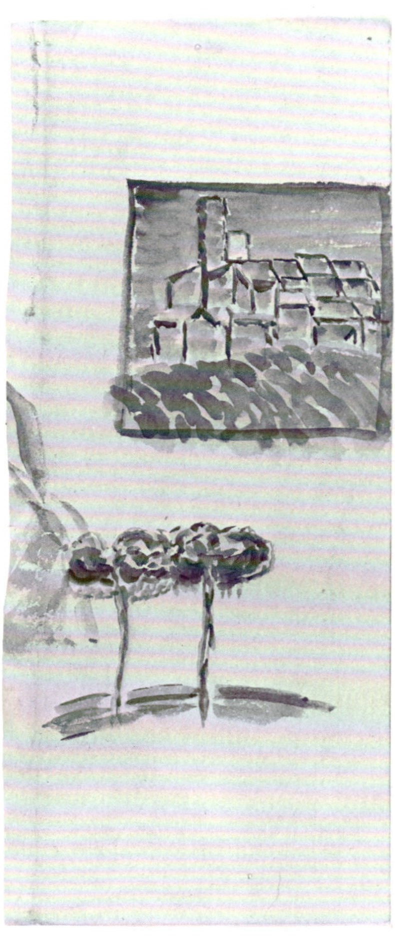

Sketch for a Hilltown and Trees, ca. 1927-29
CR 2323
Watercolor on paper (12½ x 5⅞ in.; 31.7 x 14.9 cm)
Williams College Museum of Art, Gift of Mrs. Charles Prendergast (87.5.11)
INSCRIPTIONS
Unsigned
PROVENANCE
The artist; to Mrs. Charles Prendergast, 1948; to present collection, 1987
EXHIBITIONS
1988a Williams College (no #)

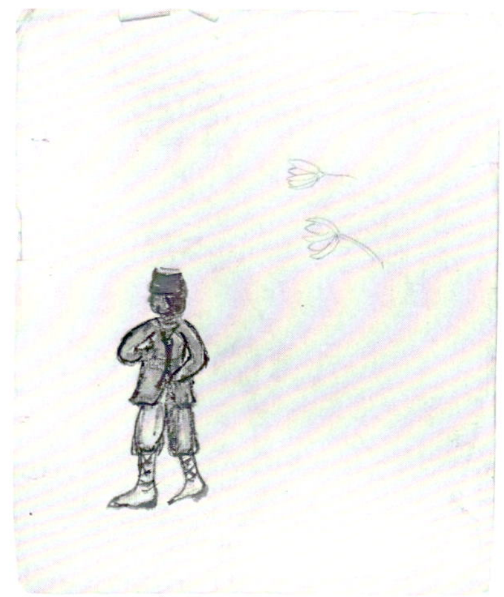

(recto) *Study of Algerian*, ca. 1927-29
CR 2350
Charcoal and tempera on paper (11¾ x 9 in.; 29.8 x 22.8 cm)
Williams College Museum of Art, Gift of Mrs. Charles Prendergast (87.5.7)
INSCRIPTIONS
Unsigned
verso, l.r. (in Eugénie Prendergast's hand): study of algerian
PROVENANCE
The artist; to Mrs. Charles Prendergast, 1948; to present

collection, 1987

verso: Untitled (study of flower, leaves)
Charcoal

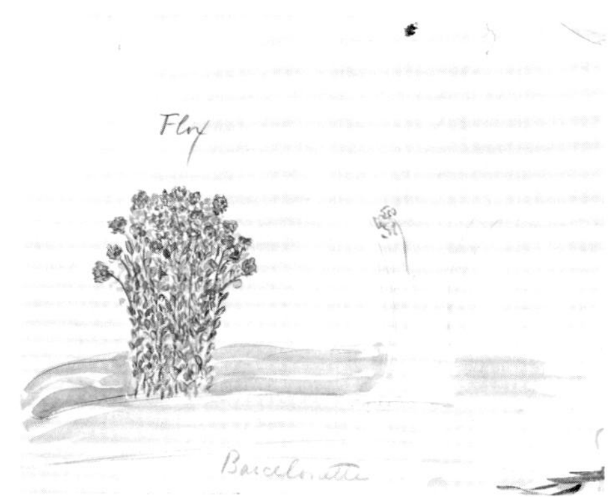

Phlox, ca. 1927-29
CR 2351
Watercolor and pencil on paper (8¾ x 11¾ in.; 22.2 x 29.9 cm)
Williams College Museum of Art, Gift of Mrs. Charles Prendergast (87.5.15)

INSCRIPTIONS
u.l.: Flox
l.c.: Barcelonette

PROVENANCE
The artist; to Mrs. Charles Prendergast, 1948; to present collection, 1987

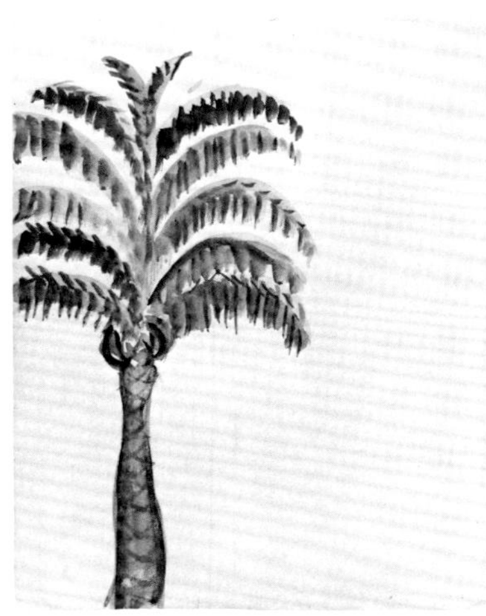

Palm Tree, ca. 1927-29
CR 2352
Watercolor and pencil on paper (13⅜ x 10¼ in.; 34.0 x 26.0 cm)
Williams College Museum of Art, Gift of Mrs. Charles Prendergast (87.5.3)

INSCRIPTIONS
Unsigned

PROVENANCE
The artist; to Mrs. Charles Prendergast, 1948; to present collection, 1987

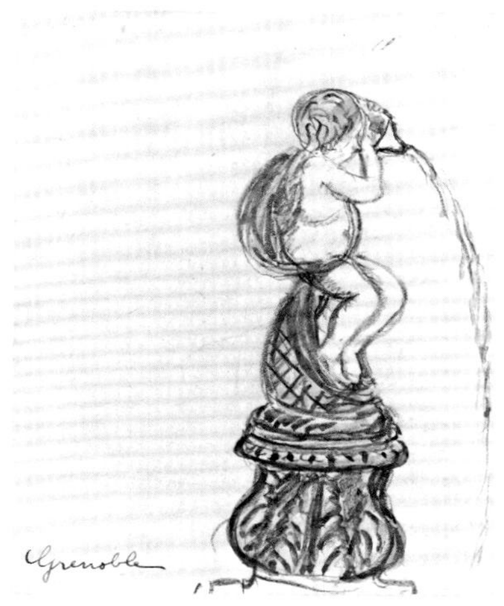

The Fountain, ca. 1927-29
CR 2353
Ink, colored pencil, and watercolor on blue paper (5¼ x 4⅛ in.; 13.3 x 10.5 cm)
Williams College Museum of Art, Gift of Mrs. Charles Prendergast (87.5.9)

INSCRIPTIONS
l.l. in black ink: Grenoble
verso, l.c.: The Fountain

PROVENANCE
The artist; to Mrs. Charles Prendergast, 1948; to present collection, 1987

EXHIBITIONS
1988a Williams College (no #)

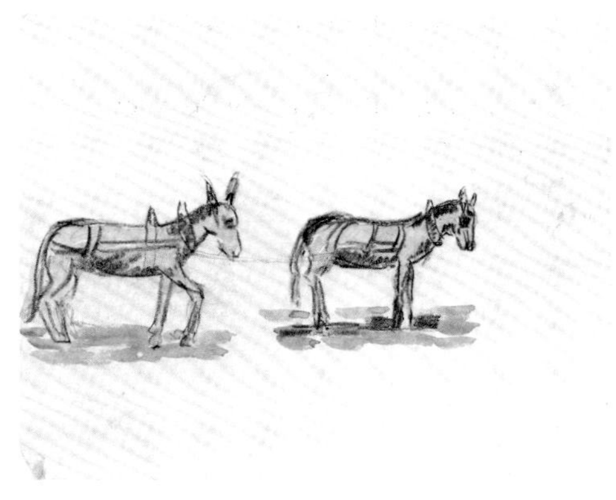

Burros, ca. 1927-29
CR 2354
Watercolor and pencil on paper (7⅞ x 9¾ in.; 20.0 x 24.8 cm)
Williams College Museum of Art, Gift of Mrs. Charles Prendergast (87.5.10)

Inscriptions
Unsigned
verso, l.c.: burrows

Provenance
The artist; to Mrs. Charles Prendergast, 1948; to present collection, 1987

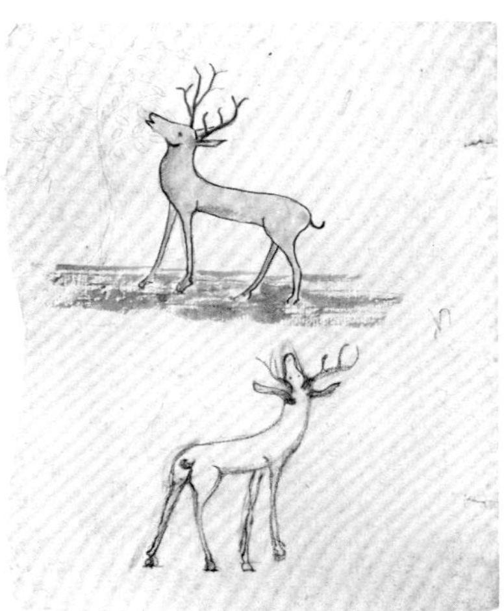

(recto) *Studies of Deer* with Eugénie Prendergast, ca. 1927-29
CR 2355
Watercolor, ink, and pencil on paper (11¼ x 9 in.; 28.6 x 22.9 cm)
Williams College Museum of Art, Gift of Mrs. Charles Prendergast (87.5.8)

Inscriptions
Unsigned
verso, l.r.: Eugénie

Provenance
The artist; to Mrs. Charles Prendergast, 1948; to present collection, 1987

verso: *Studies of Deer*, with Eugénie Prendergast
Watercolor and pencil

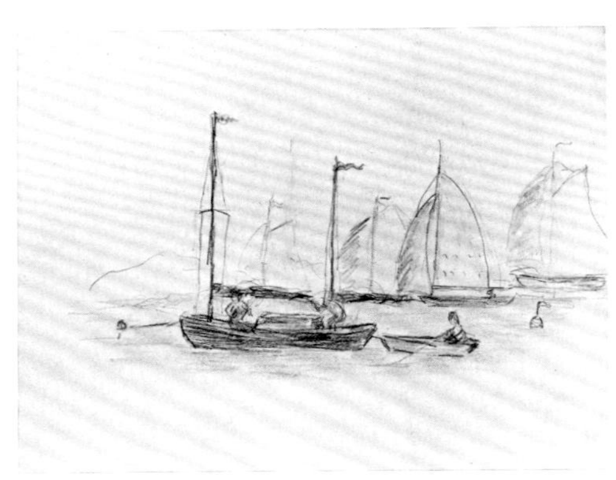

(recto) *Sailboats*, ca. 1927-29
CR 2356
Colored pencil on paper (9 x 11⅞ in.; 22.9 x 30.2 cm)
Williams College Museum of Art, Gift of Mrs. Charles Prendergast (87.5.4)

Inscriptions
Unsigned
verso, l.r. in pencil: beach hotel
l.l. (in Eugénie Prendergast's hand): C.P. per E.P.

Provenance
The artist; to Mrs. Charles Prendergast, 1948; to present collection, 1987

verso: *Beach Hotel*
Colored pencil

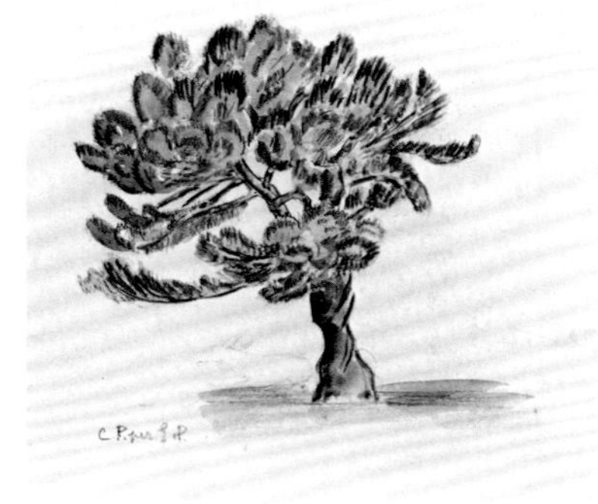

Blue Tree, ca. 1927-29
CR 2357
Watercolor and pencil on paper (8⅞ x 9½ in.; 22.5 x 24.1 cm)
Collection of Mrs. Charles Prendergast

Inscriptions
l.l. in pencil (in Eugénie Prendergast's hand): C.P. per E.P.

Provenance
The artist; to present collection, 1948

Exhibitions
1963b Davis Galleries (#20)

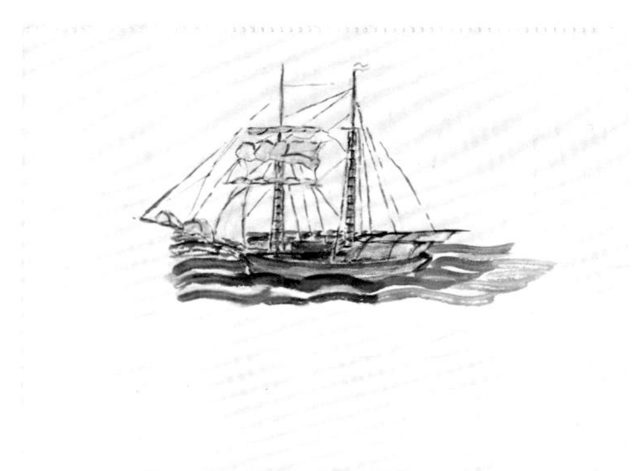

Study of a Boat, ca. 1927-29
CR 2358
Watercolor, ink, and pencil on paper with perforated edge (9½ x 12⅝ in.; 24.1 x 32.1 cm)
Williams College Museum of Art, Gift of Mrs. Charles Prendergast (87.5.5)

INSCRIPTIONS
Unsigned

PROVENANCE
The artist; to Mrs. Charles Prendergast, 1948; to present collection, 1987

EXHIBITIONS
?1963b Davis Galleries (#21)

THESE UNFINISHED SKETCHES date from Prendergast's trips to France in 1927 and 1929. Many are inscribed with the site name, for example, "Barcelonette," "Grenoble," and "Cannes." They apparently were done for his own pleasure while traveling. None of the various motifs appear in later panels or watercolors.

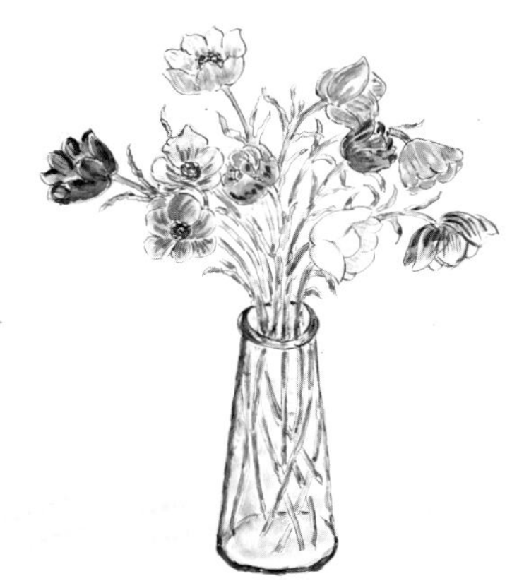

Sketchbook, ca. 1927-29
CR 2414
7 pencil and watercolor drawings (10¼ x 13¾ in.; 26.0 x 34.9 cm)
Williams College Museum of Art, Gift of Mrs. Charles Prendergast (85.23.3)

PROVENANCE
The artist; to Mrs. Charles Prendergast, 1948; to present collection, 1985

BIBLIOGRAPHY
AAA Roll #3583, begin frame 0480

EXHIBITIONS
1989a Williams College (no #); 1989b Williams College (no #)

TECHNICAL NOTES
The sketchbook has cardboard front and back covers; printed on the front cover is "Carnet Croquis." The pages are stapled underneath the green tape binding; the binding is split. The pages are perforated at the binding edge for easy removal. Many sheets are loose; others have been removed from the sketchbook at the perforation. Twenty-one pages remain, showing five sketches; there are also two loose pages not originally from this sketchbook.

MOST OF THE PAGES in this sketchbook are blank, although some of these show the smudging of drawings that have been removed. Two of the drawings are related to Prendergast's favorite French hill-town subjects: one is faintly drawn and shows an aqueduct, the other is loose, not originally from this book. It depicts, in watercolor and charcoal, a hilly landscape with buildings, telephone poles, and trucks. Prendergast's use of twentieth-century motifs is not known to occur elsewhere in the hill-town scenes. He made over two dozen hill-town drawings that are notable, instead, for their timelessness.

There are two drawings in watercolor and pencil of flowers, one an exquisite, stylized arrangement in a vase. The remaining three drawings are faint and indistinct pencil studies.

Marion M. Goethals

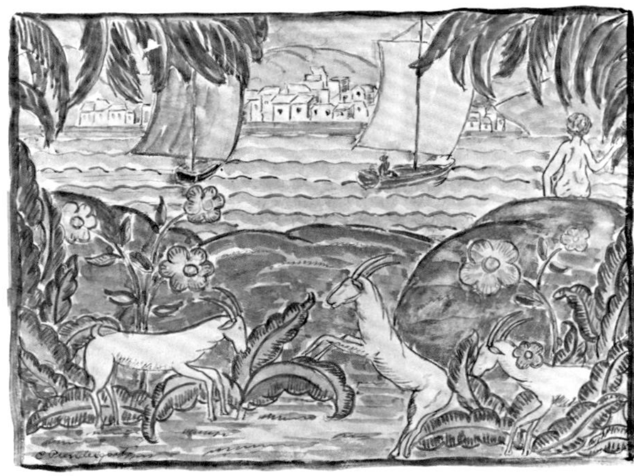

Beach Scene with Prancing Goats, ca. 1927-29
CR 2362
Watercolor, pencil, and ink on paper (10¼ x 13⅜ in.; 26.0 x 34.0 cm)
Williams College Museum of Art, Gift of Arthur T. Norman (86.10)

INSCRIPTIONS
l.l. in black ink: C Prendergast

PROVENANCE
Arthur T. Norman; to present collection, 1986

EXHIBITIONS
1988a Williams College (no #); 1989b Williams College (#34); 1990 Williams College (no #)

AFTER HIS SECOND TRIP to France in 1929, Prendergast began to sketch from nature more often and to produce scenes of identifiable modern life. But following his first trip in 1927, he was still interested in adapting his sketches of French towns to his longstanding vision of an idyllic or fantasy world. The panel *Hill Town* (CR 2260, Addison Gallery of American Art), for example, shows the city of Cannes forming a backdrop for horseback riders, maidens, bathers, and dancers cavorting among deer and other forest animals. *Beach Scene with Prancing Goats* has this same mixture of a quiet French seaside town with goats, nude bathers, and exotic flora and fauna, and very likely dates from the period between Prendergast's first and second trips to France. A more elaborate exploration of this theme can be found in a similar watercolor, *Allegory* (CR 2363, The Metropolitan Museum of Art, Robert Lehman Collection).

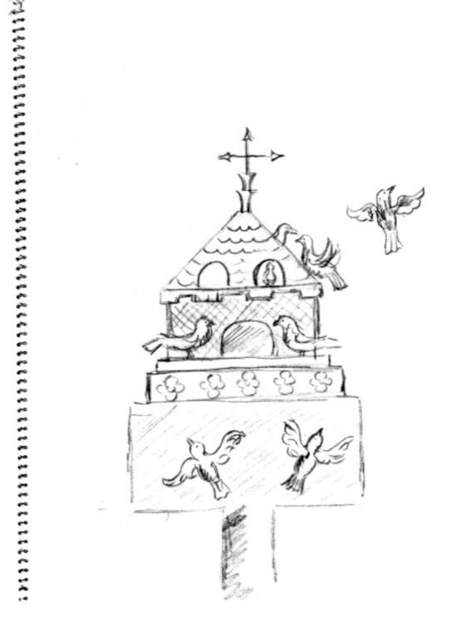

Sketchbook, ca. 1929
CR 2415
19 pencil, watercolor, and crayon drawings (12⅝ x 9⅝ in.; 32.1 x 24.4 cm)
Williams College Museum of Art, Gift of Mrs. Charles Prendergast (85.23.4)

INSCRIPTIONS
on first page: Charles Prendergast/ Madison Hotel/ 143 Boulevard Saint Germain/ Paris

PROVENANCE
The artist; to Mrs. Charles Prendergast, 1948; to present collection, 1985

BIBLIOGRAPHY
AAA Roll #3583, begin frame 0490

EXHIBITIONS
1989a Williams College (no #); 1989b Williams College (no #)

TECHNICAL NOTES
This is a spiral-bound notebook with cardboard front and back covers; printed on the cover is "Croquis Dessin, Marque Déposée [seal] Breveté France & étranger." There are fifteen pages in the book, and two loose sheets not originally from this sketchbook. Most of the first page has been cut off; the remaining portion has yellow, green, and brown watercolor strokes and an inscription in pencil: "Charles Prendergast/ Madison Hotel/ 143 Boulevard Saint Germain/ Paris." The Parisian address dates the sketchbook to a trip Charles took to France with his wife, Eugénie. Two inscriptions, presumably identifications of drawings subsequently removed, identify French towns—Grasse and St. Malo—that the couple is known to have visited in 1929. Some of

Charles's French hill-town watercolor drawings may have originated from this sketchbook.

THE DRAWINGS IN THIS SKETCHBOOK are alike in their rendering with a few exceptions: watercolors of a freighter and of a spray of flowers. Most of the rest are drawn with the same soft pencil, and in the same manner—firmly outlined and heavily shaded. There are three border designs that are figural and decorative. One of these bears a strong relationship to the panel *Promenade* (CR 2290, Private Collection) with its interspersal of trees and women in procession. The other two are similar horizontal progressions of trees and grazing animals. There are two completely composed fantasies carefully drawn in pencil. The fountain in both of them appears in two panels, *Untitled* (CR 2238, Private Collection) and *The Fountain* (CR 2263, Museum of Fine Arts, Boston).

Some of the drawings have intriguing notations that spotlight the interest of the artist in methods, materials, and other artworks as he traveled. On a page with three frame studies, Prendergast makes a reference to an Ingres portrait in the Granet collection in the museum at Aix. Other drawings may be antiquities sketched at the museum including one that has the inscription "Side of chest." In one drawing of an allover design of foliage and flowers, the artist gives instructions in the margins: "paint with water color then/ out line the lea[ves]/ paint some solid flowers on silver/ acid/ out line with black/green/pink/ stain the flowers with acid and paint leave/ some and paint on/ others."

Two of the drawings are related by their rendering of architecture, one of a birdhouse with birds and another of a cottage with flower boxes and fence. Other subjects include flowers, birds, genre figures, horses, a cow, and fish. Many of the drawings have color notations which typically indicate the artist's intent to develop the studies into finished compositions.

The two loose sheets are from different sketch pads and different time periods. One is in pencil and watercolor of a rooster in the Florida manner of the late 1940s (8-3/8 x 3-1/2 in.; 21.3 x 8.8 cm). The other sheet has nine studies of birds drawn heavily in black and blue crayon (11-3/4 x 8-7/8 in.; 30.0 x 22.6 cm) and could be from the 1920s or 1930s.

Marion M. Goethals

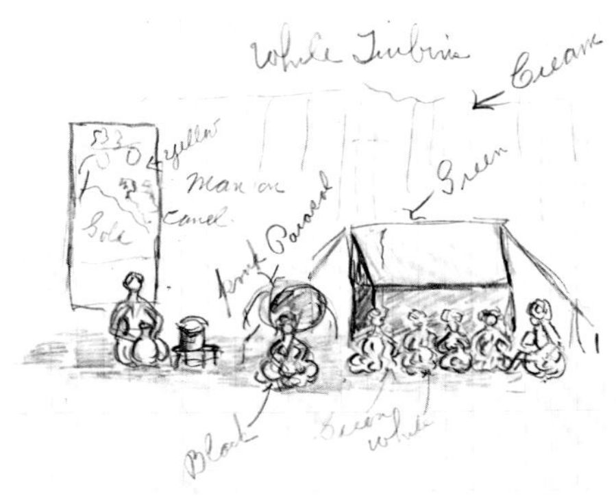

Sketchbook, ca. 1930-32
CR 2417
52 pencil drawings, on lined paper (9⅝ x 7½ in.; 24.4 x 19.0 cm)
Williams College Museum of Art, Gift of Mrs. Charles Prendergast (85.23.5)

PROVENANCE
The artist; to Mrs. Charles Prendergast, 1948; to present collection, 1985

BIBLIOGRAPHY
AAA Roll #3583, begin frame 0508

EXHIBITIONS
1988a Williams College (no #); 1989a Williams College (no #); 1990 Williams College (no #)

TECHNICAL NOTES
This book, which was produced for written exercises, is used here by the artist as a sketchbook in preparation for his largest panel, *Play, International House* (CR 2264, Collection of International House). It also includes some preparation for three other panels: *Central Park Zoo* (CR 2286, Private Collection), *The Winner* (CR 2289, The London Collection), and *Racetrack* (CR 2291, Collection of Mr. and Mrs. Arthur G. Altschul). The book has black-and-white mottled covers, long familiar to American schoolchildren. On the front is printed "Composition" with a space for the name of the owner; the paper is lined. The drawings, over fifty in all, are in pencil, although there are a few watercolor strokes.

THE MAJORITY OF THE DRAWINGS are simply drawn studies of single figures engaged in a wide variety of activities: dancing, playing instruments, sitting on benches, standing, raking. Other sketches seem to represent the working out of architectural structures—stages or platforms. Many of these figures and compositions may be found, slightly altered, in *Play, International House*, 1931. The inscriptions on the drawings are specific color notations for items of clothing, which indicate purposeful planning on Prendergast's part for finished compositions. Plans for *Play, International House* may also be found in another sketchbook (CR 2416, WCMA, p. 81).

The more complex compositions in the sketchbook reflect Prendergast's interest in the 1930s with contemporary recreational events. One drawing depicts a section of the interior of a performance tent with supports, side flaps, bleachers, and general activity. Two drawings appear to be the viewing tower that appears at the left of Prendergast's racetrack panels, *The Winner* and *Racetrack*. Another small drawing shows a grandstand; others show seals, the outdoor café from the panel *Central Park Zoo*, and a study for the buffalo mural on the café in that panel. There are also simple studies of animals: seal, bird, donkey, owl, deer, moose.

One drawing that stands apart in subject and style is a lightly sketched figure reminiscent of the central figure in *Enthroned Madonna and Child with Angels*, ca. 1915-20 (CR 2316, WCMA, p. 105); the page also has frame sketches. Only one drawing could represent an actual scheme for a panel; it compositionally recalls the spatial simplicity of certain works of the mid-1930s: in the foreground two figures stand in a yard with house and animals, in the middle ground a ship sails horizontally across the picture, hills rise in the distance.

Marion M. Goethals

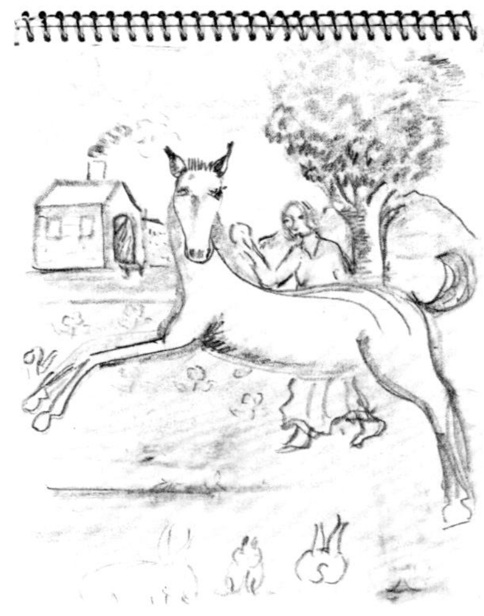

Sketchbook, ca. 1929-30
CR 2418
57 pencil and watercolor drawings (7¼ x 5⅜ in.; 18.4 x 13.6 cm)
Williams College Museum of Art, Gift of Mrs. Charles Prendergast (85.23.8)

PROVENANCE
The artist; to Mrs. Charles Prendergast, 1948; to present collection, 1985

BIBLIOGRAPHY
AAA Roll #3583, begin frame 0610

EXHIBITIONS
1988a Williams College (no #); 1989a Williams College (no #); 1989b Williams College (no #)

TECHNICAL NOTES
Because this is a sketchbook of French manufacture, and because the artist has made notations within of Parisian addresses (Colarossi and Bibliothèque du Musée des Arts Décoratifs), a portion of the over fifty pencil drawings are believed to have been made in the late 1920s when Charles traveled in France with his wife. Others probably record a visit to the Central Park Zoo and subsequent planning for the panel *Central Park Zoo*, ca. 1936 (CR 2286, Private Collection). The cover is printed "Esquisse/ Marque déposée/ Breveté/ France et Étranger/ No 1105."

IN THIS BOOK Prendergast drew delightfully conceived animals in simple, soft pencil outline. Each of these studies is on a single page unencumbered by background or setting: deer, elephant, carousel horse, rabbits, swan, zebra, donkey, baboon, mountain goat, rhinoceros, mountain lion, hippopotamus, giraffe, seals, buffalo, and owl. In the panel, however, Prendergast focused the scene on the dozens of people circulating around the seal pool rather than on the animals in the sketchbook.

The animal studies occur throughout the sketchbook, and are interspersed with outdoor scenes that relate to the zoo: a kiosk with trees, a fountain, a lake scene, an animal grazing by a building, a public walk with benches and umbrella. In one sketch, the artist works out the complicated arrangement of plaza and building that appears in the background of *Central Park Zoo*.

Other drawings in the sketchbook are independent compositions. Some are drawn more lightly and with a harder pencil—flowers in vases and an interior scene depicting figures standing in a room, one at a counter and two in doorways with their arms raised. Another drawing could be a plan for a simple panel composition; in it a leaping, stylized horse is superimposed upon a house and yard. Drawings that could have been made while in France include a fountain with figural sculpture, an architectural dome with lantern, and an elaborate gate with building and tower.

Charles Prendergast, in keeping with his uncomplicated vision, did not usually write down his thoughts about the making of art. In this little book, however, he wrote the following: "The analytical mind when it gets into art is confusing. Nature itself is so simple. The foundation of all art."

Marion M. Goethals

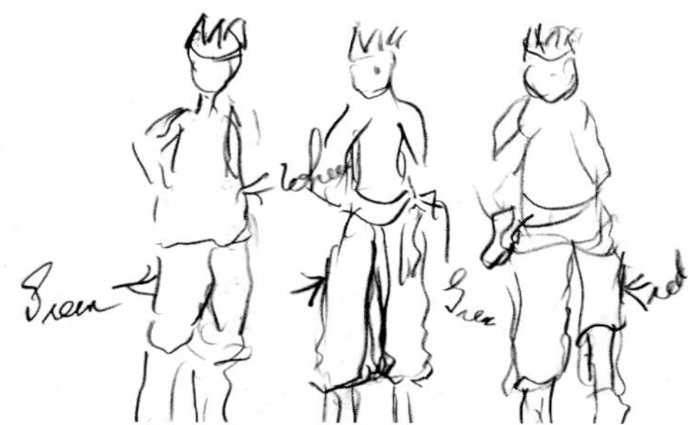

Sketchbook, ca. 1930-31
CR 2416
49 pencil drawings (7¾ x 5⅜ in.; 19.7 x 13.6 cm)
Williams College Museum of Art, Gift of Mrs. Charles Prendergast (85.23.7)

PROVENANCE
The artist; to Mrs. Charles Prendergast, 1948; to present collection, 1985

BIBLIOGRAPHY
AAA Roll #3583, begin frame 0567

EXHIBITIONS
1989a Williams College (no #)

TECHNICAL NOTES
This is a small book, probably a pad of writing paper of a type widely available, rather than an artist's sketchpad. The cover is printed "Arcadia/ Wedding Plate/ W-B 177 1/2 unruled." The pad has about seventy pages remaining, many of which are blank. The drawings are in pencil.

THE DRAWINGS IN THIS BOOK fall into two groups: the "Juno" sketches and about fifteen partial figure studies. The figure studies do not appear to relate to finished works; they are small, incompletely conceived, sketchily and briefly drawn. In addition, there are two pages with drawings that are on paper not from this pad. One (4 x 5-7/8 in.; 10.2 x 14.9 cm) is a small drawing of an exotic fish, in pencil. The other (5 x 7-5/8 in.; 12.7 x 19.4 cm) is a study in pencil on ruled paper for either of the two sculptures, *Fish* (CR 2405, Private Collection) or *Dolphin* (CR 2407, Museum of Fine Arts, Boston). A verso drawing, also in pencil, shows a figure leading a donkey and rider, another figure follows; the drawing is rubbed over with soft pencil.

The "Juno" sketches appear to be a group of studies of a theatrical performance, and are plans for the panel *Play, International House* (CR 2264, Collection of International House). There are between fifteen to twenty drawings that appear to relate to this project. Three drawings show a classical temple facade with columns and pediment, the entablature reads "JUNO." One of these is of three figures on a theatrical stage in front of the Juno temple. Elsewhere is a drawing that depicts a stage with figures in headdresses; a stage curtain seems to be indicated on the right, and the inscription reads "people in front."

The panel *Play, International House* was commissioned by Abby Aldrich Rockefeller for the International House, a student center in New York City. In preparation for the work, Prendergast was invited to spend an evening at the center enjoying multinational skits and performances by the students. The Juno temple facade from this sketchbook is altered in the panel. Rather than the sketchbook's pediment raised on four classical columns, there is a viewing box with audience. Perhaps the artist himself is among the guests portrayed in the small group.

The other drawings associated with *Play* in the sketchbook are of specific figures, their dress and props. One drawing, for instance, is of two figures in a decorative pavilion; the inscription reads "ermine red cape/ green cape/ black/ flowers white & red." Costume and color notes appear on all of the drawings; a sketch of two half-length female figures with particularly detailed notes reads "group in/ front of Juno/ red white blue/ dress suite/ girls in pink & green/ evening gowns/ tux suits with pink capes/ gold ribbon around/ head." Plans for the panel *Play, International House* may also be found in another sketchbook (CR 2417, WCMA, p. 79).

Marion M. Goethals

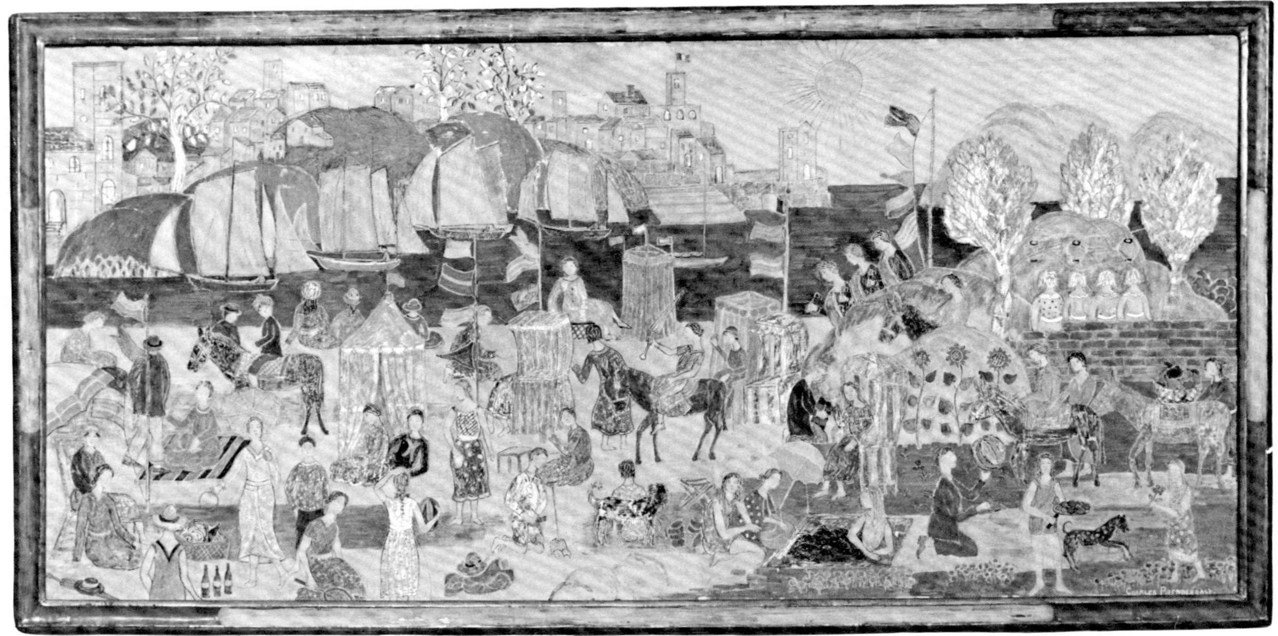

Holiday Beach Scene, ca. 1931-32
Holiday
CR 2265
Color illustration, p. 26
Frame by the artist
Incised gesso, tempera, and gold leaf on panel (27⅞ x 59 in.; 70.6 x 149.9 cm)
Williams College Museum of Art, Gift of Mrs. Charles Prendergast (86.18.63)

Inscriptions
l.r.: Charles Prendergast

Provenance
The artist; to Mrs. Charles Prendergast, 1948; to present collection, 1986

Bibliography
Art News 1935 (p. 8); Mumford 1935 (p. 69); NY Herald Tribune 1935b (p. 10); Art Digest 1947 (p. 18); ?Marlor 1984 (as *Holidays* p. 448); Antiques Arts Weekly 1986 (p. 113)

Exhibitions
1935 Kraushaar (#20 as *Holiday*); ?1936 Soc Independent Artists (#688); 1938 Addison (#9, as *Holiday*); 1947 Kraushaar (#5 as *Holiday*); 1968 Rutgers University (#24, ill. p. 63); 1969 Hirschl & Adler (#14); 1986 Williams College (no #); 1988a Williams College (no #); 1989a Williams College (no #); 1989b Williams College (#37); 1991 Williams College (no #)

Technical Notes
Numerous revisions of incised lines are apparent across the gesso-coated plywood panel. Some incisions were re-gessoed, as in the white areas of beach and sky, while other areas were just painted over, as seen in the green hills on the right. For surface variation, the artist abraded the painted and gold-leaf areas across the panel.

The modern-day subject matter of *Holiday Beach Scene* marks a departure from the earlier work of Charles Prendergast, which dealt primarily with idyllic or fantasy scenes. By representing a contemporary beach scene, the large panel has relevance to the personal lives of Charles and his brother Maurice, for whom vacations "were second in importance only to art."[1] Charles favored the fashionable French resorts of St. Malo and Cannes, both of which are referred to in *Holiday Beach Scene*. Maurice produced several St. Malo pictures after spending the summer of 1907 there. Like these works, Charles's seaside painting of over two decades later represents a populated beach decorated with striped tents and a distant view of a picturesque village. In spite of similarities with Maurice's St. Malo scenes, however, the hill town in *Holiday Beach Scene* is Cannes, a place Charles visited in 1927 and 1929. During one of these visits, he produced the watercolor entitled *Cannes* (CR 2329, Private Collection), which represents a medieval church and adjacent clock tower partially blocked by a full-blooming tree. This three-part grouping exists identically at the left edge of *Holiday Beach Scene*, which suggests the artist may have had Cannes in mind when he painted the panel.

Although Prendergast found the subject for *Holiday Beach Scene* in the real world, he included many exotic motifs that appear in his earlier fantasy work, *Hill Town*, ca. 1928 (CR 2260, Addison Gallery of American Art). Common elements in these two compositions suggest that *Holiday Beach Scene* updated the earlier fairy tale scene with the introduction of fashionable attire and popular leisure activities. In addition to their horizontal design, the panels share the motif of the medieval hill town, the varieties of trees, the poses of figures and animals, even the red brick wall. In the later work, Prendergast eliminated some of the exotic elements—the scampering wildlife and the complicated patterns of vegetation—but still used toga-clad maidens in classical poses. A young girl appears in the lower right-hand corner of both panels. In the later work, she embodies contemporary and classical styles—she wears a modern bathing suit while offering a tray of fruit. The eclectic mix of reality and fantasy in *Holiday Beach Scene* reflects a greater interest in imaginative arrangement of diverse pictorial elements than in documentation of a particular time and place.

Prendergast's compositional arrangement reveals his fascination with form and color and a disregard for locating objects in receding space. He treated figures and objects as ornaments with which to decorate a flat surface. The unusual abundance of gold leaf in *Holiday Beach Scene* emphasizes this aspect. In medieval painting, gold leaf was reserved for the sacred subjects of heaven and halos. Here it is used solely for visual effect—applied on top of painted areas for pure color or partially scraped away to highlight opaque areas. In terms of structure, he created interesting visual patterns by grouping objects in threes and fours. In just one small area on the right we see three red lanterns hanging above the golden heads of four women, above them are three bushy trees silhouetted against three pink hills. Prendergast further creates this sense of patterning by treating every figure on the beach with equal size and clarity. Rather than recede into space, objects appear vertically stacked, from the people in the foreground right up to the hill town in the distance. In *Holiday Beach Scene*, Prendergast's playful arrangement of form and color, and of reality and fantasy, suggests something ultimately optimistic—a freshness and purity, an untarnished view of the world.

Susan Imbriani

1. Basso 1946b, p. 29.

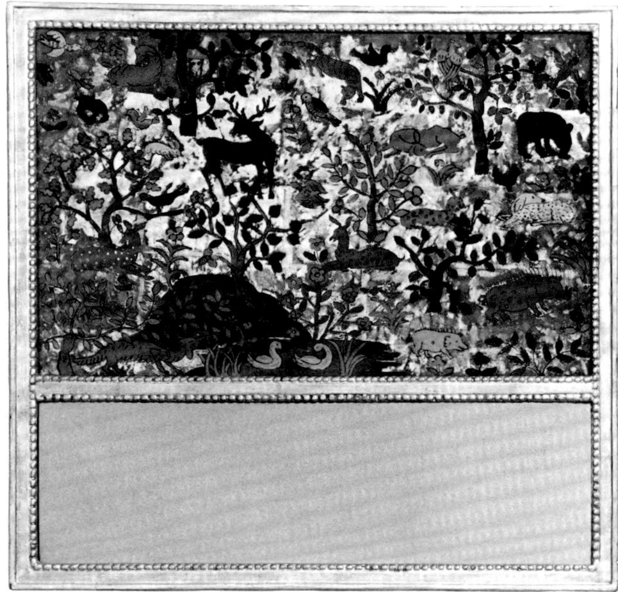

Animal Decoration on Glass, with mirror,
ca. 1928-32
CR 2262
Frame by the artist
Reverse painting with silver and gold leaf on glass, with mirror, in gessoed, carved, and gilded wooden frame (overall 23⅞ x 24 in.; 60.6 x 60.9 cm; painted panel 15 x 22 in.; 38.1 x 55.9 cm)
Collection of Mrs. Charles Prendergast

Inscriptions
Unsigned

Provenance
The artist; to present collection, 1948

Exhibitions
1937 Kraushaar (#15)

Technical Notes
This square Sheraton-style mirror is comprised of two glass panes—a reverse painting on glass and a mirror—separated horizontally by a thin wooden muntin. Both painting and looking glass are simply framed with a 1-inch-thick gessoed, carved, and gilded molding; the piece has neither cornice nor apron. Construction is modest—nails and glue used in combination with lap and mitered joinery; the wooden framing elements are probably of white pine or poplar.

In this instance, Prendergast chose to decorate the larger, upper register of his mirror with a scene replete with small animals and birds and to use the technique of reverse painting on glass. Though a time-honored method, reverse painting is a cumbersome technique: parts of a picture that would normally be painted last, must be painted first; alterations cannot be made; erasing and overpainting are impossible. What results however are colorful images characterized by tremendous luminosity when viewed from the front.

The art of reverse painting on glass readily lends itself to multiple production—one key design serving as the basis for innumerable replicas. Prendergast's *Animal Decoration on Glass, with mirror* is one of a group of three similar mirrors all based on the composition of a larger, earlier panel, *Golden Fantasy* (CR 2257, The Fuller Collection). (The others are *Animals in a Wood*, CR 2259, Collection of Mimi and Sanford Feld; and *The Zoo*, CR 2261, Collection of Margot Newman Stickley.) The artist cropped this original panel to the right, deleting several deer, birds, a rabbit, and some trees, and applied the balance of his pastoral vision to three mirrors, in reverse. He made subtle design adjustments—the inclusion of more trees and a hillock behind the small pond to the center—as well as some judicious color choices.

Sources for Prendergast's imagery are most likely found in eastern-Mediterranean and Persian textiles and ceramics, in particular the traditions of floral and hunting carpets wherein exotic beasts, birds, and flowers co-exist beneath a sylvan canopy.[1]

Prendergast may have as well looked to biblical tales as inspiration: to the Creation, Garden of Eden, and Jacob stories found in the Book of Genesis and to the gospel of Peter (Acts 10: 9-16). However, his adaptation of time-honored themes and vocabulary is most likely filtered through the lens of medieval art and folk imagery based loosely on biblical themes and popular epics or myths.

Vivian Patterson

1. Persian "hunting" carpets, the genre most similar in design to Prendergast's forest scene, usually depict animals in a frenzy of activity. Apparently, the Persian mode of hunting was such that "drivers" herded prey toward net enclosures wherein occured a mass melee of killing. Prendergast greatly tempered his scene with deer, rabbit, and fowl drawn in a variety of peaceful attitudes.

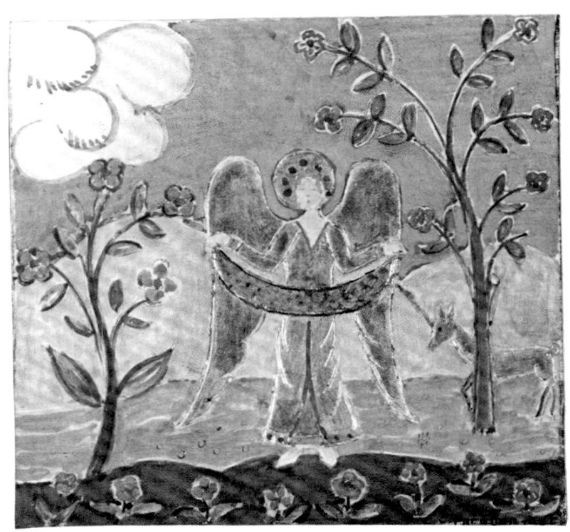

Christmas Card, 1932
CR 2365
Watercolor and gold leaf on incised gesso on paper
(7 x 7 in.; 17.8 x 17.8 cm)
Collection of Mrs. Charles Prendergast

INSCRIPTIONS
l.r.: C. Prendergast

PROVENANCE
The artist; to present collection, 1948

EXHIBITIONS
1984a Williams College (#7)

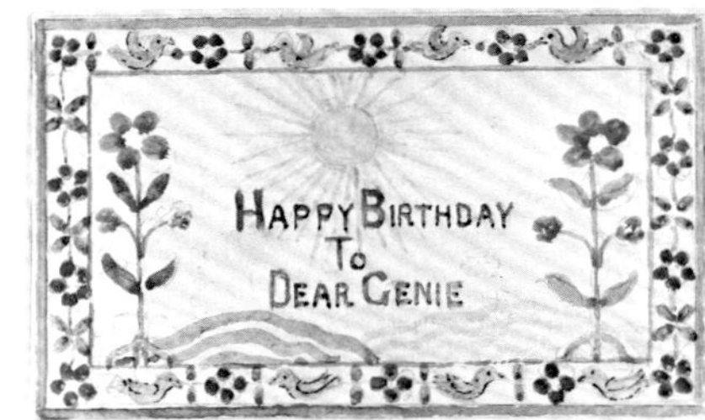

a

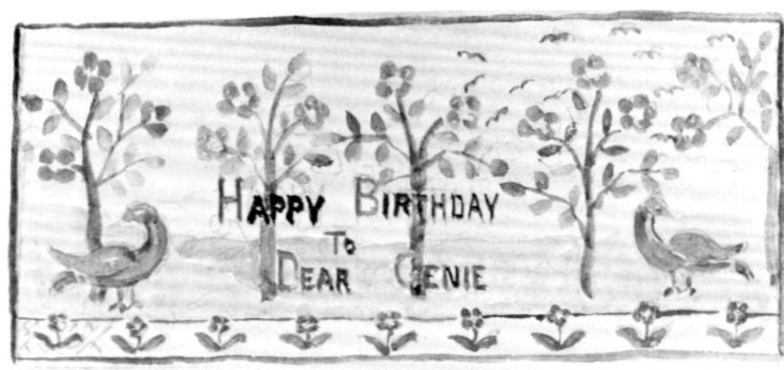

b

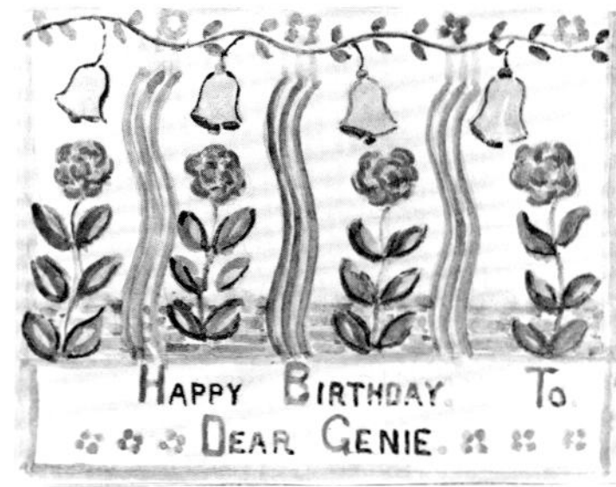

c

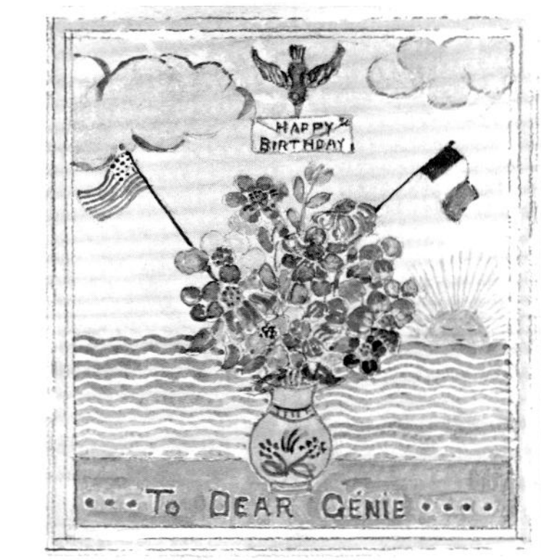

d

Four Birthday Cards
not catalogued
Watercolor and pencil on paper
a. (3½ x 5⅞ in.; 8.9 x 14.9 cm)
b. (3⅜ x 7⅜ in.; 8.6 x 18.7 cm)
c. (5⅝ x 7⅛ in.; 14.3 x 18.1 cm)
d. (6¾ x 5¾ in.; 17.2 x 14.6 cm)
Williams College Museum of Art, Gift of Mrs. Charles Prendergast (85.22.14, 15, 16, 17)

INSCRIPTIONS
Happy Birthday to Dear Genie

PROVENANCE
The artist; to Mrs. Charles Prendergast, by 1948; to present collection, 1985

LIKE MANY ARTISTS, Prendergast often decorated letters and made special greeting cards by hand. His most elaborate known today is the gessoed and gilded *Christmas Card*, which was never sent. The design of an angel holding an outstretched banner was taken directly from the far left panel of Prendergast's carved chest (CR 2398, Collection of Mrs. Charles Prendergast, p. 59), which was always prominently displayed in Mr. and Mrs. Prendergasts' living room.

After his marriage in 1925, Prendergast often designed birthday cards for his wife Eugénie (Genie). In one instance he showed the French and American flags in reference to the union of their nationalities. The fronts of four of these cards are now preserved in the Williams College Museum of Art.

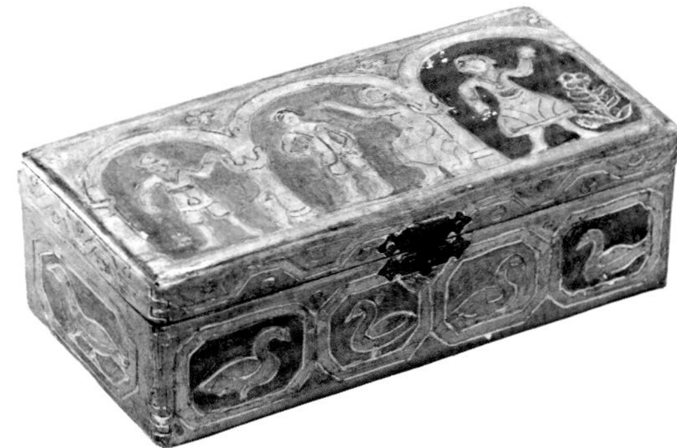

Box, ca. 1932
CR 2400
Tempera and gold leaf on incised, gessoed wood (2¾ x 7½ x 3½ in.; 6.9 x 19.1 x 8.9 cm)
Williams College Museum of Art, Gift of Mrs. Charles Prendergast (86.18.18)

INSCRIPTIONS
Unsigned

PROVENANCE
The artist; to Mrs. Charles Prendergast, 1948; to present collection, 1986

EXHIBITIONS
1968 Rutgers University (#63, ill. p. 101); 1969 Hirschl & Adler (#46); 1984a Williams College (#27); 1986 Williams College (no #); 1988b Williams College (#90); 1989a Williams College (no #); 1989b Williams College (#49); 1990 Williams College (no #)

TECHNICAL NOTES
The soft wood of this box has been incised and the whole subsequently covered with gesso, gold leaf, and tempera. The inside of the box has been gilded, and the inside of the lid has been painted with a floral design.

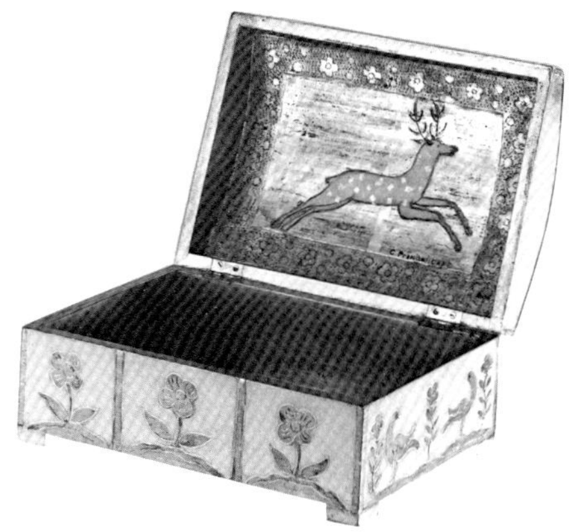

Small Chest, ca. 1934
CR 2402
Gold leaf on incised, gessoed wood (4 x 10 x 7 in.; 10.2 x 25.4 x 17.8 cm)
Collection of Mrs. Charles Prendergast

INSCRIPTIONS
incised inside cover, l.r.: C. Prendergast

PROVENANCE
The artist; to present collection, 1948

BIBLIOGRAPHY
Kay 1968 (p. 41; ill.)

EXHIBITIONS
1968 Rutgers University (#64, ill. p. 101); 1969 Hirschl & Adler (#47)

TECHNICAL NOTES
The exterior of the box has gilded deer, trees, flowers, and birds against a white gesso background. The interior, in contrast, has a white gesso deer against a background of gold leaf.

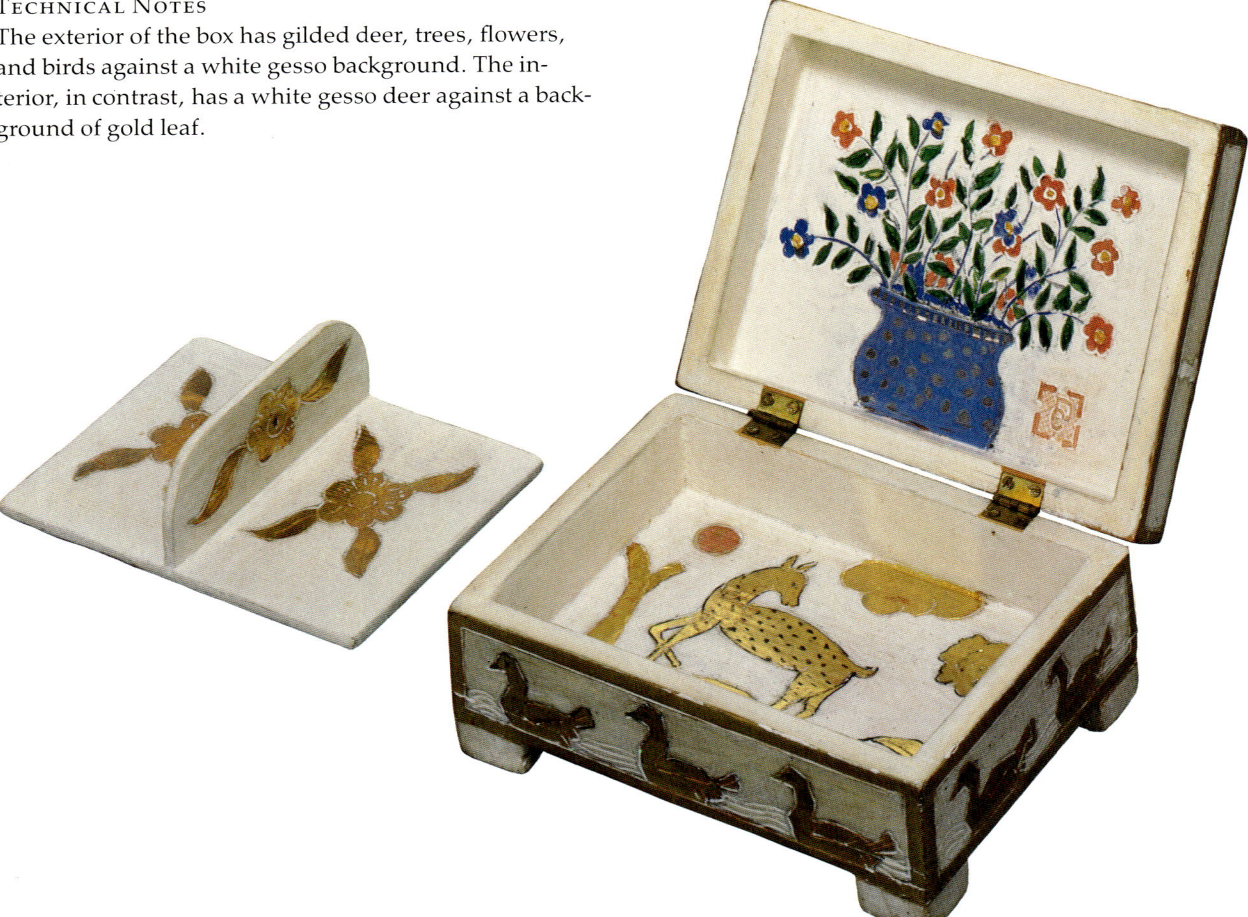

Box, ca. 1934
CR 2404
Tempera and gold leaf on incised, gessoed wood (2¾ x 5¾ x 4 in.; 7.0 x 14.6 x 10.2 cm)
Williams College Museum of Art, Gift of Mrs. Charles Prendergast (86.18.19)

INSCRIPTIONS
inside lid, l.r.: CP [monogram]

PROVENANCE
The artist; to Mrs. Charles Prendergast, 1948; to present collection, 1986

BIBLIOGRAPHY
Kay 1968 (p. 41; ill.)

EXHIBITIONS
1968 Rutgers University (#65, ill. p. 102); 1969 Hirschl & Adler (#48); 1970b Society of Four Arts (#34); 1984a Williams College (#28); 1986 Williams College (no #); 1988b Williams College (#91); 1989a Williams College (no #); 1989b Williams College (#50); 1990 Williams College (no #)

TECHNICAL NOTES
This box has been decorated on the outside with gold leaf and white gesso with occasional red tempera accents. The inside continues this color scheme with a scene of a deer on the bottom of the box. The inside of the lid, however, is painted in brilliant blues and reds depicting a vase of flowers. The wooden divider intended to separate two packs of playing cards has also been decorated with gilded floral motifs.

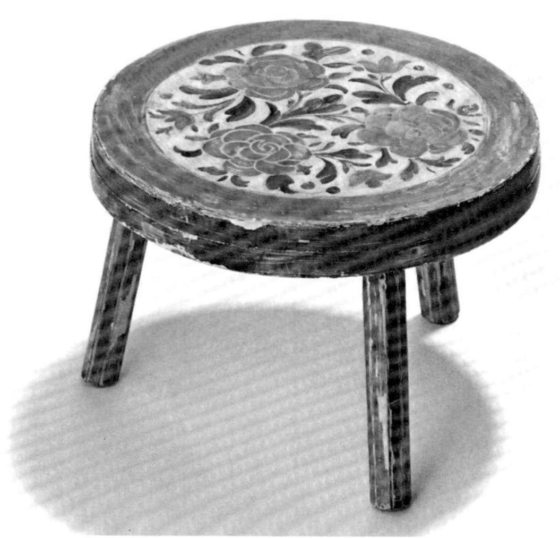

Three-legged Stool, ca. 1932-35
CR 2403
Tempera on gessoed wood (D. 8⅜ x H. 11½ in.; 21.3 x 29.2 cm)
Williams College Museum of Art, Gift of Mrs. Charles Prendergast (86.18.24)

INSCRIPTIONS
Unsigned

PROVENANCE
The artist; to Mrs. Charles Prendergast, 1948; to present collection, 1986

EXHIBITIONS
1984a Williams College (#30); 1989a Williams College (no #); 1992 Williams College (no #)

TECHNICAL NOTES
The stool is made of a reddish wood that has been coated with a thick layer of gesso and then painted. Alternating red and gold stripes decorate the legs, while on the seat a design of red flowers is surrounded by a gold-colored border. The abrasion of the gesso and darkening of the white background behind the flowers is so consistent, it appears to be deliberate.

IN THE 1930s Prendergast produced a number of decorative objects including boxes, stools, and small tables. Rather than making the objects himself, he typically acquired a manufactured or second-hand box or stool and then decorated it with incised, painted, and gilded gesso. The motifs he favored were animals, flowers, and figures in folk costume, giving the objects a primitive or folk art appearance. While the motifs on these boxes cannot be traced to a specific source, it is very likely that he derived them from books or articles on what was commonly referred to as "peasant art," such as *Peasant Art in Russia* (1912), which has been preserved from his own library, or Kathleen Mann's later guide for artists, *Design from Peasant Art* (New York: Macmillan, 1939), which illustrates traditional motifs and ways of adapting them to contemporary decorative objects.

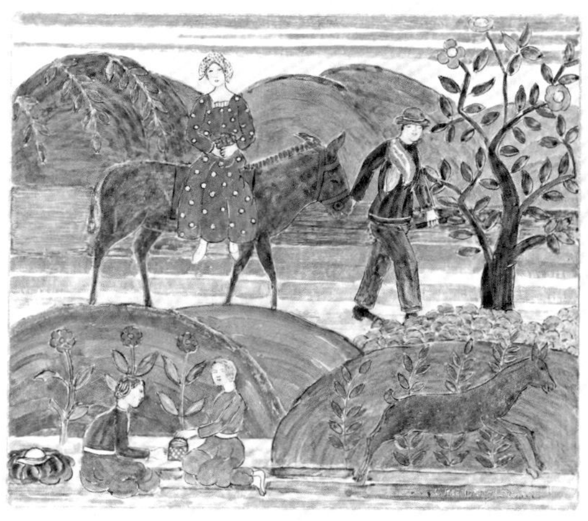

Donkey Rider #2, ca. 1936
CR 2282
Color illustration, p. 47
Frame by the artist
Incised gesso, tempera, and gold leaf on panel (16 x 17¾ in.; 40.6 x 45.1 cm)
Williams College Museum of Art, Gift of Mrs. Charles Prendergast (86.18.27)

INSCRIPTIONS
l.r. incised: C. Prendergast

PROVENANCE
The artist; to Mrs. Charles Prendergast, 1948; to present collection, 1986

BIBLIOGRAPHY
Durkin 1989 (back cover; ill.)

EXHIBITIONS
?1937 Kraushaar (#12); ?1938 Addison Gallery (#16, as *Donkey Rider*); 1984a Williams College (#9); 1985 Williams College (no #); 1986 Williams College (no #); 1988a Williams College (no #); 1989a Williams College (no #); 1989b Williams College (#40); 1990 Williams College (no #)

TECHNICAL NOTES
White gesso was applied with medium thickness to a plywood panel. The composition was then incised in the not-yet-hardened gesso creating broad outlines that define the forms. In certain areas a red-hued gold leaf was applied first and then the tempera was layered over

the leaf. This technique creates a shimmering effect that enlivens the surface of the work. In contrast, in other areas gold leaf mixed with gum arabic was applied over a surface already covered with tempera such as the polka dots decorating the woman's dress. The golden deer, the man's trousers and shirt, the hands of the female rider, and the flowers were all originally burnished to a high gloss. On the reverse of the panel appears the beginnings of a second composition that is contemporaneous with the work on the front. The artist may have used this unfinished image as a preliminary study in which he tested the thickness of the gesso and the application of gold leaf. From the rudimentary lines that were incised into the gesso it is possible to read two figures paddling a canoe.

THOUGH THE CHOICE of subject matter in *Donkey Rider #2* clearly relates this work to the earlier panel, *Donkey Rider*, ca. 1915-17 (CR 2228, WCMA, p. 64), there are important differences that distinguish this later work and suggest that the artist was using this familiar motif to develop a new style. The long linear sweeps, which unite the internal space of the earlier compositions and indicate the importance of the decorative surface pattern, have been replaced in *Donkey Rider #2* by a more rigidly structured composition in which the figures are contained within clearly defined blocks of space.[1] *Donkey Rider #2* can be divided visually into four equal sections that are related to one another by an implied narrative and balanced by the equal placement of figures.

The device of the layered hills, which divide the composition and create an implied middle ground, are derived from Italian primitive painters like Giotto.[2] The Prendergast brothers did have in their possession several illustrations of Giotto's frescos in the Arena Chapel at Padua, and it is probable that Charles visited the chapel during his 1911 visit to Italy. Giotto's *The Flight to Egypt* suggests a specific source for the donkey-rider motif. Though the woman in Prendergast's work does not hold a baby, she presses her hands against her stomach, possibly implying pregnancy.

A year later Prendergast returned to the donkey-rider motif and depicted a scene identical to *Donkey Rider #2* in the third panel of a large folding screen (CR 2284, Private Collection). In this screen he also incorporated *The Rider* (CR 2283, Private Collection) and *Going to Market* (CR 2281, Private Collection), two other incised panels that he made during the period 1935-36. The inclusion of these three smaller panels within the larger work suggests that Prendergast may have used these three earlier works to chart his ideas for the larger screen.

The seeming simplicity of Prendergast's design—the broad outlines and simplified forms—also suggests contemporary illustrations in children's literature. Though it was not possible to find a direct source for the donkey-rider motif, many of the elements of Prendergast's style link him to illustrators popular in the 1930s, such as Wanda Gag and Lynd Ward.

Rachel B. H. Petrik

1. Wattenmaker 1968, p. 32.
2. Ibid., p. 9.

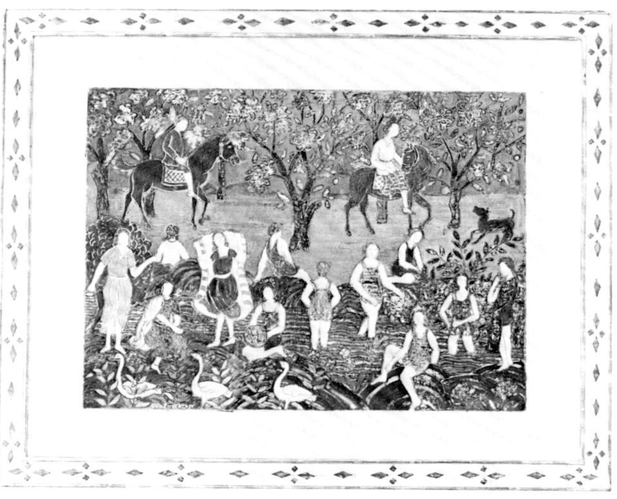

Bathers, ca. 1940
CR 2301
Frame by the artist
Incised gesso, tempera, and gold leaf on panel (26¼ x 32¼ in.; 66.7 x 81.9 cm; framed)
Collection of Mrs. Charles Prendergast

INSCRIPTIONS
l.l.: C. Prendergast

PROVENANCE
The artist; to present collection, 1948

BIBLIOGRAPHY
Wattenmaker 1968 (p. 34)

EXHIBITIONS
1941 Kraushaar (#10); 1954 Kraushaar (#26); 1968 Rutgers University (#45, ill. p. 83); 1969 Hirschl & Adler (#32)

TECHNICAL NOTES
The Masonite panel has been gessoed and the background painted in a rich green. Traces of gold leaf can be found in upper zone of the composition obscured by the tempera of the foliage of the trees.

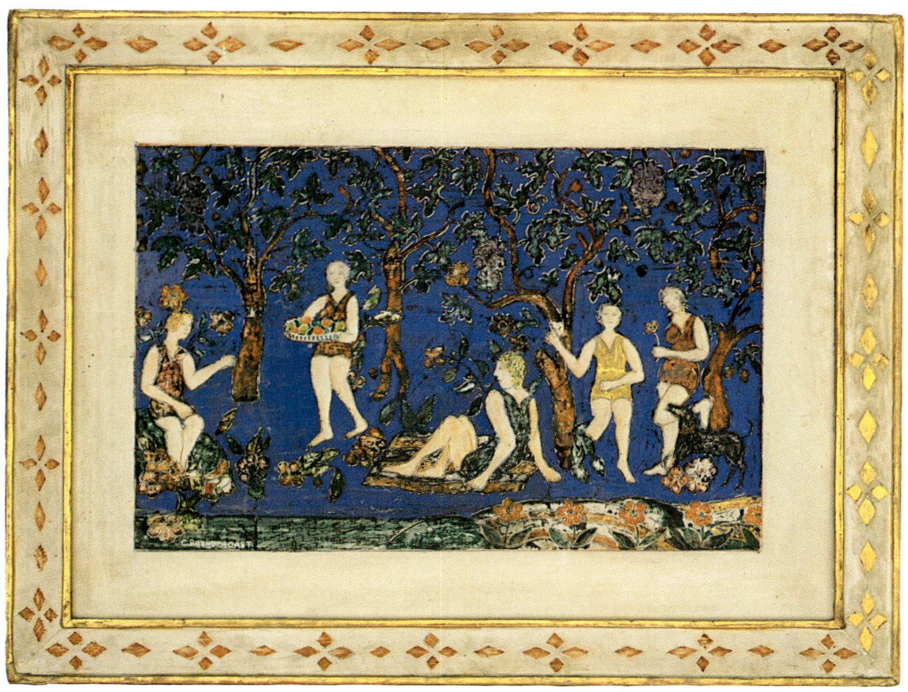

Bathers Under the Trees, ca. 1940
CR 2300
Frame by the artist
Incised gesso, tempera, and gold leaf on panel (22⅜ x 29 in.; 56.9 x 73.7 cm)
Williams College Museum of Art, Gift of Mrs. Charles Prendergast (86.18.13)

INSCRIPTIONS
l.l. incised: C. Prendergast

PROVENANCE
The artist; to Mrs. Charles Prendergast, 1948; to present collection, 1986

BIBLIOGRAPHY
Winter Park Topics 1947 (p. 1; ill.); Breuning 1947 (p. 18); Wattenmaker 1968 (p. 34)

EXHIBITIONS
1941 Kraushaar (#8, ill.); 1947 Kraushaar (#12); 1968 Rutgers University (#44, ill. p. 83); 1969 Hirschl & Adler (#31); 1970b Society of Four Arts (#32); 1983a Williams College (#32); 1984a Williams College (#13); 1986 Williams College (no #); 1989a Williams College (no #); 1989b Williams College (#36); 1990 Williams College (no #); 1992 Williams College (no #)

TECHNICAL NOTES
The rich blue tempera of the background is broken at intervals by the highly burnished red trees and bathing suits. Gold leaf has been applied to the bathing suit of the figure second to the right and may be found under the tempera on the hair of all the women. The composition is surrounded by a border of unpainted gesso in imitation of a mat. The support is Masonite.

The frame, by the artist, is carved and water gilt with incised lozenges, burnished gold. There are small gesso and gilding losses overall, although some losses have been overpainted.

THESE TWO SCENES of women bathing in a woodland setting, created at approximately the same time and framed alike, are Prendergast's only exploration of this popular theme. The two panels suggest the influence of both Maurice Prendergast and Cézanne, but cannot be traced to specific works by either of Prendergast's two heroes. Charles Prendergast has included some of his favorite symbolic motifs to give the works an air of fantasy, such as the swans, the long-stemmed red flowers, and the basket of fruit held as an offering by a figure in each composition. But the fantasy aspect is balanced by details of ordinary life, such as the bathing suits that each one modestly wears and the beach towels that they sit on or wrap around their shoulders. A sketch of a beach scene showing similar fashions and poses may be found in Prendergast's "Sketchbook B" (CR 2410, Museum of Fine Arts, Boston), indicating that the compositions may be based on drawings from life.

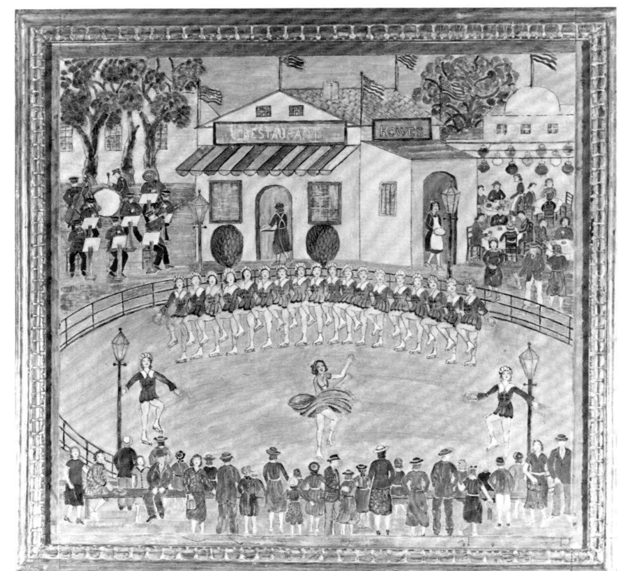

Skaters at the World's Fair, 1940
CR 2302
Color illustration, p. 48
Frame by the artist
Incised gesso, tempera, and gold leaf on panel (30¼ x 31½ in.; 76.8 x 80.0 cm)
Williams College Museum of Art, Gift of Mrs. Charles Prendergast in honor of Dr. John W. Chandler, President of Williams College 1973-1985
(83.20.3)

INSCRIPTIONS
l.l. incised: C. Prendergast 1940

PROVENANCE
The artist; to Mrs. Charles Prendergast, 1948; to present collection, 1983

BIBLIOGRAPHY
Taylor 1984 (B:3); Antiques Arts Weekly 1986 (p. 113)

EXHIBITIONS
1941 Kraushaar (#5); 1945a National Academy (#137); 1959 Davenport (#75); 1968 Rutgers University (#40, ill. p. 78); 1969 Hirschl & Adler (# 28); 1970b Society of Four Arts (#43); 1982 Parrish Museum (#82); 1983a Williams College (#34); 1984a Williams College (#11, ill.); 1986 Williams College (no #); 1988b Williams College (#84); 1989a Williams College (no #); 1989b Williams College (#31); 1990 Williams College (no #); 1992 Williams College (no #)

TECHNICAL NOTES
The composition has been painted in tempera over prepared gesso with some large areas of the rink and restaurant highly burnished. Gold leaf has been confined to the outer border, which simulates a gold mat around the picture. There are flaking paint losses exposing the white ground, possibly due to gouges or related to the artist's changes where he added gesso over dried gesso (located upper left, center musician-drummer). There are also hairline cracks in the side of the building below the sign ("Howe's") that may be due to pressure to the reverse of the Masonite panel.

The frame, by the artist, is carved and gilded. It has been burnished and some areas distressed to reveal the red bole.

THIS IS ONE OF TWO panels on the subject of the New York World's Fair that opened in Flushing Meadows Park in April of 1939. Prendergast visited the fair many times that summer and again in 1940 when it reopened for a second season. Prendergast's first panel, *World's Fair* (CR 2299, Whitney Museum of American Art), is signed and dated 1939. His second, *Skaters at the World's Fair,* is the larger of the two and is dated 1940, although sketches for it can be found in "Sketchbook C" (CR 2419, Museum of Fine Arts, Boston), which was evidently used by Prendergast to record the travels and sightseeing he and his wife engaged in with a young visitor from France in August of 1939.

Prendergast ignored the most visible symbol of the fair, the enormous sphere and spire (called the perisphere and trylon) located at the heart of the 1200-acre complex, but was captivated instead by an unusual display found in the park's amusement center, which was located across the World's Fair Boulevard (now the Long Island Expressway). This section of the fair was devoted to restaurants and entertainment, and one exhibit, called "Sun Valley," recreated a ski slope and ice skating rink in imitation of the famous Utah resort. The small rink was the site of ice skating revues that could be watched from semicircular bleachers erected on two sides. Prendergast's patient recording of the details of the restaurant setting, the musicians, and the skaters, as well as his monumentalizing of the entire scene, gives the viewer the impression that, in his ironic view, this was the major attraction of the fair.

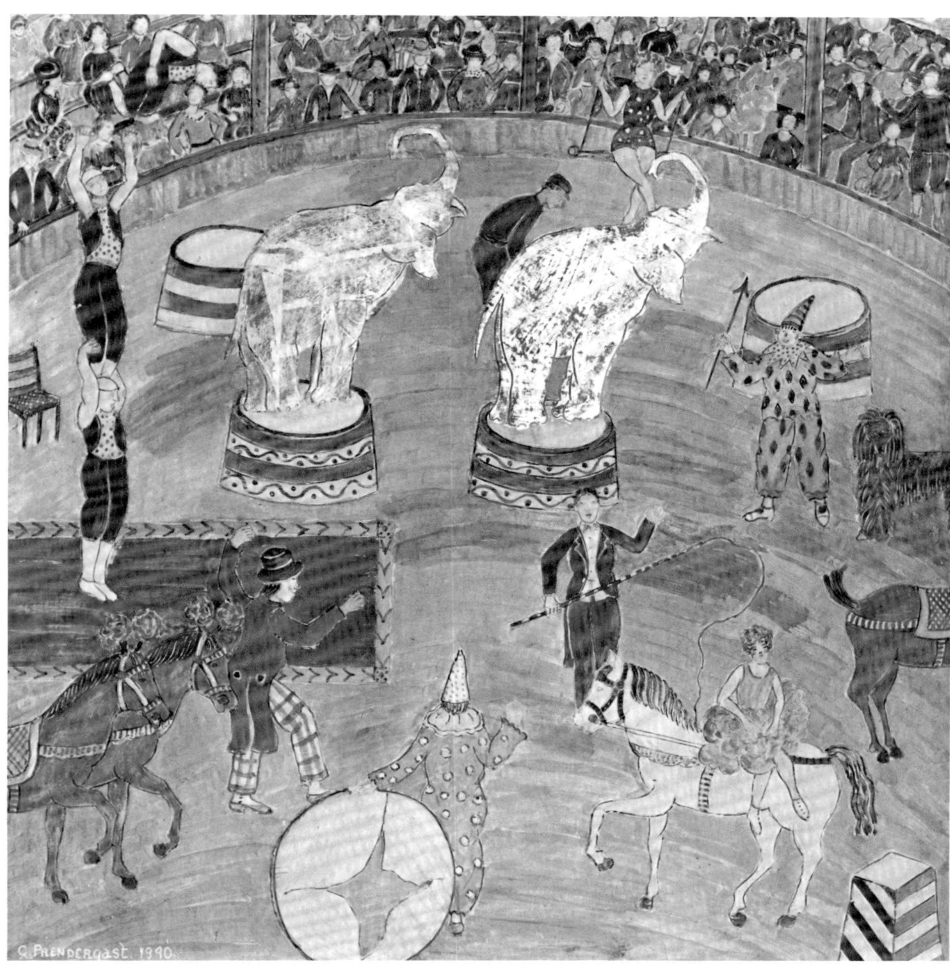

Circus, 1940
CR 2306
Color illustration, p. 31
Frame by the artist
Incised gesso, tempera, ink, and gold leaf on panel (24⅜ x 23¾ in.; 62.0 x 60.3 cm)
Williams College Museum of Art, Gift of Mrs. Charles Prendergast (86.18.34)

INSCRIPTIONS
l.l. incised: C Prendergast 1940

PROVENANCE
The artist; to Mrs. Charles Prendergast, 1948; to present collection, 1986

BIBLIOGRAPHY
Taylor 1984 (B:3); Antiques Arts Weekly 1986 (p. 113); New England Monthly 1986 (p. 96; ill.)

EXHIBITIONS
1941 Kraushaar (#13); 1954 Kraushaar (#24); 1968 Rutgers University (#41, ill. p. 79); 1969 Hirschl & Adler (#29); 1983a Williams College (#33); 1984a Williams College (#10); 1986 Williams College (no #); 1988b Williams College (#83); 1989a Williams College (no #); 1989b Williams College (#30); 1990 Williams College (no #); 1992 Williams College (no #)

TECHNICAL NOTES
The entire surface of the composition of *Circus* has a high sheen. Areas painted with tempera have been burnished as has the gold leaf that was applied to the elephants' and the horses' bridles and saddles. Gold paint has been applied to the costumes of two of the clowns and other decorative details. Contours throughout the composition have been crisply incised and often reinforced in ink.

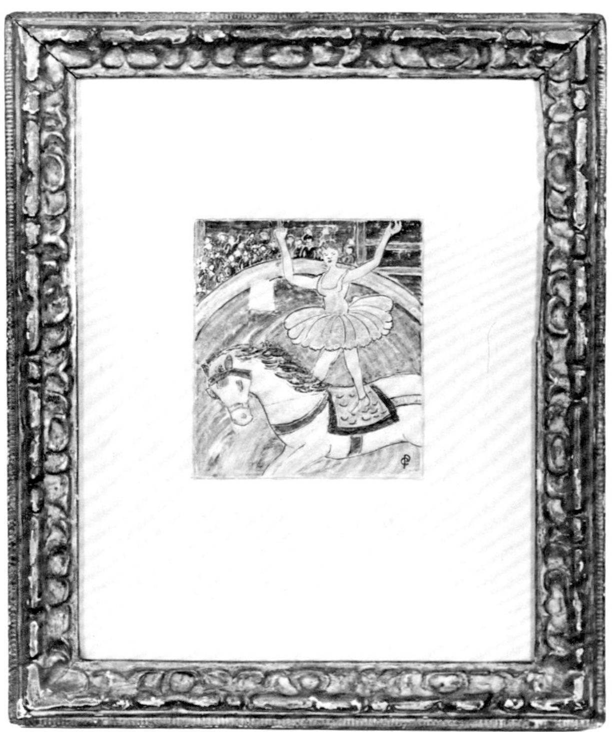

Circus Rider No. 9, ca. 1940
CR 2305
Frame by the artist
Incised gesso, tempera, ink, and crayon on panel (13½ x 10 in.; 34.3 x 25.4 cm)
Williams College Museum of Art, Gift of Mrs. Charles Prendergast (91.18.29)

INSCRIPTIONS
l.r.: CP [monogram]

PROVENANCE
The artist; to Mrs. Charles Prendergast, 1948; to present collection, 1991

EXHIBITIONS
?1941 Kraushaar (#41); 1968 Rutgers University (#43, ill. p. 8); 1969 Hirschl & Adler (#30); 1988b Williams College (#54); 1989a Williams College (no #); 1989b Williams College (#29); 1990 Williams College (no #); 1992 Williams College (no #)

TECHNICAL NOTES
Like *Circus*, this composition has a high sheen produced by burnishing the areas painted with tempera colors.

THE CIRCUS, a popular theme from the turn of the century when Maurice Prendergast made many monotypes of it, came back into vogue following an exhibition called "The Circus in Paint" at the Whitney Studio Galleries in 1929 (see above, p. 32). Prendergast, however, did not attempt the theme until 1940 when he executed four panels: *Circus*, *Circus Rider No. 9*, *Circus* (CR 2304, Collection of Libby Maynard), and *After the Show* (CR 2303, Collection of Mr. and Mrs. Charles H. Sawyer).

It is probable that these panels were inspired by a trip to the circus in the same way that Prendergast's panels of the Central Park Zoo and the New York World's Fair resulted from actual visits. From 1939 to 1941, the Prendergasts hosted the daughter of friends from France and may have taken her to see a circus performance in the Westport area or in New York. Prendergast's interpretation of the circus draws to some extent on his brother Maurice's monotypes, such as *Bareback Rider* (CR 1597, WCMA) and *Nouveau Cirque* (*Paris*) (CR 1594, Daniel J. Terra Collection, Terra Museum of American Art, Chicago), both of which were still in Charles's possession. But while the foreground elements of *Circus*—the clown, hoop, and bareback rider—may have come from Maurice Prendergast, the rest—elephants, acrobats, ringmaster, and audience—probably came from his own observations.

The title of *Circus Rider No. 9* probably comes from a misreading of an inscription on the verso of the work. It was originally exhibited as *Circus Rider*.

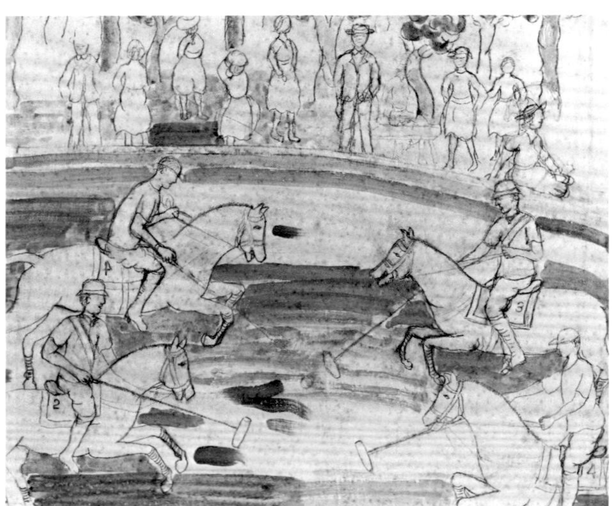

Sketch for Polo Players, No. 1, ca. 1941
CR 2368
Frame by the artist
Watercolor and pencil on incised paperboard (20 x 23¼ in.; 50.8 x 59.1 cm)
Williams College Museum of Art, Gift of Mrs. Charles Prendergast (86.18.17)

INSCRIPTIONS
Unsigned

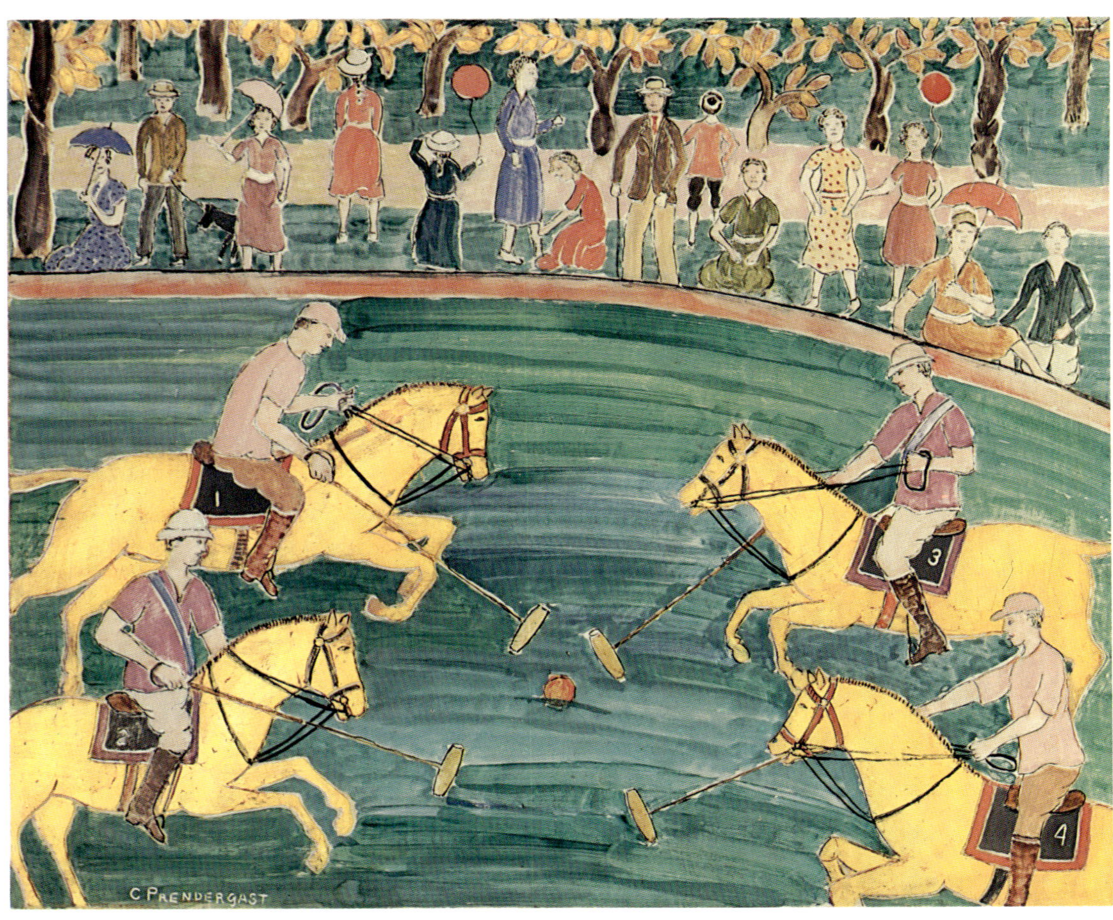

PROVENANCE

The artist; to Mrs. Charles Prendergast, 1948; to present collection, 1986

EXHIBITIONS

1968 Rutgers University (#71, ill. p. 107); 1969 Hirschl & Adler (#56); 1970b Society of Four Arts (#44, ill.); 1984a Williams College (#15); 1988a Williams College (no #); 1989a Williams College (no #); 1989b Williams College (#41); 1990 Williams College (no #)

TECHNICAL NOTES

Prendergast used a paperboard that has become discolored by mold damage or foxing.

Polo Players, No. 1, ca. 1941

CR 2307

Frame by the artist

Incised gesso, tempera, and gold leaf on panel (20 x 23¼ in.; 50.8 x 59.1 cm; sight)

Collection of Mrs. Charles Prendergast

INSCRIPTIONS

l.l. incised: C Prendergast

PROVENANCE

The artist; to present collection, 1948

Bibliography
Wattenmaker 1968 (p. 32); Taylor (B:3)

Exhibitions
1941 Kraushaar (#1); 1950 U Michigan (#32); 1959 Davenport (#74); 1968 Rutgers University (#46, ill. p. 33); 1969 Hirschl & Adler (#33); 1984 Williams College (#14)

Technical Notes
The brilliant gold leaf on the horses and autumn foliage in the background contrasts with the green of the polo field. As in *Circus*, the long strokes of the background color are curved to echo the border of the field and create a striped effect. The supporting panel is Masonite.

Like *Circus* (CR 2306, WCMA, p. 91), the *Polo Players, No. 1* composition was probably inspired by Prendergast's own experience. Another view of the polo field is offered by *Polo Players, No. 2* (CR 2310, Amon Carter Museum, Fort Worth, Texas). The subject continues Prendergast's interest in the rider theme, which dates back to his earliest works in the teens. As in those early works, Prendergast uses gold leaf to highlight the animals and give them an unexpected, almost supernatural, quality.

Sketch for Polo Players, No. 1 is unprecedented in Prendergast's work. There are no other examples of preliminary sketches that match the final composition so exactly. In this case it is possible that Prendergast was intending to finish this work, which is on gessoed paperboard, but then decided it needed a more substantial support and started over again on Masonite.

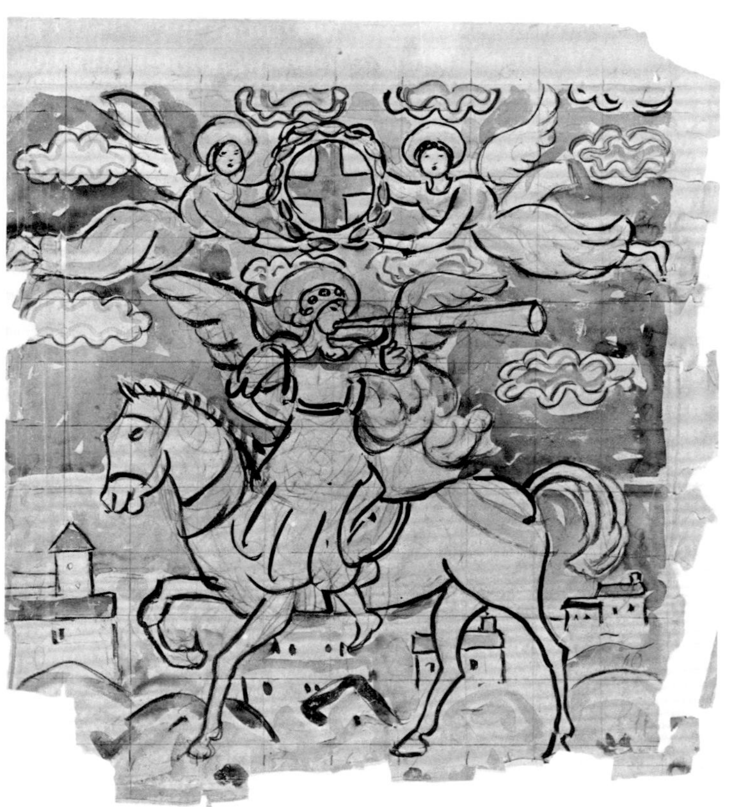

Study for Red Cross Poster, ca. 1942

CR 2370
Watercolor, pencil, and pastel on paper (22⅜ x 19¾ in.; 56.8 x 50.2 cm)
Williams College Museum of Art, Gift of Mrs. Charles Prendergast (84.8.1)

Inscriptions
Unsigned

Provenance
The artist; to Mrs. Charles Prendergast, 1948; to present collection, 1984

Bibliography
Durkin 1989 (back cover)

Exhibitions
1985 Williams College (no #); 1989b Williams College (#44)

Technical Notes
The figures are lightly sketched in graphite on paper with multiple re-workings especially in the areas of the central angel's chest, head, upper skirt, wings, and the left foreleg of the horse. A light orange-colored pastel covers the graphite under-drawing, and over the pastel are applications of watercolor. The study is squared in graphite and the reverse is covered with a black, dry medium.

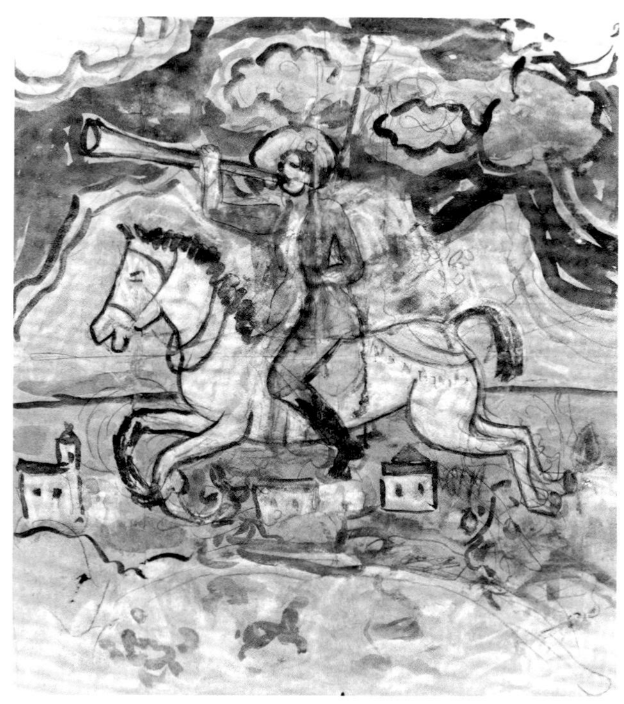

Study for Red Cross Poster, ca. 1942
CR 2369
Watercolor, pencil, and pastel on paper (24 x 21½ in.; 61.0 x 54.6 cm)
Williams College Museum of Art, Gift of Mrs. Charles Prendergast (84.8.2)

INSCRIPTIONS
Unsigned

PROVENANCE
The artist; to Mrs. Charles Prendergast, 1948; to present collection, 1984

BIBLIOGRAPHY
Durkin 1989 (back cover, ill. front cover)

EXHIBITIONS
1989b Williams College (#43); 1990 Williams College (no #)

TECHNICAL NOTES
There are multiple under-drawings in graphite, which bear no relation to the central composition, as well as numerous graphite re-workings of the central figures. A black wash outlines the equestrian figure and free applications of watercolor are applied to the garments of the figures and the background. The entire body of the horse is coated with a thin, white substance as are the walls of houses and areas of the ground. The verso of the paper is covered with a soft, black, dry medium that may have been used to transfer the finished work to another surface by tracing over the figures on the front.

BOTH STUDIES DEPICT an equestrian figure, with a long trumpet, centrally placed on the page. Behind this figure are houses, the sea, and the sky. Only *Study for Red Cross Poster* (CR 2370) has a red cross, linking the picture to its title. The red cross is inscribed within a circle and held aloft by two winged angels.[1] The composition of *Study for Red Cross Poster* (CR 2370) most closely echoes the tempera on gessoed panel painting by Charles Prendergast called *The Red Cross Poster* (see illustration; CR 2308, William Benton Museum of Art). Graphite, pastel, and watercolor are applied to paper in both of the studies, but with very different effects. The *Study for Red Cross Poster* (CR 2370) has an economy of line. There is less reworking of the under-drawing. The outlines of the figures are deliberately painted with a continuous brush stroke, seldom overlapping. When pastel is used, it is applied carefully, as with the orange outline of the horse. The *Study for Red Cross Poster* (CR 2369) is executed more freely. The graphite under-drawings are more numerous, the pastel colors are applied over each other, and the brush strokes of the watercolors vary in width and intensity of color. Because of the greater freedom in handling, there is some suspicion that this drawing may have actually been done by Maurice Prendergast thirty years earlier. But a final determination is difficult to make simply on stylistic grounds, and until conclusive evidence is found it will be treated as a

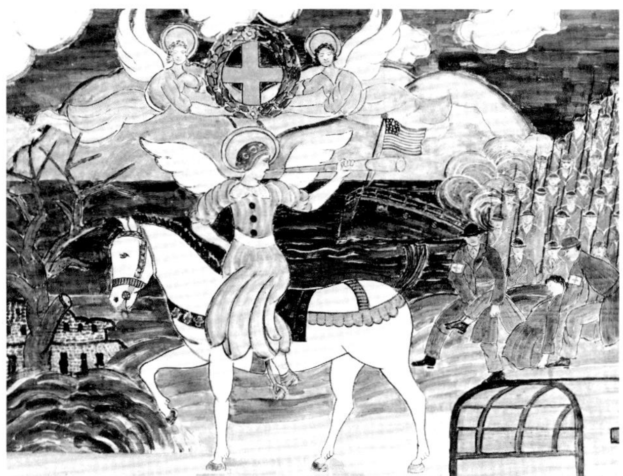

Charles Prendergast, *The Red Cross Poster*, 1942, (23 x 28¾ in.) tempera on gessoed panel, The William Benton Museum of Art, The University of Connecticut, Gift of Mrs. Eugénie Prendergast (74.8.1)

 preliminary study by Charles Prendergast for *The Red Cross Poster.*

The decision to use a winged equestrian figure as the central image for the poster may derive from a number of sources. The allegory of the rider is a major motif in the Prendergast brothers' oeuvre. The frequency of equestrian figures in both Charles's and Maurice's work probably has roots in the Arts and Crafts Movement. The symbol of St. George on a horse, slaying the dragon, was often used as a metaphor in Victorian times for a long-vanished, golden age of chivalry.[2] The dragon would have personified the industrialization of the modern world, which was the cause of terrible wars. Although there are no documents that illuminate Charles's spiritual inclinations, the winged, trumpet-blowing equestrian figure may have been inspired by biblical references to the use of trumpets in war.

The equestrian figure is clearly female in the final version of Charles's poster. Two women who played great roles on the battlefield probably inspired Prendergast to paint a female equestrian figure: Florence Nightingale (1820-1910) and Clara Barton (1821-1912). Of the two brave nurses, Clara Barton-—an American born in Oxford, Massachusetts—is credited with founding the American Red Cross. Her devotion to the wounded in the American Civil War earned her the title "Angel of the Battlefield."[3] Charles has possibly depicted the central equestrian figure as a tribute to Barton.

Charles Prendergast apparently designed *The Red Cross Poster* for a national contest sponsored by the American Red Cross in 1942. The American Red Cross fell under the Section of Fine Arts, a subgroup of the Public Buildings Administration (PBA); the PBA in turn, was part of the government umbrella organization called the Federal Works Agency (FWA) located in Washington, D.C. It was the FWA that provided up to three thousand dollars to purchase visual works depicting the Red Cross activities. The deadline for submission of art work was March 18, 1942. While the choice of subject matter was not specified, the designs were supposed to reflect "ordinary people carrying out their everyday services" for the Red Cross.[4] There were 2,038 entries received from 1,264 artists, of which 70 were purchased by a jury.[5] The chosen works were on view May 2-30, 1942, at the National Gallery of Art in Washington, D.C. in the exhibition "Paintings, Posters, Watercolors and Prints Showing the Activities of the American Red Cross." Charles Prendergast's name was not among the list of winners, but he may have been one of the entrants.

It is instructive to compare Prendergast's poster with those of the Work Projects Administration (WPA). Most of the WPA posters measured 22 x 14 inches, featured simple verbal messages with flat, silk-screen-printed colors, and displayed a balanced, centered design.[6] Such posters are products of mass production whereas Prendergast's *The Red Cross Poster* is not a poster at all, but a gessoed panel.

Claudia Hill

1. The image of two flying, winged angels bearing a medallion inscribed with a cross is repeatedly seen in Byzantine mosaics from San Vitale. Prendergast owned a book with illustrations of this image from San Vitale. See Ricci 1907, pp. 28, ill. 12; 92, ill. 91; 96, ill. 95; 97, ill. 98.
2. Durkin 1989.
3. Prendergast may have read the article "Angel of the Battlefield" by Eleanor C. Fishburn and Mildred Sandison Fenner (Fishburn 1942, pp. 85-86). In the Archives of the National Gallery of Art is an "April 12, 1942, Release from the Federal Works Agency, Public Buildings Administration, Section of Fine Arts" describing a Red Cross competition for visual works that included "historical pictures of Clara Barton, Founder of the American Red Cross."
4. Watson 1942, p. 76.
5. Art Digest 1942, p. 9.
6. For additional reading on the WPA poster movement and criteria for WPA posters see Denoon 1987.

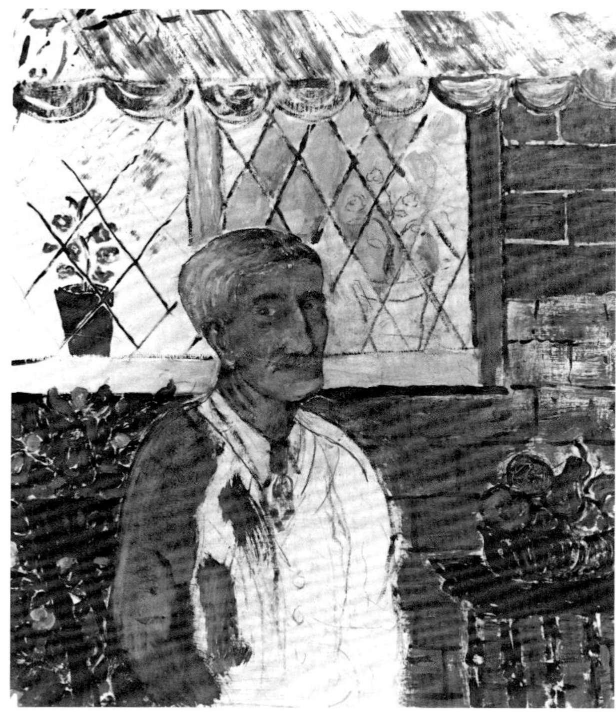

Study for Self-Portrait, ca. 1942
CR 2371
Pencil, black chalk, and enamel paint on gessoed paper (30¼ x 24¾ in.; 76.8 x 62.9 cm)
Williams College Museum of Art, Gift of Mrs. Charles Prendergast, 1984 (84.8.3)

INSCRIPTIONS
Unsigned

PROVENANCE
The artist; to Mrs. Charles Prendergast, 1948; to present collection, 1984

EXHIBITIONS
1984b Williams College (#23); 1988a Williams College (no #); 1989a Williams College (no #); 1990 Williams College (no #); 1992 Williams College (no #)

TECHNICAL NOTES
Under-drawings, probably of black chalk and graphite, are visible beneath layers of an enamel paint on gessoed paper. Small, hesitating brush strokes of pale pink, orange, yellow, and white paint appear to cover the most completed parts of the work—the face and neck of the figure. The background, sometimes colored with thick coats of paint that is cracking and flaking in some areas, appears to have been painted from the bottom upward. The wide, streaky applications of muddled light green, brown, and pink paint on the unfinished awning give the feeling of indecision on the part of the artist.

IT WAS MANDATORY that Charles Prendergast present a portrait of himself to the National Academy of Design (NAD) following his election to Associate status (ANA) on March 17, 1939.[1] The portrait did not have to be painted by the artist, but customarily they were. There was a loosely binding agreement with the NAD that the portrait be submitted one year from the date of election or the election would be void. However, the time limit for submission of Prendergast's portrait was evidently ignored, since Charles Prendergast finished his self-portrait four years after his election. It was "presented to the NAD committee and he was declared a duly qualified Associate of the National Academy of Design-painter class."[2]

The *Study for Self-Portrait* was a difficult undertaking for a number of reasons. To the best of our knowledge, Prendergast had never before painted a portrait from life.[3] Health problems may also have plagued him, preventing him from completing the self-portrait in a timely fashion. In addition, he was inexperienced with using an oil-based medium for the *Study for Self-Portrait* and eventually resorted to tempera in his finished *Self-Portrait* (see fig. 26, p. 32; CR 2309, National Academy of Design).

Prendergast depicts himself as an elderly man, seated and turned in a three-quarter pose. His face has a blank, mask-like expression. Portraits and sketches of Charles by others display more animation than he does in his self-portrait.[4] He may have relied on the many photographs taken of him standing in front of his house in Westport, Connecticut. Prendergast was frequently photographed on the lawn near the striped awning that shades the diamond leaded windows of his house. The folk or naive element of the self-portrait is in keeping with the style that he employed in the 1930s and 1940s.

Claudia Hill

1. The NAD painters who supported Prendergast's election to ANA status were all Associates, and most achieved full membership (NA) by the time Prendergast received his ANA. They were Gifford Beal, George Elmer Browne, Arthur Covey, Sidney Dickinson, Walter Farndon, Salvatore Lascari, and Jonas Lie.

2. Correspondence from George Lober of the NAD to Prendergast dated May 4, 1943 confirming the committee's acceptance of the self-portrait on Tuesday, April 20, 1943, is found in the Documents and Letters Pertaining to Charles Prendergast, Prendergast Archive and Study Center, WCMA. Prendergast later acknowledged receiving the NAD bibliography card, biographical sheet, Associate's ribbon, qualifying

letter, and possibly the certificate by a postcard postmarked May 18, 1945. However, in the Minutes for the NAD meeting on April 20th, 1943, Prendergast is nominated to ANA status in the "Architect" class!

3. An exception might be Charles Prendergast's *Welcome to America* (CR 2367, Private Collection). The title of the work and the date, July 1939, is written below three figures. It is likely that the figure of a man is a self-portrait, the woman holding a bouquet of flowers is Prendergast's wife, Eugénie, and the second woman with the suitcase is Antoinette Maynard. Antoinette traveled from France to visit the Prendergasts, and this work probably heralded her arrival to the United States.

4. Prendergast's friend, Virginia Clark, painted a full-length portrait of him in 1923 (see fig. 43, p. 49). This painting is presently in the Museum of Fine Arts, Boston (1974.605), a gift of Mrs. Charles Prendergast to the Museum in 1974. In addition, there are three published sketches of Prendergast: a sketch of Prendergast appears on the first page of each part of Hamilton Basso's two-part article on Charles Prendergast's life (see Basso 1946a, p. 24, and Basso 1946b, p. 28), and a third sketch (which pre-dates the other two by more than twenty years, but the depiction of Prendergast does not deviate from them) is on the first page of Pach 1923, p. 10.

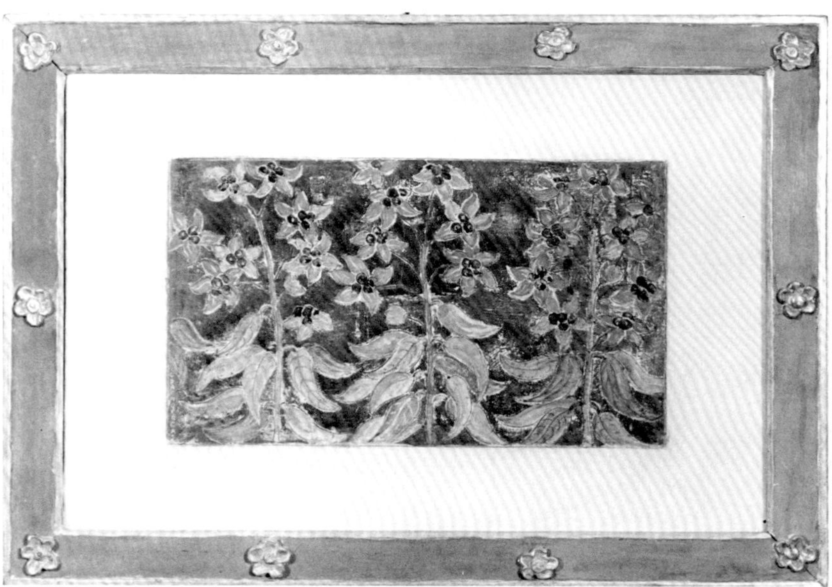

Glory Bower, ca. 1946-47
CR 2314
Frame by the artist
Incised gesso and tempera on panel (15 x 21 in.; 38.1 x 53.3 cm)
Collection of Mrs. Charles Prendergast

INSCRIPTIONS
l.l.: C. Prendergast

PROVENANCE
The artist; to present collection, 1948

BIBLIOGRAPHY
Gengarelly 1989 (p.41; ill.)

EXHIBITIONS
1947 Kraushaar (#20); 1968 Rutgers University (#50, ill. p. 88); 1969 Hirschl & Adler (#37); 1984a Williams College (#17); 1988b Williams College (#86)

TECHNICAL NOTES
The three stems of the bell-like flower, "Glory Bower," have been painted on an incised gesso panel of Masonite.

CHARLES PRENDERGAST did three large-scale horizontal panels of flowers. Two titled *Zinnias* (CR 2267, Private Collection; CR 2270, Private Collection) have been dated to the 1930s in conjunction with a number of flower still lifes Prendergast executed and exhibited at that time. *Glory Bower* was not exhibited until 1947, thus suggesting that it belongs to the mid-1940s.

Flowers were always a favorite motif of Prendergast, whether they were featured in the carving of a decorative object like a frame, were used alone as a still life, or formed part of a larger composition. He not only saw them as symbols of springtime, fruitfulness, and rebirth, but he personally loved gardening and filled the grounds around his house in Westport with flowers.

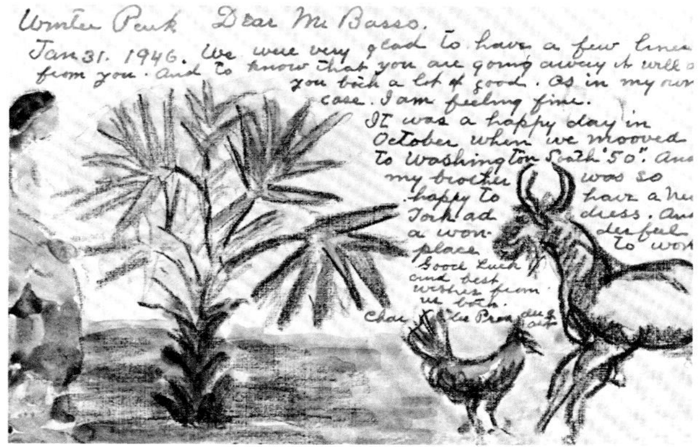
Winter Park Dear Mr Basso.
Jan 31. 1946. We were very glad to have a few lines
from you. And to know that you are going away it will do
you back a lot of good. As in my own
case. I am feeling fine.
It was a happy day in
October when we mooved
to Washington South "50". And
my brother was so
happy to have a New
York ad dress. And
a won derful
place to work
Good Luck
and best
wishes from
us both.
Charlie Prenderg ast

Illustrated letter to Hamilton Basso, January 31, 1946
CR 2384
Watercolor on paper (5¼ x 7¾ in.; 13.3 x 19.7 cm)
Williams College Museum of Art, Gift of Etolia S. Basso (83.28)

Inscriptions
Winter Park Dear Mr. Basso./ Jan 31. 1946. We were very glad to have a few lines/ from you. And to know that you are going away it will do/ you back a lot of good. As in my own/ case. I am feeling fine./ It was a happy day in October when we mooved [sic] to Washington South "50". And/ my brother was so happy to have a New York address. And/ a wonderful/ place to work/ Good luck/ And best/ wishes from us both./ Charlie Prenderg/ast

Provenance
The artist; to Mr. and Mrs. Hamilton Basso, 1946; to present collection, 1983

Exhibitions
1988a Williams College (no #); 1990 Williams College (no #)

Technical Notes
The ink-pen writing was applied after the watercolor sketch as indicated in the area to the right of the tree as well as around the rooster's head where the writing partially covers the watercolor.

Charles Prendergast wrote the letter to Hamilton Basso while on a rest cure in Winter Park, Florida, in the winter of 1946. At this time, Hamilton Basso, a writer from *The New Yorker*, was preparing a two-part biographical sketch of Prendergast for the magazine entitled "Profiles: A Glimpse of Heaven I and II" for the July 27 and August 3 issues. Prendergast's letter was probably one of a number of correspondences between the two men in addition to personal interviews.

The Bassos and the Prendergasts met in Weston, Connecticut, sometime between 1943, when the Bassos moved there, and 1946 at the home of a mutual friend, Van Wyck Brooks. According to Mrs. Basso, her husband was charmed by Charles Prendergast, and he liked the work of the Prendergast brothers. Charles was apparently very pleased with Basso's *New Yorker* piece and, in appreciation, he gave Hamilton Basso Maurice Prendergast's *Donkey Rider* (CR 1376, Private Collection).[1]

Basso's articles provide us with perhaps the most comprehensive account of Charles Prendergast's life and career as well as information about his brother Maurice. For example, the letter recalls Charles's and Maurice's move from Boston to their New York apartment at 50 Washington Square in 1914. Prendergast writes, "And my brother was so happy to have a New York address," which correlates to Basso's second article in which he described the moving day in October: "'Thank God!' said Maurice when the lease was signed. 'At last we have a New York address!' They shook hands on it."[2]

In Charles Prendergast's illustrated letter to Hamilton Basso, the artist integrated the text into the pictorial elements. He did so by filling the sky of the watercolor scene in with writing. Apparently Prendergast illustrated the Florida picture before he wrote the letter, which is suggested in two ways. To begin with, the size of the script decreases significantly from the top of the page to the bottom, indicating that Prendergast conformed his writing to the allotted space. Secondly, due to this limitation, Prendergast's signature overlaps the painted ground slightly around the rooster's tail and head.

Despite the visual interrelation between text and illustration in Prendergast's letter to Basso, the scene does not depict the contents of the letter. However, it would seem that the pictorial elements of the letter were not entirely coincidental given Basso's and Prendergast's shared interest in southern subjects.

The figures illustrated in the letter—a black woman, a rooster, and a goat—were a result of Prendergast's sojourn in Florida where he completed eighteen watercolor sketches. His works from this series depict everyday rural, southern black life. Basso, a native of New Orleans, wrote eleven novels on the South. In his first article on Prendergast, Basso quotes the artist's reason for portraying people of African descent in all but one of his Florida watercolors: "They have more character from an artist's point of view than a white man. The men dress in such a manly way - in real, pure colors. And what material for a sculptor, especially their faces, men and women both! The colors of the women's clothes are wonderful. I got all excited over their Negroes. I even got excited by their roosters."[3] As Basso points out, "the exception was a bright, splashy, impression of two roosters set to gaff each other."[4] Prendergast includes such a rooster in his letter to Basso.

Illustrated letters and greeting cards were not uncommon among artists in Charles Prendergast's circle. Contemporaries such as Walt Kuhn often sent illustrated greetings, for example, the 1937 Christmas card he made with his daughter Brenda. (Collection of National Museum of American Art, Smithsonian Institution, 1980.124.32) Many such correspondences were sent by Prendergast to his friends, as in his playfully illustrated New Year's message to Brenda Kuhn in 1921 (CR 2320, Collection of Barbara and Lawrence B. Salander).

Molly Donovan

1. From a conversation with Etolia S. Basso, December 2, 1992.
2. Basso 1946b, p. 34.
3. Basso 1946a, p. 28.
4. Ibid.

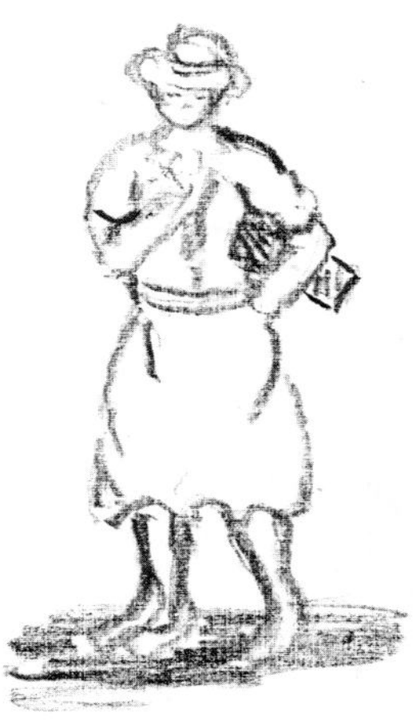

Sketchbook, ca. 1946
CR 2420
25 pencil, crayon, and watercolor drawings (8 x 5 in.; 20.3 x 12.7 cm)
Williams College Museum of Art, Gift of Mrs. Charles Prendergast (85.23.6)

PROVENANCE
The artist; to Mrs. Charles Prendergast, 1948; to present collection, 1985

BIBLIOGRAPHY
AAA Roll #3583, begin frame 0545

EXHIBITIONS
1988a Williams College (no #); 1989a Williams College (no #); 1990 Williams College (no #)

TECHNICAL NOTES
The cover of this small stationery pad is printed with the words "LUXOR Linen Finish. Made in U.S.A. M-1020 1/2." There are twenty-two pages remaining in the pad (two of these are loose), and a backing cardboard.

THIS SKETCHBOOK DATES from the Prendergasts' trip to Florida in 1946. It has two loose pages with detailed, finished scenes. One is in colored crayon, of orange pickers in an orchard with baskets; the other, in pencil, depicts what could be an agricultural packing plant.[1]

The other sketches in this book, slightly over twenty, are primarily in black crayon, with some in colored crayon, some in watercolor, and a few in pencil. They are firmly drawn, and are primarily of figures in simple poses, in groups and singly. The usual affection for animals is evidenced by birds and dogs, and a rooster. The rooster was a favorite motif of Prendergast in the Florida works; it appears often with wings flapping, adding liveliness and humor to the scenes.

Several drawings, now dispersed, likely come from this sketchbook. They are *Street Scene, Florida* (CR 2372, Mattatuck Museum), *Orange Pickers, Florida* (CR 2376, Private Collection), *Illustrated letter to Hamilton Basso* (CR 2384, WCMA p. 99), and *Jubilant Figure* (CR 2389, Private Collection). *Series of Negroes, Florida* (CR 2387, Collection of Howard Kopet), with its cutout figures, was probably constructed from pages of this book. The similar use of crayon and watercolor, the small size of the sheets, and the distinctive weave of the paper revealed by the crayon strokes all point to this sketchbook as the original source.

Marion M. Goethals

1. These two scenes were microfilmed (Archives of American Art) with WCMA 85.23.7, which begins at frame 0567 of roll #3583.

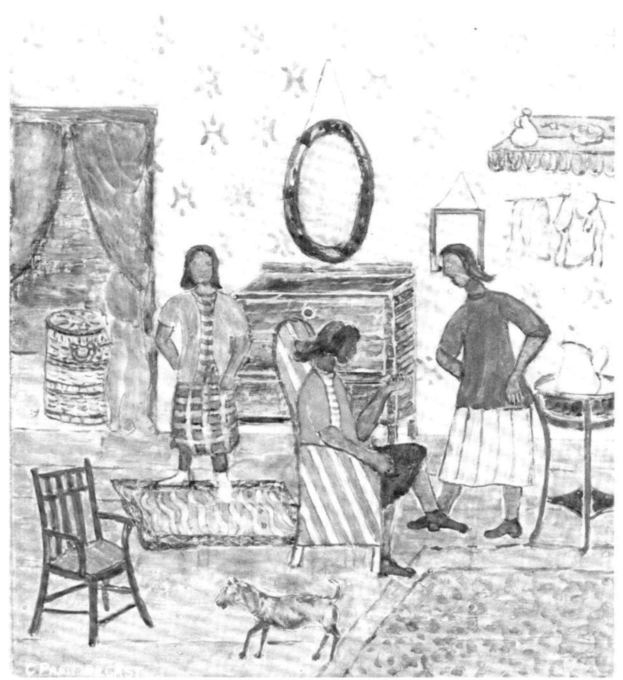

Interior, Florida, ca. 1946-47
CR 2311

Frame by the artist
Incised gesso and tempera on panel (21 x 17 in.; 53.3 x 43.2 cm)
Williams College Museum of Art, Gift of Mrs. Charles Prendergast (86.18.14)

INSCRIPTIONS
l.l.: C. Prendergast

PROVENANCE
The artist; to Mrs. Charles Prendergast, 1948; to present collection, 1986

EXHIBITIONS
1947 Kraushaar (#15); 1954 Kraushaar (#32); 1968 Rutgers University (#49, ill. p. 87); 1969 Hirschl & Adler (#36); 1970b Society of Four Arts (#37); 1983a Williams College (#36); 1984a Williams College (#16, ill.); 1986 Williams College (no #); 1988a Williams College (no #); 1989a Williams College (no #); 1990 Williams College (no #)

TECHNICAL NOTES
This work shows evidence of several changes Prendergast made in the composition. Ultraviolet light reveals that the desk in the background was originally a high chest of drawers covering the area where the mirror now hangs. Changes were also made in the furnishings in the foreground area. The supporting panel is Masonite.

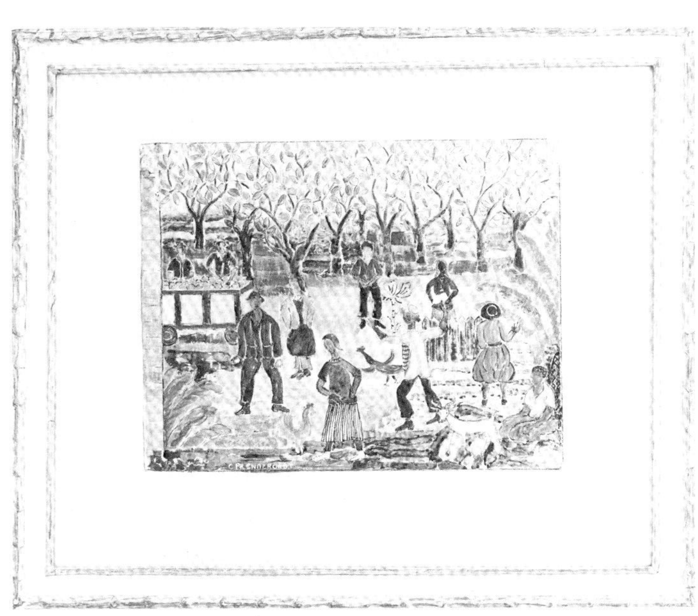

Florida Grove, ca. 1946-47
CR 2315
Color illustration, p. 33
Frame by the artist
Incised gesso and tempera on panel (11 x 13¾ in.; 27.9 x 34.9 cm)
Collection of Mrs. Charles Prendergast

INSCRIPTIONS
l.l.: C. Prendergast

PROVENANCE
The artist; to present collection, 1948

BIBLIOGRAPHY
Goldin 1976b (p. 63; ill.)

EXHIBITIONS
1947 Kraushaar (#17); 1968 Rutgers University (#48, ill. p. 86); 1969 Hirschl & Adler (#35); 1988b Williams College (#85)

TECHNICAL NOTES
The edge of a gray wall visible along the left inch of the

composition appears to be an afterthought because of the awkward transition along the ground line and the addition of oranges and leaves at the top. Prendergast may have extended the composition to achieve a more balanced effect. He used a Masonite panel as a support.

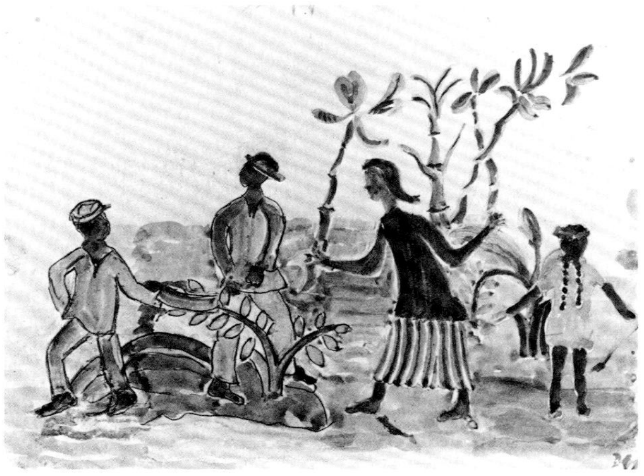

Florida, ca. 1946-47
CR 2379
Watercolor on paper (8⅜ x 11 in.; 21.3 x 27.9 cm)
Collection of Mrs. Charles Prendergast

INSCRIPTIONS
Unsigned

PROVENANCE
The artist; to present collection, 1948

EXHIBITIONS
1969 Hirschl & Adler (#57)

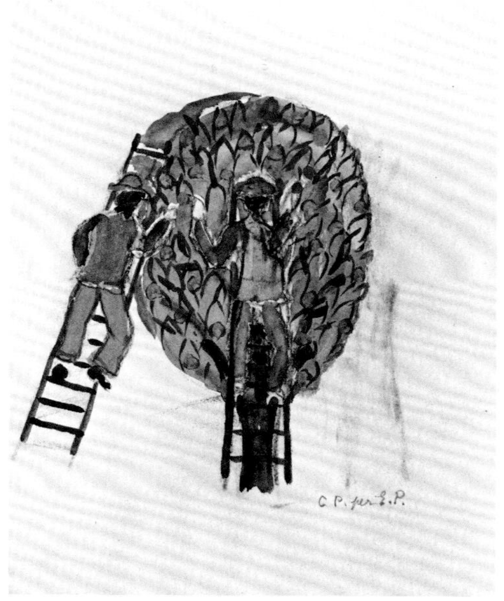

Two Orange Pickers, ca. 1946-47
CR 2382
Watercolor and charcoal on paper (11¾ x 9 in.; 29.8 x 22.9 cm)
Williams College Museum of Art, Gift of Mrs. Charles Prendergast (87.5.6)

INSCRIPTIONS
l.r. (in Eugénie Prendergast's hand): CP. per E.P.

PROVENANCE
The artist; to Mrs. Charles Prendergast, 1948; to present collection, 1987

DURING PRENDERGAST'S STAY in Florida in the winter of 1946, he was inspired to make a series of watercolor sketches of the black community in and around Winter Park. Nineteen sketches and one sketchbook (CR 2420, WCMA, p. 100) from this series are known today. *Florida* and *Two Orange Pickers* represent the kinds of subjects Prendergast was interested in: residential life in the black ghettos and the laborers in the orange groves. The sketches suggest that Prendergast worked either at the site (being driven around in a car) or immediately upon returning to his temporary studio.

In Florida and after his return to Westport, Prendergast worked on four panels based on these sketches: *Interior, Florida*, *Orange Grove* (CR 2312, whereabouts unknown), *Orange Pickers, Florida* (CR 2313, North Carolina Museum of Art), and *Florida Grove*.

Interior, Florida is Prendergast's only known interior genre scene. A watercolor sketch, *#27 Florida Series* (CR 2381, Chestnut Hill College) provided the poses for two of the figures, indicating that Prendergast was working from firsthand experience of this house. The addition of the figure on the right (which was adapted from other outdoor sketches) and the many changes in the furnishings of the house (barely visible as pentimenti) suggest, however, that Prendergast developed the finished composition from his imagination.

Prendergast composed the outdoor subjects so that they cast the Florida scenes in familiar guise. Decorative trees form a stylized background, single figures are scattered throughout the tilted foreground space, and birds, goats, and containers of oranges give these panels his longstanding favorite theme of fruitfulness. According to Mrs. Charles Prendergast, this was the last panel completed by the artist.

APPENDIX A

Contents of the Studio:
Unfinished Works and Tools

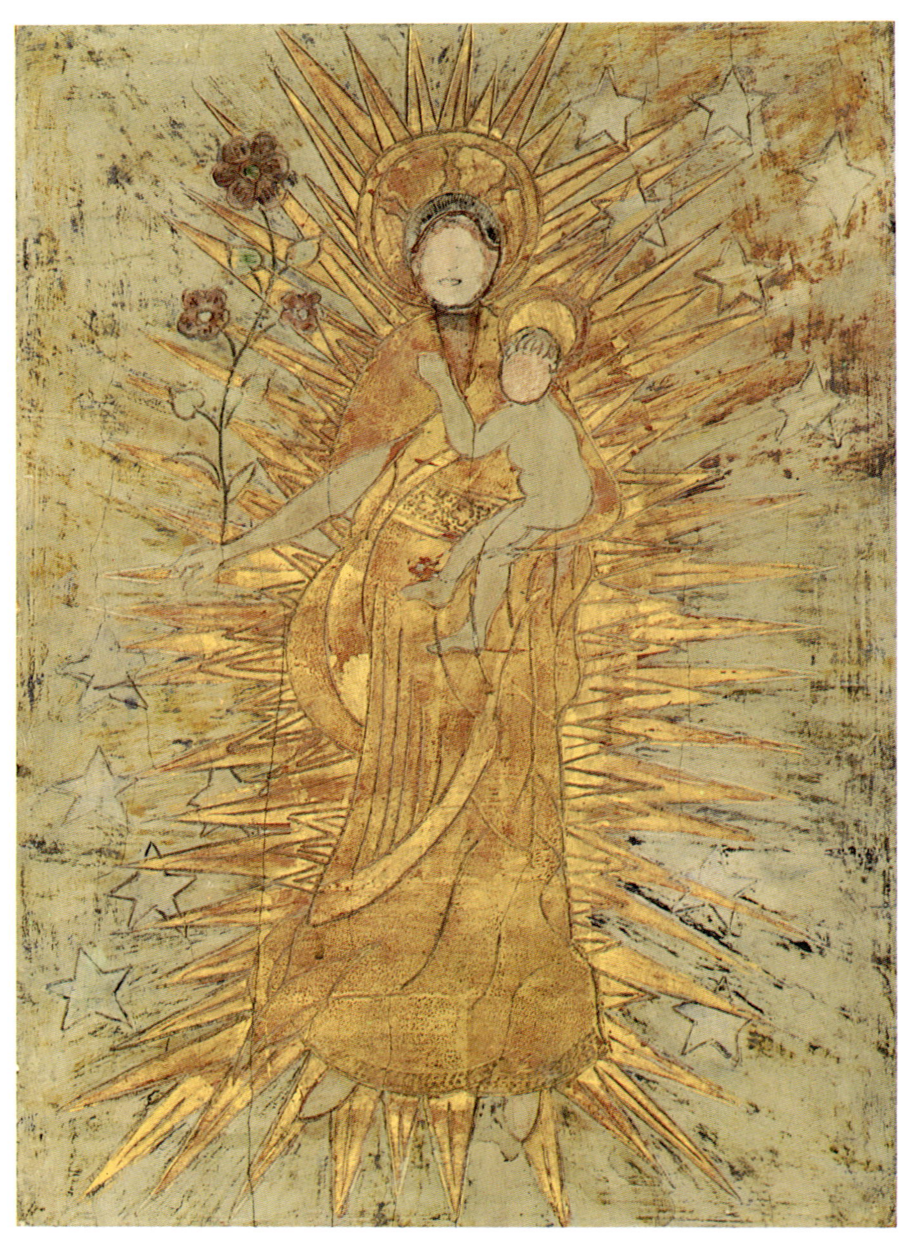

Madonna and Child, ca. 1915-20
CR 2214
Incised gesso, tempera and gold leaf on panel (17½ x 12½ in.; 44.5 x 31.8 cm)
Williams College Museum of Art, Gift of Mrs. Charles Prendergast (91.18.28)

Inscriptions
Unsigned

Provenance
The artist; to Mrs. Charles Prendergast, 1948; to present collection, 1991

Bibliography
Wattenmaker 1968 (pp. 26, 30); Komanecky 1984 (p. 193)

Exhibitions
1968 Rutgers University (#2, ill. p. 40); 1970b Society of Four Arts (#39); 1989b Williams College (#26); 1990 Williams College (no #)

Technical Notes
The plywood support has been coated with gesso on both sides. Both the paint and gold leaf appear to have been abraded by the artist to the point of removing most of the color and exposing the red bole below the gold leaf. In spite of the high degree of completion, the fact that color has been applied to the faces but not the other flesh areas indicates that this is an unfinished panel.

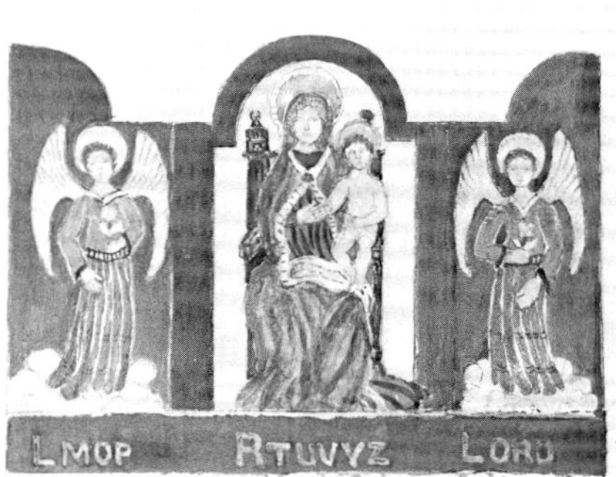

Enthroned Madonna and Child with Angels, ca. 1915-20
CR 2316
Tempera and pencil on gessoed matboard (12¼ x 12½ in.; 31.1 x 31.8 cm)
Williams College Museum of Art, Gift of Mrs. Charles Prendergast (87.5.12)

Inscriptions
LMOP RTUVYZ LORD

Provenance
The artist; to Mrs. Charles Prendergast, 1948; to present collection, 1987

Exhibitions
1989a Williams College (no #)

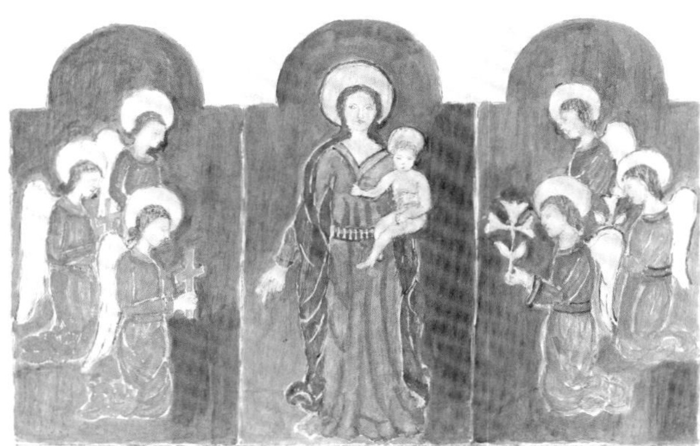

Madonna and Child with Angels, ca. 1915-20
CR 2317
Tempera and pencil on gessoed matboard (12 x 13⅝ in.; 30.5 x 34.6 cm)
Williams College Museum of Art, Gift of Mrs. Charles Prendergast (87.5.13)

Inscriptions
Unsigned

Provenance
The artist; to Mrs. Charles Prendergast, 1948; to present collection, 1987

Exhibitions
1989a Williams College (no #)

This group of three Madonnas represents Prendergast's most faithful rendition of traditional Christian imagery. It falls into a larger group of works on Christian subjects including *Calling of Saints Peter and Andrew* (CR 2217, Collection of Evelyn R. Tecosky), the gilded figurines *Eve* (CR 2390, WCMA, p. 60) and *Angel* (CR 2392, WCMA, p. 61), the *Decorated Mirror with Two Figures* (CR 2231, WCMA, p. 66), and the *Chest* (CR 2398, Collection of Mrs. Charles Prendergast, p. 59) that Prendergast adopted with relatively few alterations. Prendergast's Irish Catholic background may have given him a special appreciation of these images, but it would be going too far to say that he used them specifically to convey Catholic dogma. Rather, they can be more reasonably attributed to Prendergast's love of all art of the past and his attempt to recreate a mixture of long-forgotten cultures and

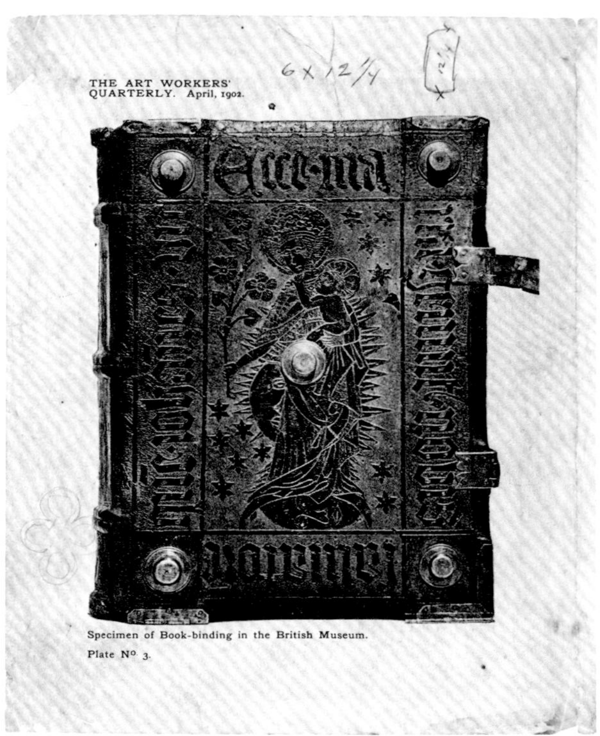
THE ART WORKERS' QUARTERLY. April, 1902.

Specimen of Book-binding in the British Museum.

Plate No 3.

Specimen of book-binding in the British Museum, illustrated (plate no. 3) in *The Art Workers' Quarterly*, April 1902, Williams College Museum of Art, Prendergast Archive and Study Center

ideas through his own evocative and anachronistic objects.

This is especially evident in the gilded panel of the standing Madonna (CR 2214). This treatment of the Madonna holding a nude child and posed against a star-studded sky is an adaptation of the Apocalyptic Woman "clothed in the sun" described in Revelations 12:1: "And a great portent appeared in heaven, a woman clothed with the sun, with the moon under her feet, and on her head a crown of twelve stars." Prendergast copied the image almost exactly from an illustration in *The Art Workers' Quarterly* (April 1902) captioned "Specimen of Book-binding in the British Museum"[1] (see illustration). Prendergast altered the traditional iconography by changing the curved disc of the sun, seen behind the Madonna's right leg in *The Art Workers' Quarterly*, into a curved fold of drapery and by eliminating the half moon traditionally found under her feet. Prendergast used the red flower that the Madonna holds often in his work, indicating that it had for him a general significance as an offering of love and a symbol of rebirth (see Prendergast's *Eve*).

1. Prendergast was also familiar with other versions of this Madonna type. A very dramatic tapestry showing the Madonna in life size also haloed by flames is illustrated as plate 381, "Interior of the Volkskunst Museum at Kieff," in Holme 1912. A similar image is found in a book well known to the Prendergasts: Toesca 1912, p. 564, fig. 467, Jacopino Cietario, *Madonna*. Maurice Prendergast noted the title of the book and made a series of sketches from plates (although not fig. 467) sometime after his return from Italy in 1912 ("Sketchbook #46," CR 1502, Museum of Fine Arts, Boston).

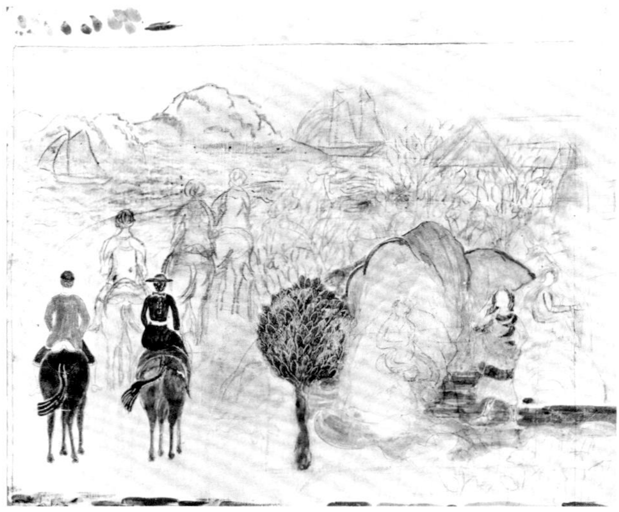

Untitled, unfinished panel, ca. 1933-36

CR 2280

Tempera, gold leaf and pencil on gessoed panel (19⅞ x 24 in.; 50.5 x 61.0 cm)

Williams College Museum of Art, Gift of Mrs. Charles Prendergast (84.8.4)

INSCRIPTIONS

Unsigned

PROVENANCE

The artist; to Mrs. Charles Prendergast, 1948; to present collection, 1984

EXHIBITIONS

1989a Williams College (no #)

TECHNICAL NOTES

The Masonite panel has been coated with a thick layer of gesso on both sides. The design has been transferred onto the gesso surface by tracing the lines of a drawing, the back of which has been covered with charcoal or graphite. Gold leaf has been applied to the tree and tempera has been applied to a few figures in the foreground. A border has been drawn around the composition suggesting that Prendergast might have intended to cut it down to a small size at a later date. Test strokes of color can be found outside the limits of the border and on the back.

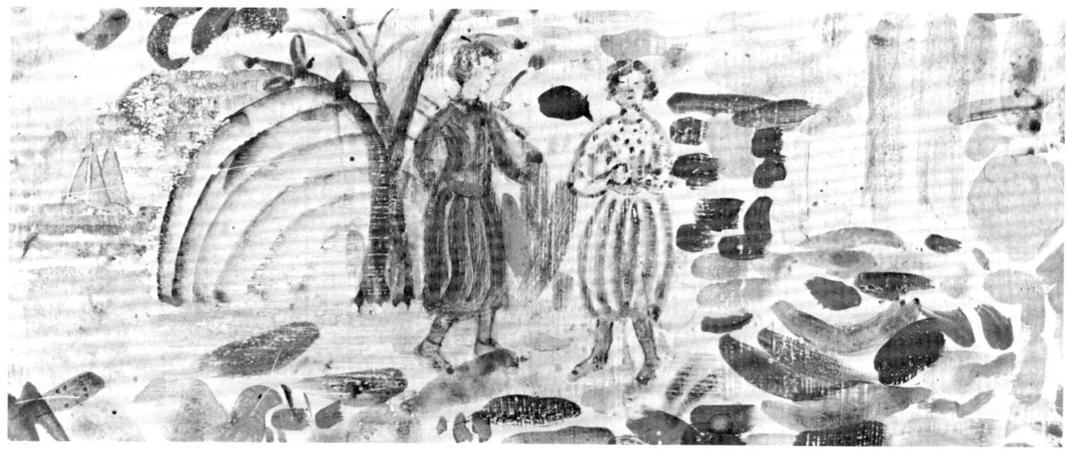

Two Figures by the Sea, ca. 1936-38
CR 2287
Tempera on gessoed panel (6⅜ x 15½ in.; 16.2 x 39.4 cm)
Collection of Mrs. Charles Prendergast

INSCRIPTIONS
l.r. in pencil: CP

PROVENANCE
The artist; to present collection, 1948

verso: Tree, girl, balloons, castle
Tempera and silver leaf

TECHNICAL NOTES
Both sides of this panel are covered with test strokes of color, as well as studies of trees, figures, and a sailboat. A small squared-off area on the verso contains a sketch for an entire composition with figure, tree, and castle in a landscape.

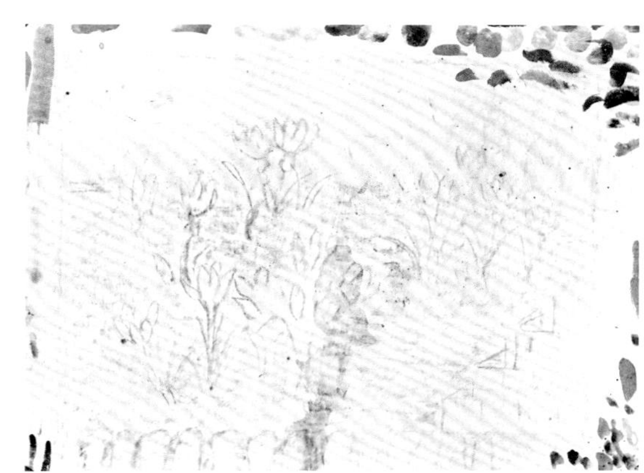

Unfinished panel, ca. 1940-47
not catalogued
Tempera and pencil on gessoed Masonite (9⅝ x 13¼ in.; 24.5 x 33.7 cm)
Williams College Museum of Art, Gift of Mrs. Charles Prendergast (92.20)

INSCRIPTIONS
verso, l.l. in pencil: red dress/ black coat

PROVENANCE
The artist, to Mrs. Charles Prendergast, 1948; to present collection, 1992

TECHNICAL NOTES
This panel was cut from a larger piece of Masonite after gesso had been applied to both front and back. A drawing of a flower garden has been applied to the surface gesso through a transfer method. Tempera colors in shades of reds, pinks, oranges, blues and greens have been tested around the edges and on the verso of the panel.

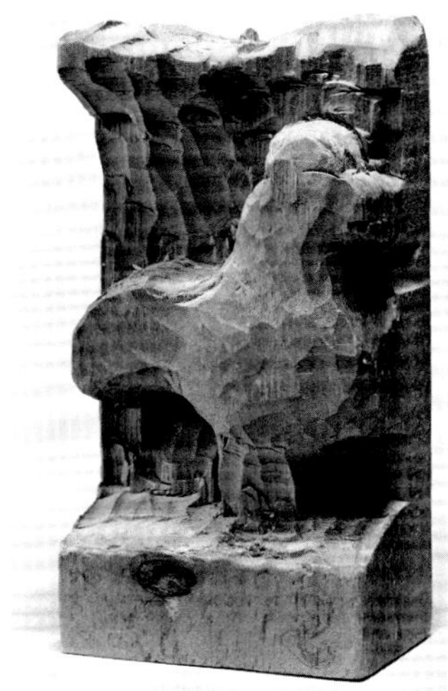

Unfinished figure of a rooster, ca. 1947-48
not catalogued
Carved wood (8¼ x 4 x 2⅜ in.; 21.0 x 10.2 x 6.0 cm)
Williams College Museum of Art, Anonymous Gift (85.45.1)

INSCRIPTIONS
Unsigned

Provenance
The artist; to Mrs. Charles Prendergast, 1948; to present collection, 1985

Exhibitions
1984a Williams College (#31); 1990 Williams College (no #)

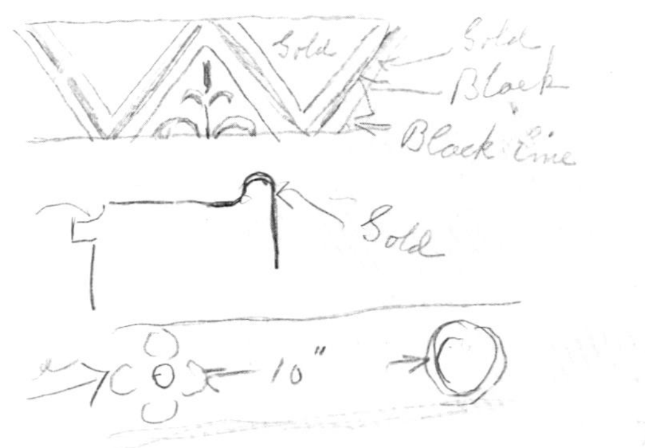

(recto) *Frame Sketch*
not catalogued
Pencil on paper (5¼ x 7¼ in.; 13.3 x 18.4 cm)
Williams College Museum of Art, Gift of Mrs. Charles Prendergast (85.22.12)

Inscriptions
Unsigned

Provenance
The artist; to Mrs. Charles Prendergast, 1948; to present collection, 1985

Exhibitions
1989b Williams College (#24)

verso: *Frame Sketch*
Pencil

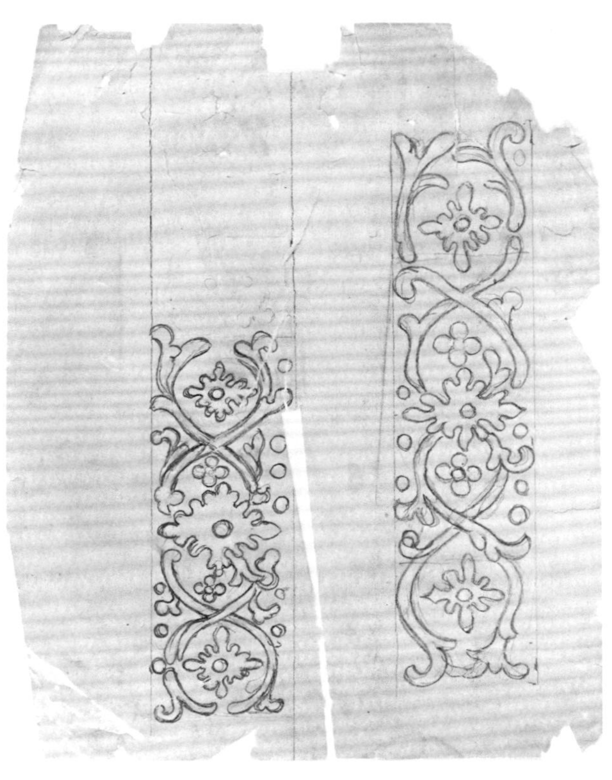

Frame Sketch
not catalogued
Pencil on paper (10⅜ x 7⅞ in.; 26.4 x 20.0 cm)
Williams College Museum of Art, Gift of Mrs. Charles Prendergast (85.22.13)

Inscriptions
Unsigned

Provenance
The artist; to Mrs. Charles Prendergast, 1948; to present collection, 1985

Exhibitions
1988b Williams College (#93)

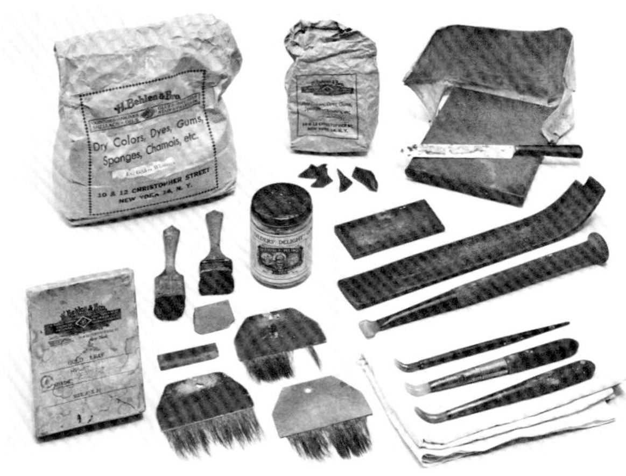

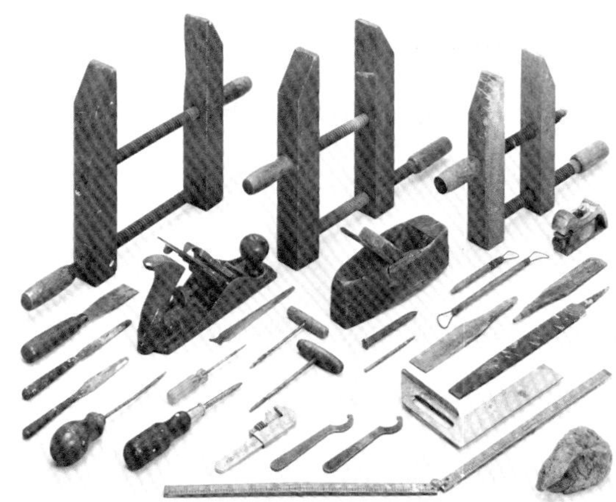

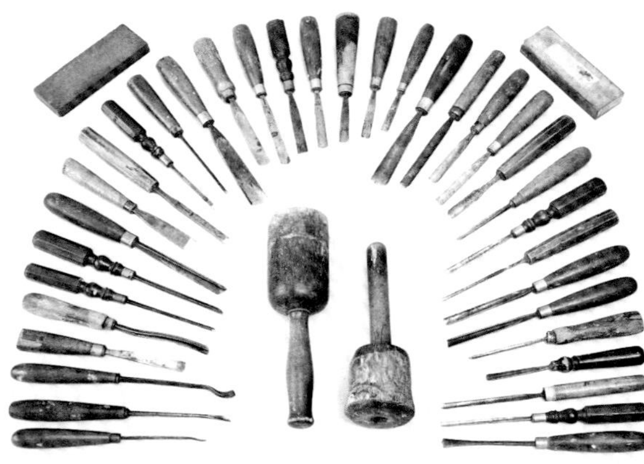

Charles Prendergast's Tools and Materials
not catalogued
3 wooden vises
½ bag plaster for gesso, H. Behlen & Bro. 10 & 12 Christopher St. New York 14, New York
cushion for cutting gold leaf
wood block covered with leather with parchment screen attached
knife for cutting gold leaf
3 brushes for moving gold leaf
cloth
box of gold leaf, H. Behlen & Bro. 10 & 12 Christopher St. New York 14, New York
wood palette 9¾ x 7½ inches
bag of hanging clips
jar of gold size, Heins' "Gilders' Delight," John J. Heins, New York
bag of glue for gesso, H. Behlen & Bro. 10 & 12 Christopher St. New York 14, New York
2 brushes
2 palette knives
2 mallets
3 planes
5 wetstones
sponge
4 burnishers
file
leather strip
folding ruler
4 hinges
large square edge
wrench
36 wood carving tools, several of English and French manufacture
3 putty knives
2 punches
2 screw-hole starters
2 clay carving tools
7-inch square
broken brass letter opener
2 ratchets
wood handle for unidentified tool
2 small paddle-shaped objects with orange tips
Williams College Museum of Art, Prendergast Archive and Study Center, Gift of Mrs. Charles Prendergast

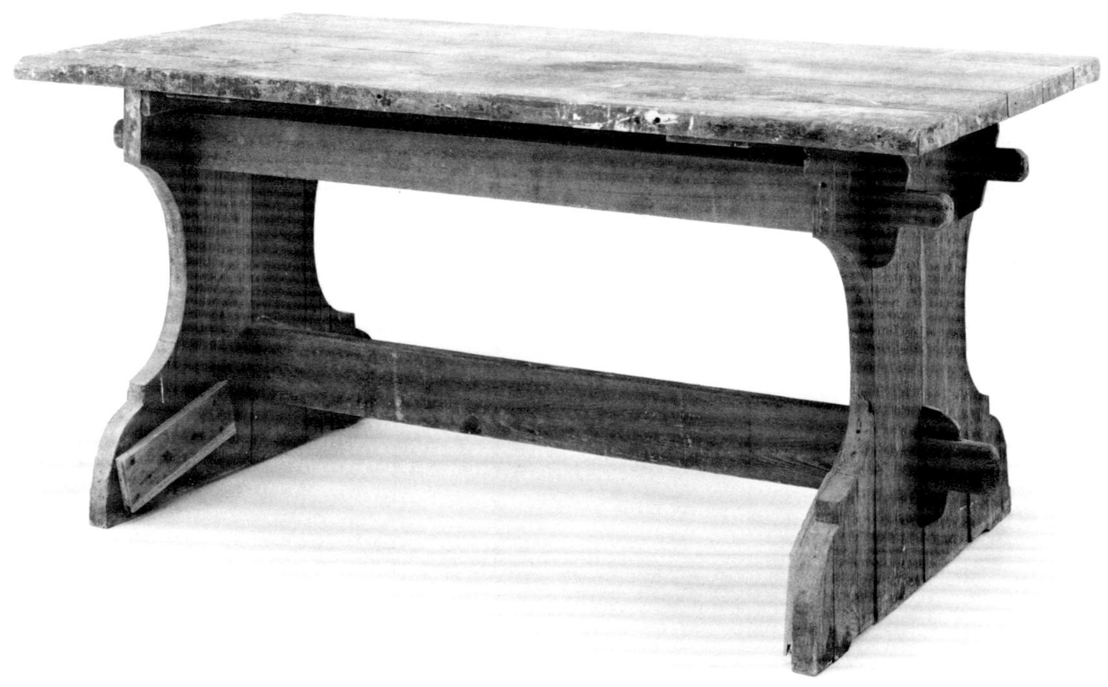

Charles Prendergast's Work Table, ca. 1900-25
not catalogued
Oak (35½ x 72½ x 36¾ in.; 90.2 x 184.2 x 93.4 cm)
Williams College Museum of Art, Prendergast Archive and Study Center, Gift of an anonymous friend of Charles Prendergast

PROVENANCE

The artist; to Mrs. Charles Prendergast, 1948; to private collection; to present collection, 1992

TECHNICAL NOTES

This work table used by the Prendergast brothers bears no marks or inscriptions. The table is similar to mission-style library trestle tables made between 1900-25. It has a rectangular top made of five boards with plain outer edges. The top is set on two pairs of plain vertical supports made up of four boards each. These supports end in slightly curved feet. Three boards are mortised through the vertical supports (two at the top and one lower) with keys as reinforcements. There is some nail construction, but the table can be dismantled into six pieces. The vertical legs and underside of the table top have been reinforced. The table top is rough, and worn from use.

APPENDIX B

Books from the Prendergasts' Library Now in the Prendergast Archive and Study Center

Addison Gallery of American Art. *Handbook of the Addison Gallery of American Art*. Andover, Mass.: Addison Gallery of American Art, 1939.

———. *The Prendergasts: Retrospective Exhibition of the Work of Maurice and Charles Prendergast*. Andover, Mass.: Addison Gallery of American Art, 1938.

The Adventures of Gil Blas of Santillane. London: E. Newbery, 1788.

Album delle Catacombe di S. Callisto. [Rome]: R.R. P.P. Trappisti, n.d.

American Institute for Persian Art and Archaeology. *Persian Fresco Paintings*. New York: American Institute for Persian Art and Archaeology, 1932.

Ashbrook, Frank G. *The Blue Book of Birds of America*. Racine, Wis.: Whitman Publishing Co., 1931.

———. *The Green Book of American Birds*. Racine, Wis.: Whitman Publishing Co., 1931.

Baedecker, Karl. *Italy: From the Alps to Naples*. 2nd ed. Leipzig: Karl Baedecker, 1909.

———. *Italy: Handbook for Travellers (Northern Italy)*. Leipzig: Karl Baedecker, 1895.

———. *Southern France including Corsica: Handbook for Travellers*. 6th ed. Leipzig: Karl Baedecker, 1914.

Basso, Hamilton. *Charles Prendergast*. Plandome, N.Y.: G. Alan Chidsey, 1947. [Copy of Basso's two-part article "Profile: A Glimpse of Heaven-I, -II" in *The New Yorker*, July 27 and August 3, 1946, bound into a book by G. Alan Chidsey.]

Berenson, Bernhard. *The Florentine Painters of the Renaissance*. New York: G. P. Putnam's Sons, 1907.

———. *The Venetian Painters of the Renaissance*. 3rd ed. New York: G. P. Putnam's Sons, 1906.

Bertini, Emma. *Italian Companion and Interpreter*. 8th ed. Florence: Felice le Monnier, 1921.

Beauties of the Waverly Novels. Boston: Samuel G. Goodrich, 1828.

Bibliotheque Universelle et Historique de l'Année 1688: Tome Huitième. Amsterdam: Wolfgang, Waesberge, Boom and van Someren, 1688.

Blanchard, Raoul, and D. Faucher. *Cours de Géographie: La France et Ses Colonies*. Paris: Librairie Gedalge, 1923.

Breuning, Margaret. *Maurice Prendergast*. American Artists Series. New York: Whitney Museum of American Art, 1931.

Brooks, C. Harry. *The Practice of Autosuggestion*. New York: Dodd, Mead, and Co., 1922.

Burnand, R. *Reims: La Cathédrale*. Paris: Berger and Leurault, n.d.

Cadot, Michel, ed. *Madame de Sévigné: Lettres*. Paris: Librairie A. Hatier, n.d.

Cezanne Mappe. Munich: R. Piper & Co., 1912.

Chateaubriand. *Voyage en Italie: Peintures et Dessins de Corot*. Le sixième de la Collection du Bouquet, 2nd ed. Edited by H. L. Mermod. Geneva: Albert Kundig, 1947.

Clement, Clara Erskine. *Handbook of Legendary and Mythological Art*. New York: Hurd and Houghton, 1871.

Collingwood, W. G. *The Art Teaching of John Ruskin*. London: Percival and Co.; New York: G. P. Putnam's Sons, 1891.

Colombe, Le Docteur Gabriel. *Le Palais des Papes d'Avignon*. Paris: Henri Laurens, 1927.

Conrad, Joseph. *The Arrow of Gold*. New York: Doubleday, Page and Co., 1919.

Cousin, J.-A. P. *Voyages Gastronomique au Pays de France: Paris et la région parisienne*. Paris: Ernst Flammarion, 1925.

Davidson, trans. *First Six Books of Virgil's Aeneid*. Philadelphia: David McKay, 1896.

de Dillmont, Thérèse. *Encyclopédie des Ouvrages de Dames*. Alsace, France: Mulhouse, n.d.

de Saint Pierre, J. B. H. *Paul and Virginia*. New York: Appleton and Co., n.d.

de Saint Pierre, Jacques-Bernardin-Henri. *La Chamière Indienne*. Paris: Chez P. Fr. Didot le jeune, 1791.

Delle Poesie Meliche di Giuseppe Battista. Parte 1. Venice: Presso Abbondio Menafoglio et Valentino Mortali, 1666.

Douglas, Frederick, and Rene d'Harnoncourt. *Indian Art of the United States*. New York: Museum of Modern Art, 1941.

Edgarton, S. C. *The Flower Vase: Containing The Language of Flowers and Their Poetic Sentiments*. Lowell, Mass.: Merrill and Heywood, 1847.

Ehl, Heinrich. *Deutsche Steinbildwerke der Frühzeit*. Berlin: Verlog Ernst Wosmuth A. G., n.d.

English-French Conversational Dictionary. 2nd ed. London: Richard Jäschke, n.d.

Faure, Elie. *History of Art: Ancient Art*. New York and London: Harper Brothers, 1921.

Fazzini, Lillian Davids. *Indians of America*. Racine, Wis.: Whitman Publishing Co., 1935.

Federal Writer's Project of the Works Progress Administration. *Florida: A Guide to the Southernmost State*. New York: Oxford University Press, 1939.

Fels, Florent. *Les Vielles Tapisseries Française*. Paris: Les Editions G. Cres & Cie, 1924.

Galsworthy, John. *The Forsyte Saga*, Vol. 1, *The Man of Property*. Collection of British and American Authors, Tauchnitz Edition, vol. 4733. Leipzig: Bernhard Tauchnitz, 1926.

________. *The Forsyte Saga*, Vol. 2, *Indian Summer of a Forstye; In Chancery*. Collection of British and American Authors, Tauchnitz Edition, vol. 4734. Leipzig: Bernhard Tauchnitz, 1926.

Geller, G. J. *Sarah Bernhardt*. Paris: Librairie Gallimard, 1931.

Gone Astray. New York: John Lane Co., 1918.

Goodrich, Lloyd. *American Watercolor and Winslow Homer*. Minneapolis: Walker Art Center, 1945.

Guérinet, Armand, ed. *Matériaux et Documents d'Art Décoratif: Étoffes Byzantines*. Paris: Librairie d'Architecture & d'Art Décoratif, [1922].

Guide Michelin Régional: Bretagne. Clermont-Ferrand, France: Michelin et Cie, 1929-30.

Guillaume Tell. Program for opera by Rossini. [Paris]: Academie National de Musique et Danse, November 15, 1929.

Hines, Duncan. *Adventures in Good Eating*. Bowling Green, Ky.: Adventures in Good Eating, Inc., 1939.

Holme, Charles, ed. *Peasant Art in Russia*. New York: The Studio, Ltd., 1912.

Holmes, C. J. *Constable*. London: Sign of the Unicorn, 1901.

Holy Bible. London and New York: Oxford University Press, n.d.

Hugo, Victor. *Quatrevingt-treize*. Paris: Nelson Éditeurs, 1930.

Hunt, Violet. *The Wife of Rosetti: Her Life and Death*. New York: E. P. Dutton and Co., Inc., 1932.

Japanese Design Book of Flowers. [19th century]

Jäschke, Richard, comp. *English-Italian Conversational Dictionary*. London: W. Lockwood and Co., n.d.

John Quinn: Collection of Paintings, Watercolors, Drawings, and Sculpture. Huntington, N.Y.: Pidgeon Hill Press, 1926.

Junta de Museus. *Frontals Romànics Catalans del Museus d'Art de Catalunya*. Barcelona: Junta de Museus, 1934.

LaFollette, Suzanne. *Art in America*. New York and London: Harper and Brothers, 1929.

Le Musée du Mont-Saint-Michel. *Le Mont-Saint-Michel et ses Merveilles, d'Après des Notes du Marquis de Tombelaine*. Paris: Le Musée du Mont-Saint-Michel, n.d.

Mack, Gerstle. *Paul Cézanne*. New York: Alfred A. Knopf, 1935.

________. *Toulouse-Lautrec*. New York: Alfred A. Knopf, 1938.

The Maritime Provinces: A Handbook for Travellers. Boston: James R. Osgood and Co., 1875.

Markevitch, Z. B. *Steppes d'Ukraine*. Montreal: Editions Beauchemin, 1944.

Maspero, G. *Art in Egypt*. New York: Charles Scribner's Sons, 1912.

The Masterpieces of Peter Breugel. New York: Frederick A. Stokes Co., n.d.

Mayer, Frederick. *The Louvre*. Paris: Société Anonyme de Publications Anglo-Américaines, n.d.

Meier-Graefe, Julius. *Die Moderne Impressionismus*. Die Kunst by Richard Muther. Berlin: Julius Bard Verlag, n.d.

Metropolitan Museum of Art. *The Unicorn Tapestries: A Picture Book*. New York: Metropolitan Museum of Art, 1938.

Meyer, Peter. *Art in Switzerland: from the Earliest Times to the Present Day*. London: Nicholson and Watson, 1946.

Milton's Poetical Works with Life. London and Edinburgh: T. Nelson & Sons, 1861.

Moore, George. *Confessions of a Young Man*. 1886. Edited and annotated. Leipzig: Bernhard Tauchnitz, 1904.

Morley, John. *Rousseau*. Vol. 1. London: MacMillan and Co., 1886.

Motifs Japonais. Enluminure exécutée par l'Atelier Ferrariello. Levallois, France: H. Guillaume, n.d.

Motta, Enrico. *Venice Seen by the Painter*. Novara, Italy: The Uffici Press, n.d.

Murray, Alexander S. *Manual of Mythology*. Philadelphia: David McKay, 1895.

Museum of Modern Art. *Cézanne, Gauguin, Seurat, Van Gogh: First Loan Exhibition*. New York: Museum of Modern Art, 1929.

———. *Italian Masters Lent by the Royal Italian Government*. New York: Museum of Modern Art, 1940.

Neuhaus, Eugene. *World of Art*. New York: Harcourt, Brace and Co., 1936.

Nitti, Francesco. *Escape*. New York: G. P. Putnam's Sons, 1930.

*Oeuvres Complètes de M. le C. de B****. Vol. 1. London: L'Académie François, 1786.

*Oeuvres Complètes de M. le C. de B****. Vol. 2. London: L'Académie François, 1786.

Pach, Walter. *Ananias or the False Artist*. New York and London: Harper and Brothers, 1928.

———. *Queer Thing, Painting*. New York and London: Harper and Brothers, 1938.

Peattie, Donald Culross. *Trees You Want to Know*. Racine, Wis.: Whitman Publishing Co., 1934.

Peltier, C. and P. H. Gay. *Cours de Langue Française*. Paris: Librairie Ch. Delagrave, n.d.

Pène du Bois, Guy. *William J. Glackens*. American Artist Series. New York: Whitney Museum of American Art, 1931.

Pène du Bois, Henri, ed. and trans. *French Maxims of Art*. New York: Brentano's, 1894.

Persian Painting from Miniatures of the XIII-XVI Centuries. New York and Toronto: Iris Books, Oxford University Press, 1945.

Phillips, Duncan. *A Collection in the Making*. New York: E. Weyhe; Washington, D.C.: Phillips Memorial Gallery, 1926.

Picture Book of Flowers and Birds. Tokyo: n.p., 1884.

Pope, Alexander. *The Rape of the Lock*. London and New York: John Lane, 1902.

Poux, Joseph. *La Cité de Carcassonne*. Toulouse, France: Imprimerie et Librairie Edourd Privat, 1925.

Queen Mathilde's Tapestry. U.S.: Delandes, 1910.

The Redcoat Press. Westport, Conn.: Redcoat Press, May 1940.

Reed, Chester A. *Flower Guide: Wildflowers East of the Rockies*. Rev. ed. Garden City, N.Y.: Doubleday, Doran and Co., Inc., 1930.

Ricci, Corrado. *Art in Northern Italy*. New York: Charles Scribner's Sons, 1911.

———. *Ravenna*. Artistic Italy, vol. 2. Bergamo, Italy: Instituto Italiano d'Arti Grafiche, 1907.

Richter, Gisela M. A. *Metropolitan Museum of Art: The Classical Collection*. New York: Metropolitan Museum of Art, 1917.

Ricordo di Roma: Parte 1.

Ricordo di Roma: Parte 2.

Rorimer, James. *The Cloisters*. New York: Metropolitan Museum of Art, 1938.

Rothenstein, William. *Men and Memories*. New York: Coward-McCann Inc., 1931.

Rousseau, J. J. *Pensées*. Paris: Payot et Cie., n.d.

Sand, George. *Francis the Waif*. London: George Routledge & Sons, 1889.

Shakespeare's Sonnets, Passionate Pilgrim, Etc. Philadelphia: David MacKay, n.d.

Souvenir Rouen.

Street, Julian. *Abroad and at Home*. With pictorial sidelights by Wallace Morgan. New York: The Century Co., 1915.

Thode, Henry. *Giotto*. Bielefeld and Leipzig: Verlag von Velhagen und Klasing, 1910.

Titmarsh, M. A. *The Paris Sketchbook*. London: George Routledge and Sons, 1886.

Vollard, Ambroise. *Paul Cézanne*. Paris: Les Editions G. Cres et Cie, 1924.

Voltaire. *Candide*. New York: Three Sirens Press, 1930.

———. *Histoire de Charles XII*. Paris: Didot, 1817.

Weege, Fritz. *Etruskische Malerei*. Halle, Germany: Max Niemeyer Verlag, 1921.

Whistler, James McNeill. *The Gentle Art of Making Enemies*. New York: John W. Lovell Co., 1890.

Whitney Museum of American Art. *Maurice Prendergast Memorial Exhibition*. New York: Whitney Museum of American Art, 1934.

———. *William Glackens Memorial Exhibition*. New York: Whitney Museum of American Art, 1939.

Yonge, C. D., trans. *Select Orations of Marcus Tullius Cicero*. Philadelphia: David McKay, 1896.

Zetland, Marquis of, ed. *The Letters of Disraeli to Lady Chesterfield and Lady Bradford*. Vol. 2. New York: D. Appleton and Co., 1929.

AMERICAN ARTIST 1941
"John S. de Martelly describes his painting methods." *American Artist* 5 (March 1941): 4.

AMERICAN ART NEWS 1909
"Picture Framing Reform." *American Art News* 7 (April 17, 1909): 6.

ANDERSON 1990
Anderson, Ross. "Charles Prendergast." In *Maurice Brazil Prendergast, Charles Prendergast: A Catalogue Raisonné*, Carol Clark, Nancy Mowll Mathews, and Gwendolyn Owens. Munich: Prestel-Verlag; Williamstown, Mass.: Williams College Museum of Art, 1990.

ANTIQUES ARTS WEEKLY 1986
"Williams College to Show Prendergast Collection." *Antiques & The Arts Weekly* (Oct. 31, 1986): 113.

ART DIGEST 1942
"For the Red Cross." *Art Digest* 16 (May 15, 1942): 9.

ART DIGEST 1948
"Charles Prendergast." *Art Digest* 22 (Sept. 15, 1948): 16.

ART NEWS 1935
"Charles Prendergast: Kraushaar Galleries." *Art News* 34 (Nov. 2, 1935): 8.

ART NEWS 1938
"The Brothers Prendergast in Review." *Art News* 37 (Oct. 8, 1938): 14-15, 19.

ART WORKERS' QUARTERLY 1902
The Art Workers' Quarterly (April 1902).

BASSO 1946a
Basso, Hamilton. "Profiles: A Glimpse of Heaven-I." *New Yorker* 22 (July 27, 1946): 24-28, 30.

BASSO 1946b
Basso, Hamilton. "Profiles: A Glimpse of Heaven-II." *New Yorker* 22 (Aug. 3, 1946): 28-32, 34, 36, 37.

BENTON 1969
Benton, Thomas Hart. *An American in Art, A Professional and Technical Autobiography*. Lawrence, Kans.: University of Kansas Press, 1969.

BERMAN 1990
Berman, Avis. *Rebels on Eighth Street: Juliana Force and the Whitney Museum of American Art*. New York: Atheneum, 1990.

BINYON 1916
Binyon, Laurence. "A Group of Japanese Screen-Paintings in the Freer Collection in Washington." *Art in America* 4, no. 5 (Aug. 1916): 328-39.

BOSTON MFA 1911
Bulletin of the Museum of Fine Arts, Boston. 1911.

BOSTON MFA 1915
Bulletin of the Museum of Fine Arts, Boston. 1915.

BRAUN 1985
Braun, Emily, and Thomas Branchick. *Thomas Hart Benton: The America Today Murals*. Williamstown, Mass.: Williams College Museum of Art, 1985.

BREUNING 1947
Breuning, Margaret. "Decorative Art of Charles Prendergast." *Art Digest* 21 (April 1, 1947): 18.

BUTLER 1989
Butler, Joseph T. "Arts and Crafts Furniture and Charles Prendergast." In *The Prendergasts and The Arts and Crafts Movement*, W. Anthony Gengarelly and Carol Derby. Williamstown, Mass.: Williams College Museum of Art, 1989. (1988b Williams College)

CENNINI 1899
Cennini, Cennino. *The Book of the Art of Cennino Cennini. A Contemporary Practical Treatise on Quattrocento Painting*. Translated by Christiana J. Herringham. London: George Allen & Unwin, Ltd., 1899.

CHANIN 1954
C[hanin], A. L. "Charles Prendergast." *Art Digest* 28 (Jan. 15, 1954): 20.

CHRISTIAN SCIENCE MONITOR 1913
"Making Carved Frames Choice Work." *Christian Science Monitor* (Nov. 22, 1913).

CLARK, MATHEWS, OWENS 1990
Clark, Carol, Nancy Mowll Mathews, and Gwendolyn Owens. *Maurice Brazil Prendergast, Charles Prendergast: A Catalogue Raisonné*. Munich: Prestel-Verlag; Williamstown, Mass.: Williams College Museum of Art, 1990.

COMSTOCK 1935
Comstock, Helen. "The Connoisseur in America." *The Connoisseur* 98, no. 411 (Nov. 1935): 283.

COOMARASWAMY 1929
Coomaraswamy, Ananda K. *Les Miniatures Orientales de la Collection Goloubew au Museum of Fine Arts de Boston*. Paris: Ars Asiatica, 1929.

CORNING 1992
Corning Museum of Glass. *Reverse Painting on Glass: The Ryser Collection*. Corning, New York: The Corning Museum of Glass, 1992.

CRANE 1893
Crane, Walter. "Notes on Gesso Work," *Studio* 1, no. 2 (May 1893): 45-48.

CRAWFORD 1919
Crawford, M. D. C. "The Carved Gesso Panels of Charles E. Prendergast." *Country Life in America* 36 (Sept. 1919): 47-49.

DENOON 1987
Denoon, Christopher. *Posters of the WPA, 1935-1943*. Los Angeles: Wheatley Press, 1987.

DERBY 1989
Derby, Carol. "Charles Prendergast's Frames: Reuniting Design and Craftsmanship." In *The Prendergasts and The Arts and Crafts Movement*, W. Anthony Gengarelly and Carol Derby. Williamstown, Mass.: Williams College Museum of Art, 1989. (1988b Williams College)

DERBY 1990
Derby, Carol. "Charles Prendergast's Frames: Reuniting Design and Craftsmanship." In *Maurice Brazil Prendergast, Charles Prendergast: A Catalogue Raisonné*, Carol Clark, Nancy Mowll Mathews, and Gwendolyn Owens. Munich: Prestel-Verlag; Williamstown, Mass.: Williams College Museum of Art, 1990.

DUMBARTON OAKS 1973-76
Dumbarton Oaks Center for Byzantine Studies. *Literature on Byzantine Art, 1892-1967*. Vol. 2. Edited by Jelisaveta S. Allen. Dumbarton Oaks Bibliographies, Series 1. London: Mansell, 1973-76.

DURKIN 1989
Durkin, Elizabeth. *Kindred Spirits: Maurice and Charles Prendergast*. Williamstown, Mass.: Williams College Museum of Art, 1989. (1989b Williams College)

FISHBURN 1942
Fishburn, Eleanor C., and Mildred Sandison Fenner. "Angel of the Battlefield." *Journal of the National Education Association* 31 (March 1942): 85-86.

GENGARELLY 1989
Gengarelly, W. Anthony, and Carol Derby. *The Prendergasts and The Arts and Crafts Movement*. Williamstown, Mass.: Williams College Museum of Art, 1989. (1988b Williams College)

GOLDIN 1976
Goldin, Amy. "How Are the Prendergasts Modern?" *Art in America* 64 (Sept. 1976): 60-67.

GOLDWATER 1967
Goldwater, Robert. *Primitivism in Modern Art*. Rev. ed. New York: Random House, 1967.

GOOD FURNITURE 1918
Good Furniture Magazine (Sept. 1918).

GUÉRINET 1922
Guérinet, Armand, ed. *Étoffes Byzantines, Coptes, Romaines, etc. du IV au X siècle*. Matériaux et Documents d'Art Décoratif: Étoffes Byzantines. Paris: Librairie d'Architecture & d'Art Décoratif, [1922].

GUGGENHEIM 1922
Solomon R. Guggenheim Foundation. *Kandinsky: Painting on Glass*. New York: Solomon R. Guggenheim Foundation, 1966.

HALL 1974
Hall, James. *Dictionary of Subject and Symbols*. New York: Harper & Row Publishers, 1974.

HIRSCHL & ADLER 1972
Hirschl & Adler Galleries, Inc. *The Early Paintings of Max Kuehne*. New York: Hirschl & Adler Galleries, Inc., 1972.

HOEPLI 1912
Hoepli, Ulrico. *Lombardia*. Milan: Ulrico Hoepli, 1912.

HOLME 1912
Holme, Charles, ed. *Peasant Art in Russia*. New York: The Studio, Ltd., 1912.

HUDSON 1919
Hudson, Pedro Hernandez. "Los Paneles de Yeso Tallado de Carlos E. Prendergast." *La Revista del Mundo* 6 (Nov. 1919): 86-89.

JOHNSON 1979
Johnson, Diane Chalmers. *Art Nouveau*. New York: Abrams, 1979.

KAY 1968
Kay, Jane Holtz. "Charles Prendergast, Museum of Fine Arts, Boston, Massachusetts; October 2-November 3 (1968)." *Craft Horizons* 28 (Nov.-Dec. 1968): 41.

KOMANECKY 1984
Komanecky, Michael, and Virginia Fabbri Butera. *The Folding Image: Screens by Western Artists of the Nineteenth and Twentieth Centuries*. New Haven: Yale University Art Gallery, 1984. (1984 Yale)

KUEHNE 1932
Kuehne, Max. "On the use of gesso." *Arts Weekly* (March 26, 1932): 61.

LAUZON 1990
Lauzon, Lorraine. "Prendergast exhibit features gentle world." *The Catholic Observer* (Nov. 2, 1990): 28.

LEBRUN 1968
LeBrun, Caron. "The Fine Art of Framing and Then Some: Charles Prendergast Show at the Museum of Fine Arts." *Boston Arts* 1 (Oct. 1968): 24-28, 62-64.

LUDDINGTON 1992
Luddington, Townsend. *Marsden Hartley: The Biography of an American Artist*. Boston: Little, Brown and Co., 1992.

MARLOR 1984
Marlor, Clark S. *The Society of Independent Artists: The Exhibition Record 1917-1944*. Park Ridge, N.J.: Noyes Press, 1984.

MASPERO 1912
Maspero, G. *Art in Egypt*. New York: Charles Scribner's Sons, 1912.

MATHER 1920
Mather, Frank Jewett. "Three Florentine Furniture Panels: The Medici Desco, the Stibbert Trajan, and the Horse Race of the Holden Collection." *Art in America* 8, no. 4 (June 1920): 148-59.

MAYER 1981
Mayer, Ralph. *The Artists' Handbook of Materials and Techniques*. 4th ed. New York: Viking Press, 1981.

METCALF 1988
Metcalf, Eugene F., and Claudine Weatherford. "The Fine Art Meaning of American Folk Art." In *Folk Roots, New Roots*, Jane S. Becker and Barbara Fanco. Lexington, Mass.: The Museum of National Heritage, 1988.

MEYER 1957
Meyer, Franz Sales. *Handbook of Ornament*. New York: Dover Publications, 1957.

MEYER-RIEFSTAHL 1916
Meyer-Riefstahl, R. "Oriental Carpets in American Collections: Part I." *Art in America* 4, no. 3 (April 1916): 147-61.

MIGEON 1910
Migeon, Gaston. "Exposition des arts Musulmans á Munich." *Les Arts* (Dec. 1910): 21.

MILLIKEN 1926
Milliken, William Mathewson. "Maurice Prendergast, American Artist." *The Arts* 9 (April 1926): 180-92.

MUMFORD 1935
Mumford, Lewis. "The Art Galleries." *New Yorker* 11, no. 38 (Nov. 2, 1935): 69-70.

MURRAY 1895
Murray, Alexander S. *Manual of Mythology*. Philadelphia: David McKay, 1895.

NEW ENGLAND MONTHLY 1986
"Art of Two Brothers." *New England Monthly* 3 (Dec. 1986): 96.

NY HERALD TRIBUNE 1935
"A Modern Artist and an Old Tradition." *New York Herald Tribune* (Oct. 20, 1935): 10.

PACH 1923
Pach, Walter. "The Wizard Wood-Carver." *Shadowland* 8, no. 3 (May 1923): 10-11, 72.

PARKE-BERNET 1966
Parke-Bernet Galleries. *American Paintings and Drawings: From Various Owners*. Sale 2440 (May 13, 1966).

POPE 1902
Pope, Alexander. *The Rape of the Lock*. London and New York: John Lange, 1902.

PRENDERGAST 1909
Prendergast, Charles. "Revival of Wood-Carving." *House Beautiful* 26 (Aug. 1909): 70.

RICCI 1907
Ricci, Corrado. *Ravenna*. Artistic Italy, vol. 2. Bergamo, Italy: Instituto Italiano d'Arti Grafiche, 1907.

RICCI 1911
Ricci, Corrado. *Art in Northern Italy*. New York: Charles Scribner's Sons, 1911.

SEATON-SCHMIDT
Seaton-Schmidt, A. "An Artist Frame Maker." *Art and Progress* 1, no. 10 (Aug. 1910): 290-93.

TAYLOR 1984
Taylor, Robert. "Two Shows Worth Trip to Williams." *Boston Globe* (July 8, 1984): B:3.

THOMPSON 1956
Thompson, Daniel V. *The Materials and Techniques of Medieval Painting*. 1936. Reprint. New York: Dover Publications, 1956.

THOMPSON 1962
Thompson, Daniel V. *The Practice of Tempera Painting*. 1936. Reprint. New York: Dover Publications, 1962.

WATSON 1942
Watson, J. "The Red Cross Challenges the Artist." *Magazine of Art* 35 (Feb. 1942): 76.

WATTENMAKER 1968
Wattenmaker, Richard. *The Art of Charles Prendergast*. Boston: Museum of Fine Arts; New Brunswick, N.J.: Rutgers University Art Gallery, 1968. (1968 Rutgers University)

WEBER 1927
Weber, F. R. *Church Symbolism*. Cleveland: J. H. Jansen, 1927.

WEEGE 1921
Weege, Fritz. *Etruskische Malerei*. Halle, Germany: Max Niemeyer Verlag, 1921.

WETZEL 1915
Wetzel, Hervey E. "Persian and Indian Paintings in the Museum of Fine Arts, Boston: Part II." *Art in America* 3, no. 6 (Oct. 1915): 284-99.

WINTER PARK TOPICS 1947
"Art of Prendergasts at Research Studio." *Winter Park Topics* 14 (Jan. 31, 1947): 1.

York 1933
York, Lewis E. "Notes: Combination Gold and Silver Leafing." In *Technical Studies*, Fogg Art Museum, Harvard University, vol. 2, no. 2 (Oct. 1933): 105-6.

1935 Kraushaar
Charles Prendergast. New York: C. W. Kraushaar Art Galleries, Oct. 15-Nov. 2, 1935. Checklist.

1936 Soc Independent Artists
20th Annual Anniversary Exhibition. New York: Society of Independent Artists; Grand Central Palace, April 24-May 17, 1936. Brochure.

1937 Kraushaar
Decorative Panels by Charles Prendergast. New York: C. W. Kraushaar Art Galleries, Oct. 26-Nov. 13, 1937. Checklist.

1938 Addison Gallery
The Prendergasts: Retrospective Exhibition of the Work of Maurice and Charles Prendergast. Andover, Mass.: Addison Gallery of American Art, Phillips Academy, Sept. 24-Nov. 6, 1938. Catalogue.

1941 Kraushaar
Decorative Panels and Sculpture by Charles Prendergast. New York: Kraushaar Galleries, Dec. 8-31, 1941. Checklist.

1945a National Academy
119th Annual Exhibition of Contemporary American Painting, Sculpture and Graphic Art. New York: National Academy of Design, National Academy Galleries, March 14-April 3, 1945. Catalogue.

1947 Kraushaar
Charles Prendergast. New York: Kraushaar Galleries, March 31- April 19, 1947. Checklist.

1950 U Michigan
Sport and Circus. Ann Arbor, Mich.: Museum of Art, University of Michigan, Nov. 9-29, 1950. Brochure.

1954 Kraushaar
Charles Prendergast 1869-1948: Memorial Exhibition. New York: Kraushaar Galleries, Jan. 4-23, 1954. Brochure.

1959 Davenport
Sports and Recreation Panorama. Davenport, Iowa: Davenport Municipal Art Gallery, April 4-May 4, 1959. Brochure.

1963b Davis Galleries
Charles Prendergast: Watercolors, Carvings, Panels. New York: Davis Galleries, Oct. 22-Nov. 9, 1963. Brochure.

1968 Rutgers University
The Art of Charles Prendergast. New Brunswick, N.J.: Rutgers University Art Gallery and the Museum of

Fine Arts, Boston; MFA Boston, Oct. 2-Nov. 3, 1968, circulating. Catalogue.

1969 Hirschl & Adler
The Art of Charles Prendergast. New York: Hirschl & Adler Galleries, March 5-22, 1969. Checklist.

1970b Society of Four Arts
Six American Romantic Painters. Palm Beach, Fla.: Society of the Four Arts, March 7-29, 1970. Brochure.

1982 Parrish Museum
The Long Island Landscape 1914-1946: The Transitional Years. Southampton, N.Y.: Parrish Art Museum, June 13-Aug. 1, 1982. Catalogue.

1983a Williams College
The Art of Maurice and Charles Prendergast. Williamstown, Mass.: Williams College Museum of Art, Sept. 11-Dec. 4, 1983. Catalogue.

1984a Williams College
Charles Prendergast: Figures and Carved Panels. Williamstown, Mass.: Williams College Museum of Art, April 21-Sept. 16, 1984. Brochure.

1984b Williams College
Portraits by the Prendergasts. Williamstown, Mass.: Williams College Museum of Art, Oct. 19, 1984-March 24, 1985. Brochure.

1986 High Museum
The Advent of Modernism: Post Impressionism and North American Art, 1900-1918. Atlanta, Ga.: High Museum of Art, March 4-May 11, 1986. Catalogue.

1986 Williams College
Maurice and Charles Prendergast. Williamstown, Mass.: Williams College Museum of Art, Oct. 19, 1986-April 28, 1987. Brochure.

1988a Williams College
The Artist's Eye: Maurice and Charles Prendergast. Williamstown, Mass.: Williams College Museum of Art, May 14-Sept. 17, 1988. Checklist.

1988b Williams College
The Prendergasts & the Arts & Crafts Movement. Williamstown, Mass.: Williams College Museum of Art, Oct. 8, 1988-Jan. 8, 1989. Catalogue.

1989a Williams College
The Panels of Charles Prendergast. Williamstown, Mass.: Williams College Museum of Art, Jan. 21-Nov. 26, 1989. Checklist.

1989b Williams College
Kindred Spirits: Maurice and Charles Prendergast. Williamstown, Mass.: Williams College Museum of Art, Dec. 2, 1989-March 18, 1990. Brochure.

1990 Williams College
Charles Prendergast. Williamstown, Mass.: Williams College Museum of Art, Sept 29.-Dec. 16, 1990 and Feb. 16-April 12, 1991. Checklist.

1991 Williams College
Fugitive Colors and Other Issues in Conservation. Williamstown, Mass.: Williams College Museum of Art, Aug. 24-Nov. 3, 1991. Checklist.

1992 Williams College
The Prendergasts and the History of Art. Williamstown, Mass.: Williams College Museum of Art, April 25, 1992-Jan. 31, 1993. Checklist.

INDEX BY TITLE

Exhibition and Catalogue Project Staff

Susan Dillmann, *Editor*
Anne Dowling, *Prendergast Intern*
Ann Ugast Greenwood, *Project Coordinator*
Frances Lloyd, *Graduate Assistant to the Editor*
Nancy Mowll Mathews, *Exhibition Curator and Project Director*
Jonathon Nix, *Catalogue Design*
Timothy Sedlock, *Exhibition Installation*
The Studley Press, Dalton, Massachusetts, *Catalogue Printing*

Photography

Michael Agee: cover, pp. 2, 26-27, 38, 44 top, 46-48, 52, 61 right, 65, 70, 77 right, 78 right, 79-81, 86, 89, 100, 104, 109, 110
E. Irving Blomstrann: pp. 24, 54 left, 59 left, 60, 63, 67, 72 top right and bottom right, 73-76, 77 left, 78 left, 82, 83, 84 center and bottom, 85, 87, 91, 92 right, 94, 95 left, 97, 99, 102, 105 right, 106 right, 107 top
Geoffrey Clements: pp. 28, 30 top left, 55 left, 61 left, 92 left, 98
Helga Photographers: p. 41 top
Peter A. Juley and Son Collection, National Museum of American Art, Smithsonian Institution: pp. 17, 30 top right and bottom, 32 top
University of Connecticut Photographic Laboratory: p. 95 right
Williamstown Regional Art Conservation Laboratory: p. 44 bottom

Prendergast Foundation Board

Mrs. Charles Prendergast
Joseph T. Butler
John W. Boyd
Harold Genvert
Catherine I. Genvert
Nancy Mowll Mathews

Museum Staff

Linda Bartlett, *Accounts Secretary*
Hanne Booth, *Executive Secretary*
Amber Chand, *Museum Shop Manager*
Susan Dillmann, *Public Relations Coordinator*
Marion M. Goethals, *Curatorial Coordinator*
Ann Ugast Greenwood, *Prendergast Administrative Assistant*
Diane Hart, *Registrar*
Claudia Hill, *NEA Curatorial Intern*
Silvio Lamarre, *Security Monitor*
Bernard Lewitt, *Security Monitor*
Nancy Mowll Mathews, *Eugénie Prendergast Curator*
Robert McDonough, *Security Officer*
Vivian Patterson, *Associate Curator, Collections Management*
Judith Raab, *Assistant to the Director*
Barbara Robertson, *Education Coordinator*
Deborah Menaker Rothschild, *Associate Curator, Exhibitions*
Timothy Sedlock, *Preparator*
Linda Shearer, *Director*
Zelda Stern, *Public Relations/ Development Director*
Marilyn Superneau, *Security Monitor*
Rachel Tassone, *Data Entry Clerk*
Amy Tatro, *Secretary*
Theodore Wrona, *Fulltime Security Officer*

Visiting Committee

Suzi Stone, *Chair*
John D. Coffin, *Co-Vice Chair*
Michael S. Engl, *Co-Vice Chair*
Members: Milo C. Beach, John D. Coffin, Charles M. Collins, Mary Spivy Dangremond, Romeyn Everdell, Michael Glier, Linda B. Janovic, Elaine P. Kend, Katy Kline, Wendy Lehman Lash, William O'Reilly, Stephen D. Paine, Dorothy D. Rudolph, Stephen F. Selig, Martha D. Tucker, David P. Tunick, James N. Wood, Nicholas H. Wright

Members Emeriti: S. Lane Faison, Jr., Mrs. Charles Prendergast, Whitney S. Stoddard

Advisory Members: David S. Brooke, Director, Clark Art Institute; Samuel Y. Edgerton, Jr., Director, Graduate Program in the History of Art, Williams College; Gary C. Burger, Director, Williamstown Regional Art Conservation Laboratory; J. Hodge Markgraf, Vice President for Alumni Relations and Development, Williams College; Robert L. Volz, Custodian, Chapin Library of Rare Books, Williams College

Members Ex Officio: Francis C. Oakley, President of the College; Carol Ockman, Art History, and Barbara Takenaga, Studio Art, Co-Chairs, Department of Art; Keith C. Finan, Assistant Provost; Linda Shearer, Director, Williams College Museum of Art